POSTCARD HISTORY SERIES

Belmont

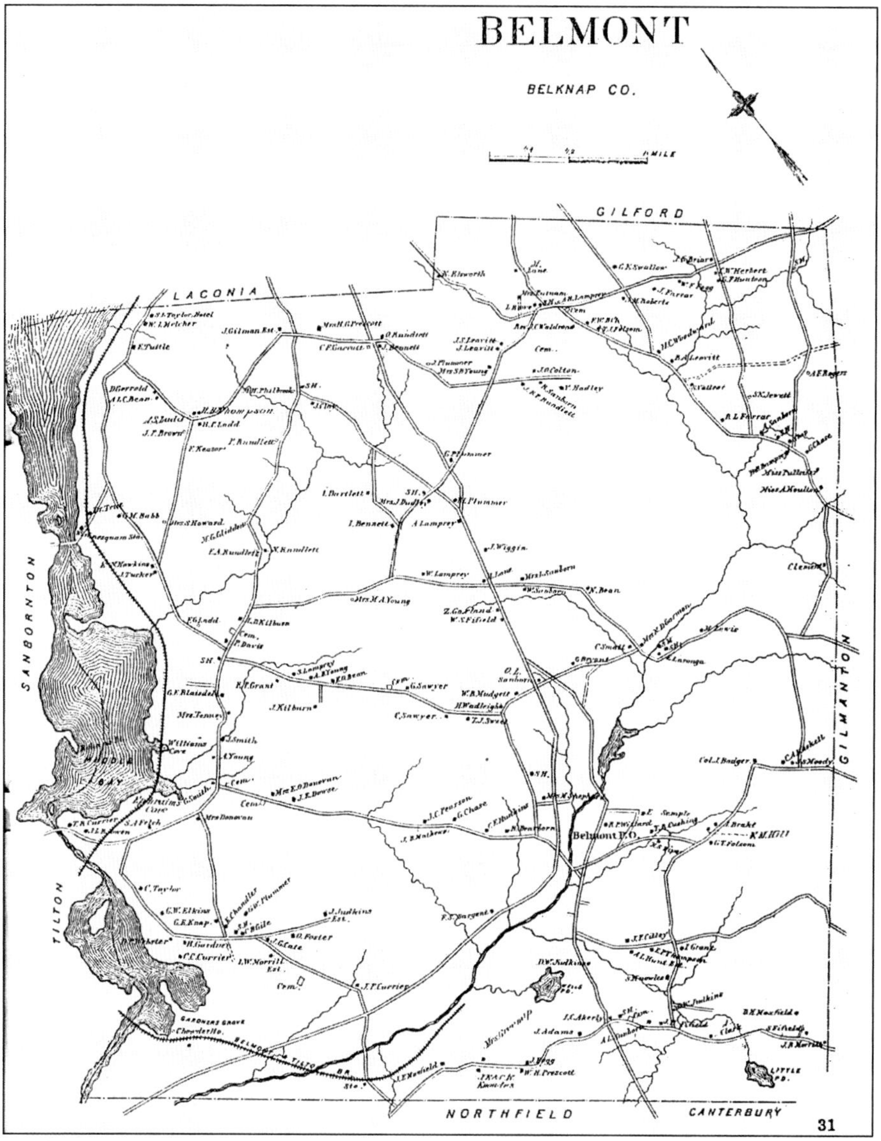

This 1892 map of Belmont contains the names of several families that were in town during this time period. The vast area of Belmont can be seen with minimal passageways used to travel upon.

On the front cover: The saw- or gristmill at the Upper, or Fellows, Dam was built after a previous structure was washed out in the freshet of 1852. In 1872, shingle-making machinery was added, and from 1876 until the structure burned on May 7, 1885, it was used for the manufacture of cases for the hosiery mill. (Author's collection.)

On the back cover: The Belmont Mill, shown here around 1909, was constructed in 1833 and was used for the manufacture of cotton sheeting until 1865 when it was converted to hosiery manufacture. By about 1900, the manufacturing complex had grown considerably. In 1992, the building was severely damaged by fire, bringing to a close manufacturing activity in Belmont Village that had spanned several generations over a period of 160 years. (Author's collection.)

POSTCARD HISTORY SERIES

Belmont

Diane M. Marden
with the Belmont Historical Society

ARCADIA
PUBLISHING

ISBN 0-7385-4584-8

Published by Arcadia Publishing
Charleston, South Carolina

Printed in the United States of America

Library of Congress Control Number: 2006926489

For all general information contact Arcadia Publishing at:
Telephone 843-853-2070
Fax 843-853-0044
E-mail sales@arcadiapublishing.com
For customer service and orders:
Toll-Free 1-888-313-2665

Visit us on the Internet at www.arcadiapublishing.com

Contents

ACKNOWLEDGMENTS

Producing this postcard history was an endeavor chosen specifically to share with all past, present, and future citizens of Belmont. Through this collection of postcards, it is hoped that those reading this will not only look at the past as a mere memory but will take all necessary actions to preserve what remains. Without the postcard collection of the author, the Belmont Historical Society, and the individuals who also shared their collections, this postcard history may not have been possible. A thank-you goes out to Brenda Paquette, Candace Daigle, Mr. and Mrs. Marshall Ford, and Carlton Bordeau for sharing their collections of Belmont. Also, a thank-you to Rick Ball for providing necessary range maps surrounding the town of Belmont for the purpose of researching parts of this publication.

A special thank-you to Wallace Rhodes, town historian, for all his wealth of information, for listening to the many questions of this author, for writing the introduction to this publication, and for assisting with the editing of the book.

A sincere appreciation to the surviving friends and families of the authors who have left great pieces of work in the past for future generations. The following publications were used as resources when researching the postcard history contained within: Rev. Moses T. Runnell's *History of Sanbornton*, volumes 1 and 2, Wallace Rhodes's *Reminiscences of a New Hampshire Town*, Daniel Lancaster's *History of Gilmanton*, Capt. William Badger's *History of Gilmanton*, and the Town of Belmont's annual reports, from 1869 to present.

The author has made a sincere attempt to continue Belmont's history by picking up where Wallace Rhodes left off in his 1969 publication. Historical information has been added in areas where known changes have occurred. Although this is not a complete collection of Belmont postcards, it does reflect the town's history through images presented within. For those collecting these wonderful postcards, the author trusts that one can identify these images and bring them home to Belmont whenever found. For those not collecting postcards, may memories be triggered throughout this publication, as memories of the past are so easily forgotten. It is hoped that some insight on Belmont's origins can be gained by readers, forever bridging the gap between past, present, and future generations.

Introduction

The first people to set foot on the soil of central New Hampshire were the original Native Americans who lived a migrant life following seasonal opportunities to capture fish and animals, which were the major part of their diet. The western edge of what was to become Belmont at the Winnipesaukee (Winnipisogee) River, or Great Bay, contains a site that was popular for thousands of years for locating weirs to catch fish as they migrated between the ocean and lakes. In his *History of Sanbornton*, Rev. Moses T. Runnell also recalls the story of a battle that was once waged on present-day Mohawk Island between the warring Pequawkets and Mohawks.

The town of Belmont's origin dates to May 20, 1727, when Lt. Gov. John Wentworth granted a charter for the town of Gilmantown to 144 individuals, of whom 24 bore the name of Gilman. In 1727, the lieutenant governor granted this and five other townships charters to vast areas of uninhabited territory in central New Hampshire east of the Merrimack and Winnipesaukee Rivers. Gilmantown itself contained 86,500 acres, or 135 square miles.

Although granted in 1727, most of this vast territory remained uninhabited other than by the sparse migrant Native American populations or by the few brave individuals who attempted to explore the territory. Years of tension between the settlers of the coastal communities and the Native Americans had come about as the result of atrocities carried out by both parties. With the culmination of the French and Indian War in 1760, the Native American population withdrew into Canada and left vast areas safe for settlement by the English. Thus in 1761, preparations were made to settle the town, and in December of that year, the first settler arrived in Gilmantown.

There is no known record of who first settled within the bounds of present-day Belmont. One can assume that settlement did not begin until after 1765 when the territory of Belmont was surveyed and divided in 100-acre lots. The two most likely parts of town to receive the first settlers were the area near the Winnipesaukee River in the western part of the town and along Province Road (State Route 107), which was surveyed in 1770 and built shortly thereafter. It is safe to say that Belmont was settled before the American Revolution, but the number of inhabitants was few. In the 1780s and 1790s, many of the current roadways in the town were laid out to connect to the scattered farms that had been established by then. There was little activity in the town other than farming.

In 1794, Joseph Fellows purchased land along the Great Brook (Tioga River) on which he built a sawmill and gristmill. The sawmill was located downstream from the Church Street Bridge, and the gristmill was located upstream at the falls. At about the same time, a roadway was built that connected to Gilmanton in the east and Sanbornton in the west by way of Union Bridge across the Winnipesaukee River. By the early 1800s, a village began to develop near the mills with the construction of a store, post office, and blacksmith shop. Thus Belmont Village, then called Fellows Mills, was born. The village population was limited to a few individuals who primarily operated businesses serving residents and nearby farms. Connection to the outside world was limited to an east–west pattern, and what was to become Main Street was merely a crude pathway connecting Union Bridge Road at the north end of the village to South Road, which was another east–west roadway. It was not until 1821 that a north–south roadway was surveyed and constructed through Belmont, connecting today's Laconia to Concord. Today's Main Street, first referred to as the Cross Road, was incorporated into this new highway.

In 1832, profound changes began to take place when William Badger and several associates received a charter from the New Hampshire legislature incorporating Gilmanton Village Manufacturing Company. The corporation soon accumulated property including the Fellows sawmill and water rights and the next year commenced construction of the brick factory building, which was to become today's Belmont Mill. Much of what constitutes today's Belmont can be traced to this development. The fortunes of the town would be linked to the mill from 1833 until 1970 when the last textile operation closed. Fortunately today the mill lives on in another incarnation.

Politically the original Gilmantown underwent two divisions. First Gilford became a separate town in 1812, and the remainder of the town was split into today's Belmont and Gilmanton in 1859. This final division was not at the request of the residents but rather appears to have come about as the result of political maneuvers in the state legislature. According to the legislative act, a new town by the name of Gilmanton was created, and the remaining portion was renamed Upper Gilmanton. As a consequence of the wording of the act, Upper Gilmanton was accorded the original incorporation date and all town records dating to 1727.

In 1869, the town warrant contained a petitioned article to change the town's name to Belmont. After being approved by the voters, the legislature approved the name change, which became effective on July 5, 1869. At first, naming the town for August Belmont, a man who had no connection to the town and never set foot in it, is hard to comprehend. Since politically the town was predominantly controlled by Democrats and August Belmont had been prominent in the party, it would have been a popular choice for them; however, the petition was authored by the town's leading Republicans who would not normally be expected to support the choice. The only probable explanation is that, although a Democrat, Belmont had been an ardent supporter of Lincoln's efforts to preserve the Union and had the Republicans' admiration. Thus the choice was popular with most all residents.

Throughout the 19th and early 20th centuries, activities of the inhabitants of the town were mostly centered around either the family farms or the mill. One little-documented activity for the farms was to take in summer boarders. Many farms with spare rooms would rent them to people living in cities so that at least the wife and children could spend a part of the summer in the country. In the village area, life centered more around the mill, which in addition to representing long hours of work provided the workers with contacts that resulted in many community activities such as establishment of the Grange, a Knights of Pythias lodge, the town band, community minstrel shows, and undoubtedly many other now-forgotten activities. The mill provided a source of cash income to many farmers' wives, which allowed families to purchase items they would never be able to purchase with the little cash that the farms generated. A significant event for the village area was the coming of the railroad in 1889. This spur ran from the main rail line in Tilton across the Winnipesaukee River into Belmont at present-day Gardner's Grove, then generally following the Tioga River to Belmont Village. In the late 1800s, the area with rail access nearest to Silver Lake originally known as Sawyer's Cove and later called Gardner's Grove developed into a summer resort having a considerable number of cottages and, depending on the time period, a bowling alley, roller-skating rink, and restaurant.

Throughout the late 19th and early 20th centuries, the town's population remained nearly constant at around 1,400 with any population growth offset with the outward migration of family members to cities or to the Midwest and West Coast. By the 1950s, significant changes took place as farming diminished and farm families sought jobs in industry outside the town. In August 1955, Belmont Hosiery Company ceased operation, and a year later, all assets were auctioned. Fenwick Hosiery Mills occupied the property until 1970 when it also closed its doors. Thus ended 135 years of textile manufacture in Belmont. The town was evolving into a bedroom community for a much more mobile population. As farms were abandoned, many were seen as opportunities for subdivision and profit. A population that had remained relatively stable for over a century began to rise, a pattern that continues to this day. With a current population approaching 8,000, the town is met with new challenges.

Sections of Belmont today continue to carry the traditional names that evolved during the 19th century, namely Belmont Village, Winnisquam (WI-nis-kwawm), Province Road, Jamestown, Gardner's Grove, and Farrarville. In recent years, the area from Mosquito Bridge on Lake Winnisquam to the Laconia line has evolved into the town's largest commercial area, and many country roads now host subdivisions where once the family farm existed.

Once abundantly available, postcards represent a valuable source of photographic material, the collection of which creates an interesting and rewarding hobby. Collectors are continually motivated to find the previously unseen card for their collections. In this volume an attempt has been made to present a photographic history of Belmont as it once was and as it evolved. There are obviously many gaps where no photographic record has been found, but a wholehearted attempt has been made to recapture Belmont's history.

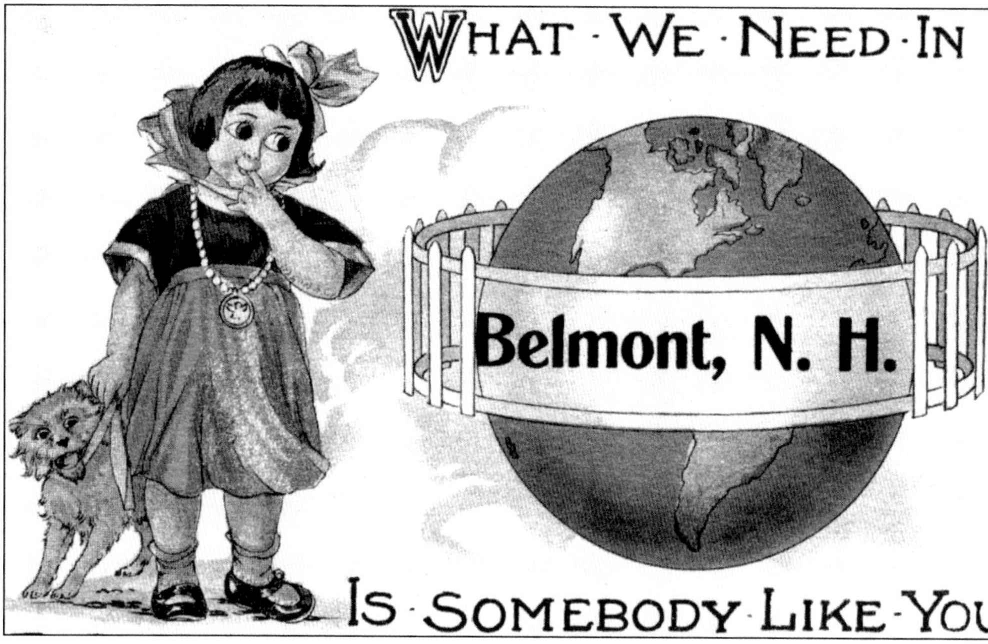

This *c.* 1913 postcard invites people from all over to come stay in Belmont, offering a special place for vacationers, loved ones, friends, and family. Many used these postcards to drop a note to someone, rather than writing a letter of any substantial length.

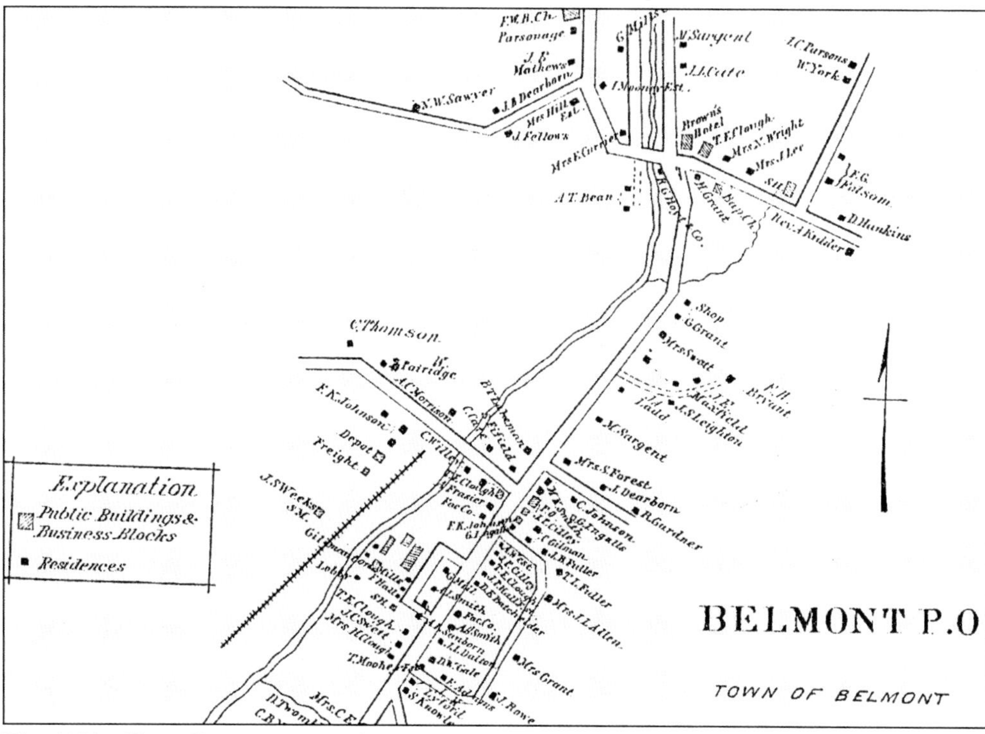

The 1892 village district map can be seen here, showing the number of inhabitants in the area at the time. Notice how Main Street turns to the left at this time and does not continue straight toward today's North Main Street.

One

WATERS AND BRIDGES

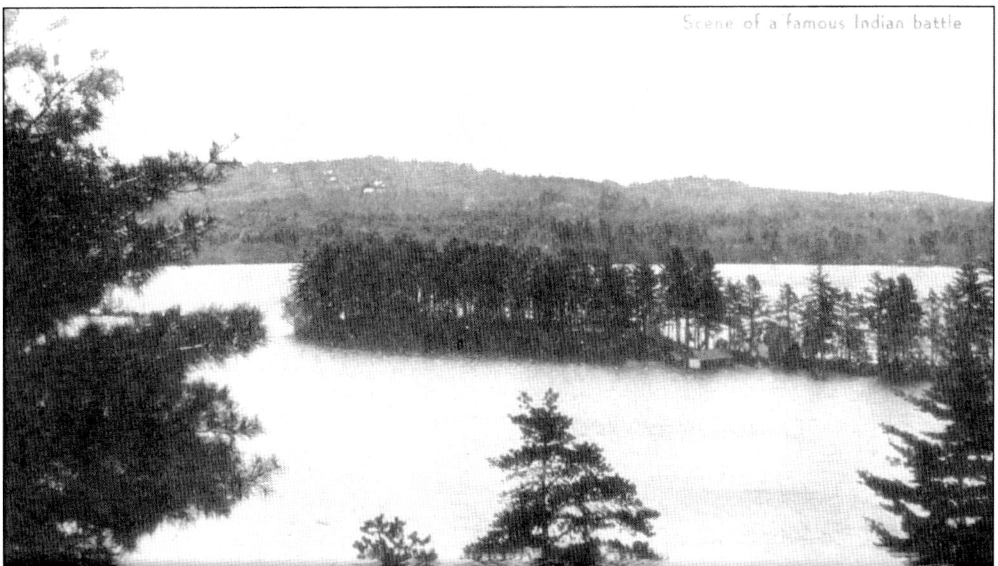

The western edge of what is now Belmont at the Winnipesaukee (Winnipisogee) River, or Great Bay, contains the site of a famous Native American battle (1676–1677). The Mohawks, known to be a formidable warlike tribe, inhabiting the borders of the Hudson River in New York were influenced by New Hampshire governor Edward Cranfield to commence a war of extermination upon the eastern Native Americans. Therefore, the Pequawkets, a group inhabiting this region, formed an alliance with the Penacooks in order to defend themselves against an unexpected invasion. The Pequawkets, a much larger group since the alliance, were attacked by surprise and driven upon a point of land in the Great Bay upon the Gilmanton shore (now Belmont). They became overpowered by the superior force of Mohawks, and their strategy was used to decoy the Pequawkets (simulating a retreat point) and brought them to victory. The place where this battle was fought is known today as Mohawk Point or Mohawk Island. In 1788, roads were constructed from Mohawk Point, up Ladd Hill, across to Mile Hill, and up Plummer Hill.

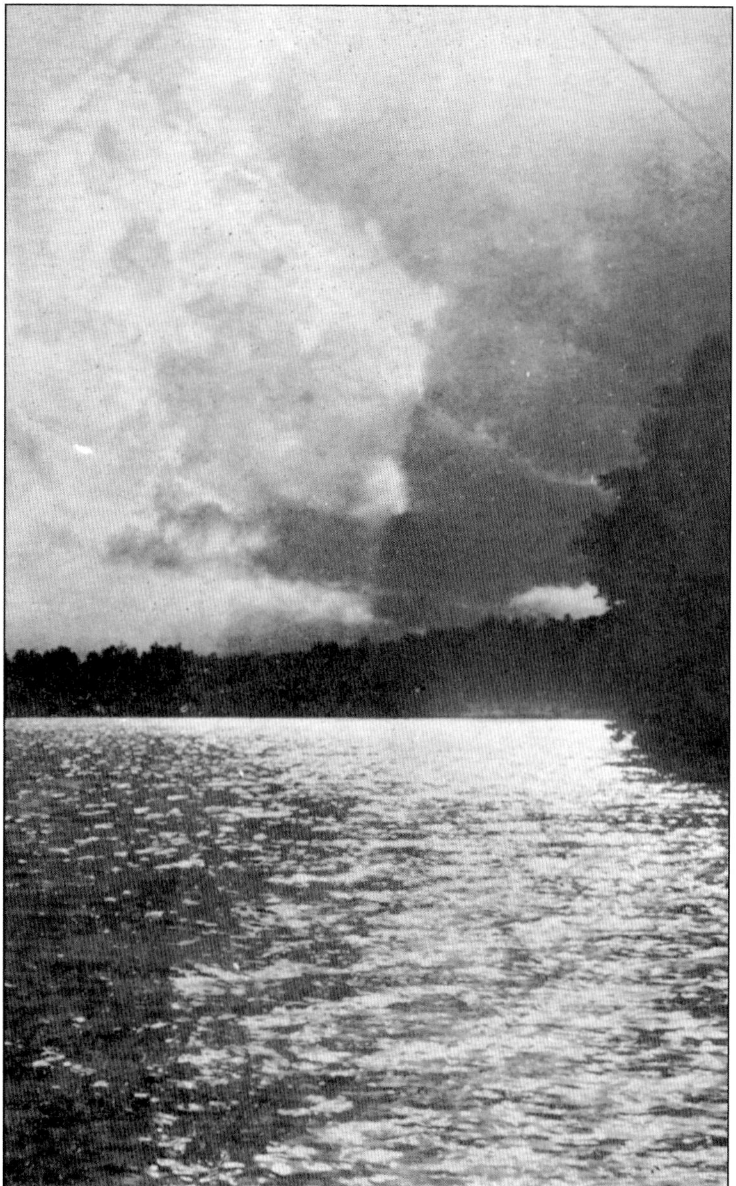

Sunset, Winnipesaukee River, Belmont, N. H.

From the dam at the outlet of Lake Winnipesaukee in the Lakeport section of Laconia, the river almost immediately enters Opechee Bay. One mile down the lake, the river exits over a dam and drops through the center of Laconia, its banks lined by industrial buildings from the 19th century originally constructed to take advantage of the river's power. The one-mile section through Laconia ends at Lake Winnisquam, the third-largest lake in New Hampshire after Winnipesaukee and Squam Lake. A five-mile stretch across Winnisquam leads to the Lochmere Dam at the lake's outlet and a short descent to Silver Lake (formerly known as Little Bay). At the natural outlet of Silver Lake, on the boundary between Belmont and Tilton, the river passes through the center of two towns, Tilton and Northfield. It then descends through a narrow valley to Franklin, dropping up to 90 feet per mile on its journey. Downstream from the center of Franklin, it joins the Pemigewasset River and forms into the Merrimack River.

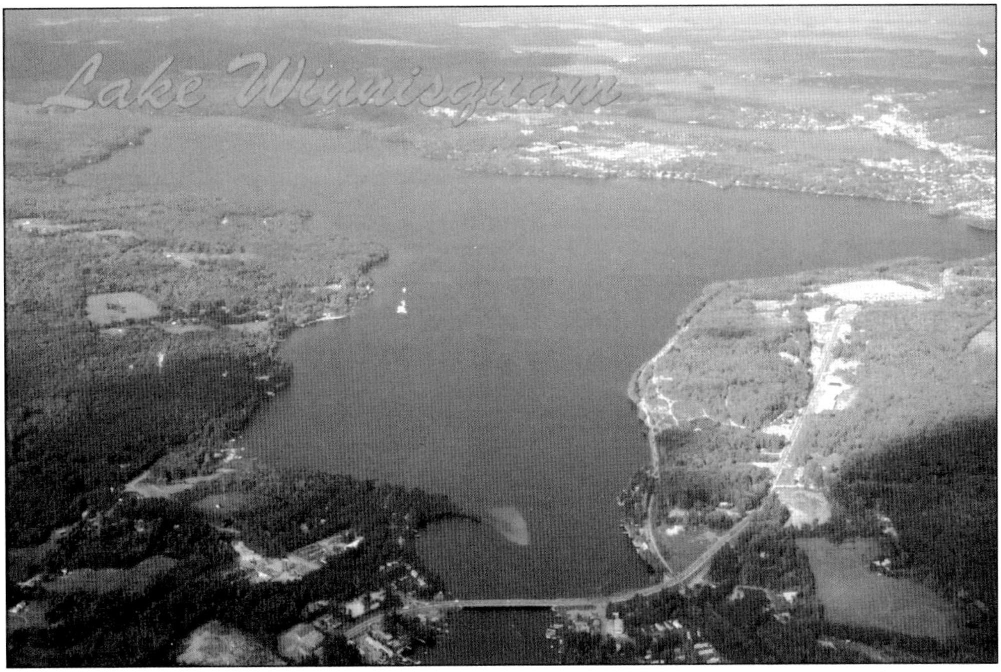

Lake Winnisquam originally had been known as the Winnipisogee Lake. It consists of 4,264 acres and borders the communities of Sanbornton, Belmont, Laconia, and Meredith. It is fed primarily by the outlet from Lake Winnipesaukee, and Winnisquam's outlet is the Winnipesaukee River, previously known as the Winnipisogee River or Great Bay, flowing through the towns of Tilton and Northfield into Franklin where it joins with the Pemigewasset River to form the Merrimack River. It is the third-largest lake in New Hampshire, with its shores hosting numerous seasonal visitors. Early Native Americans often fished here, as did the early settlers in this region.

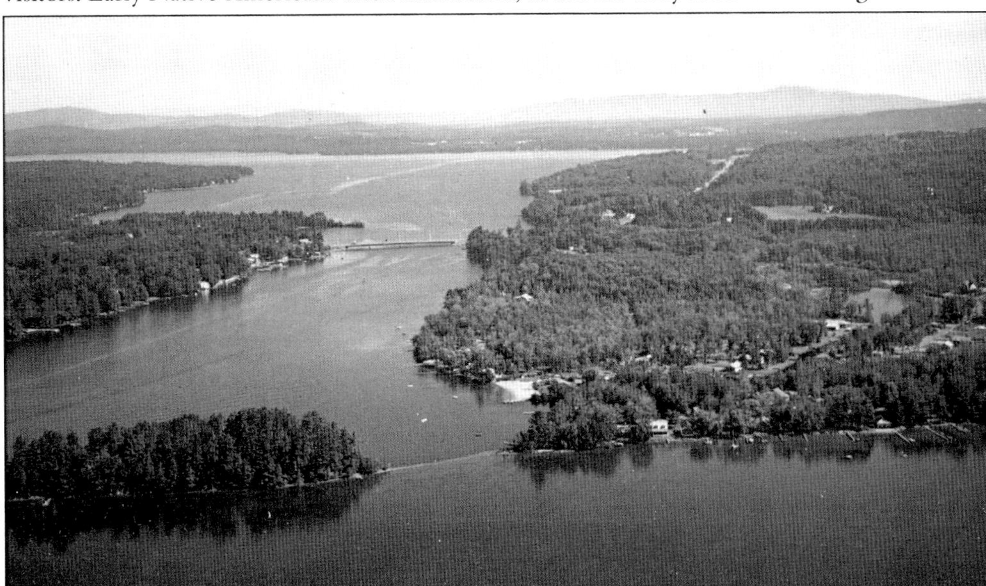

Aerial View of Lake Winnisquam, N.H.

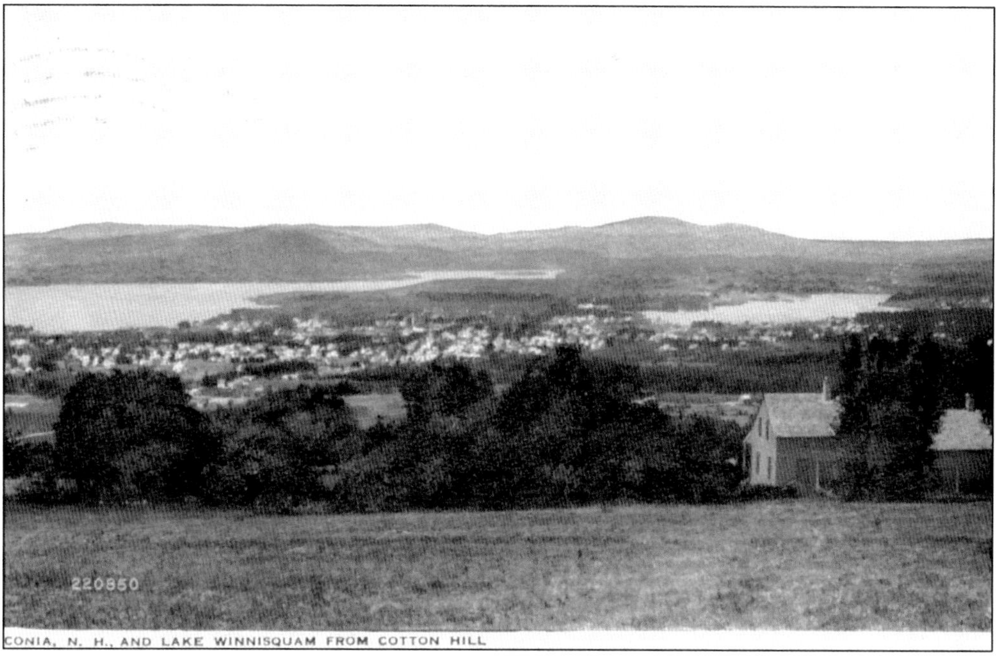

This postcard from 1919 shows the view from the top of Cotton Hill in Belmont. The home to the right still stands today in the town of Gilford, and to the middle of the postcard the city of Laconia can be seen. Cotton Hill Road was one of the early passageways to Gilford Village.

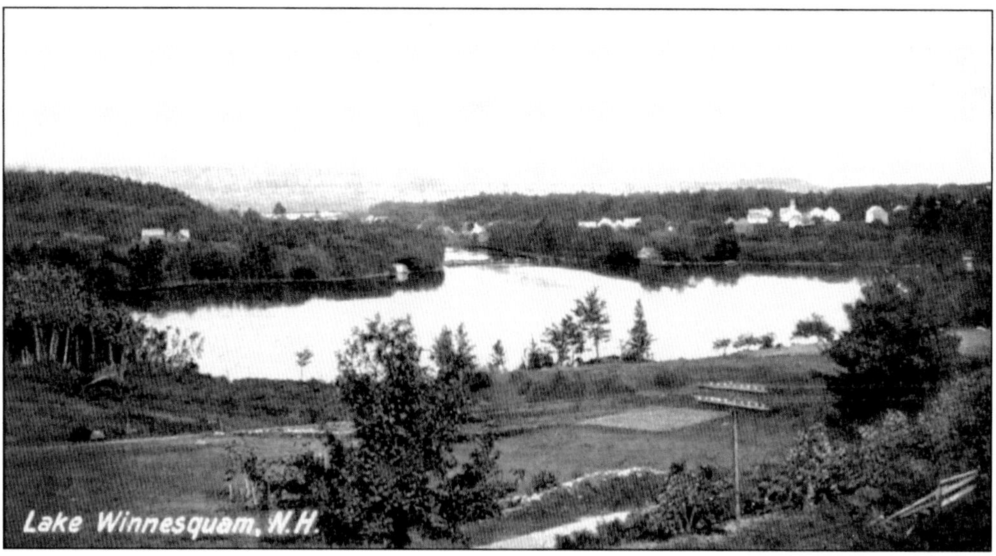

Lake Winnisquam is located in Belknap County in central New Hampshire and is bordered by the city of Laconia and town of Belmont on the east shore, and by Sanbornton and Tilton on the west shore. At the south end of the lake, a short section of the Winnipesaukee River reemerges and then enters Silver Lake, which forms the border between Belmont and Tilton.

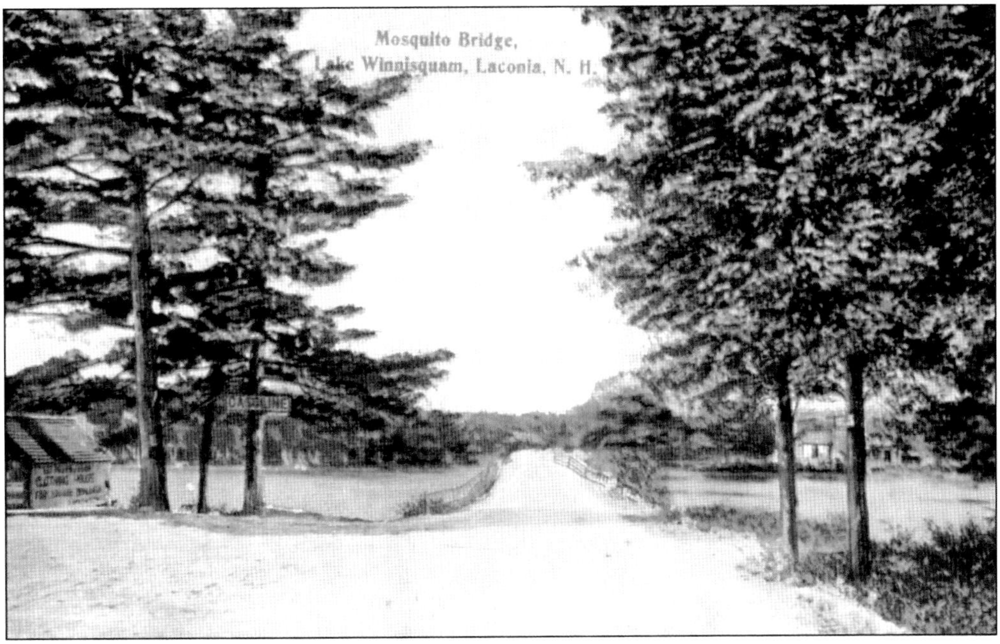

This postcard shows the approach to the Winnisquam Bridge from the Belmont side heading toward the towns of Tilton and Sanbornton. To the left is a small building that was located on the property of John Morrison, who also owned and operated a general store on the site.

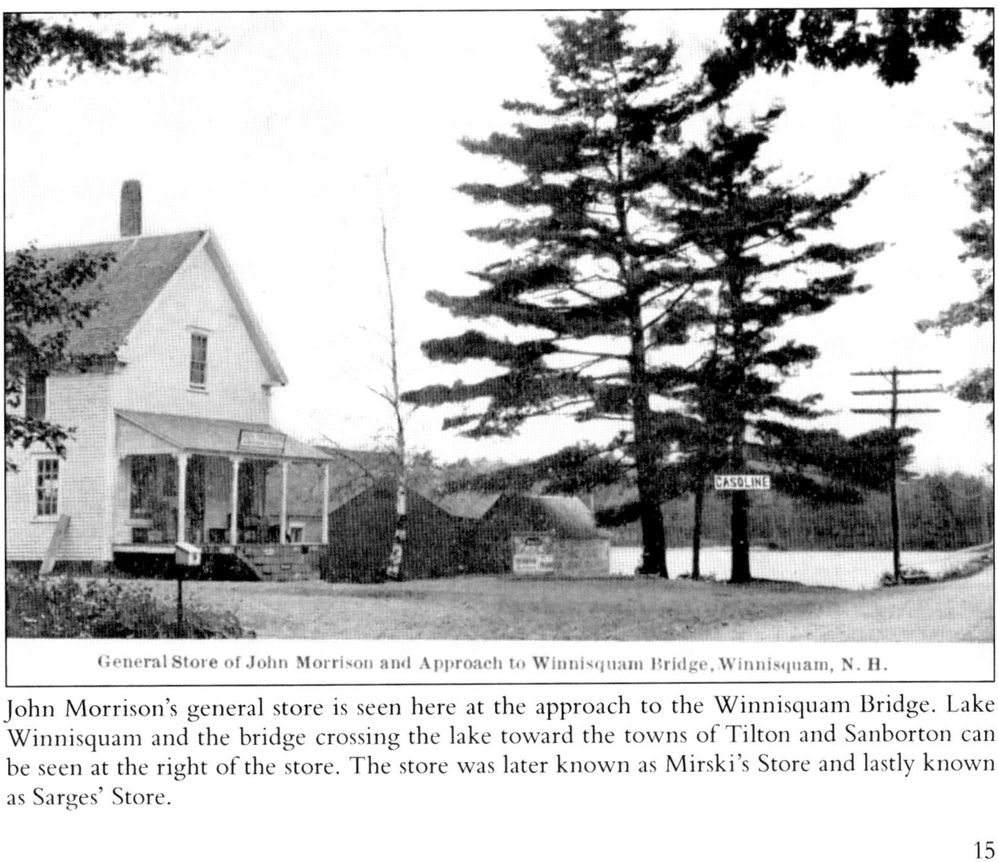

General Store of John Morrison and Approach to Winnisquam Bridge, Winnisquam, N. H.

John Morrison's general store is seen here at the approach to the Winnisquam Bridge. Lake Winnisquam and the bridge crossing the lake toward the towns of Tilton and Sanborton can be seen at the right of the store. The store was later known as Mirski's Store and lastly known as Sarges' Store.

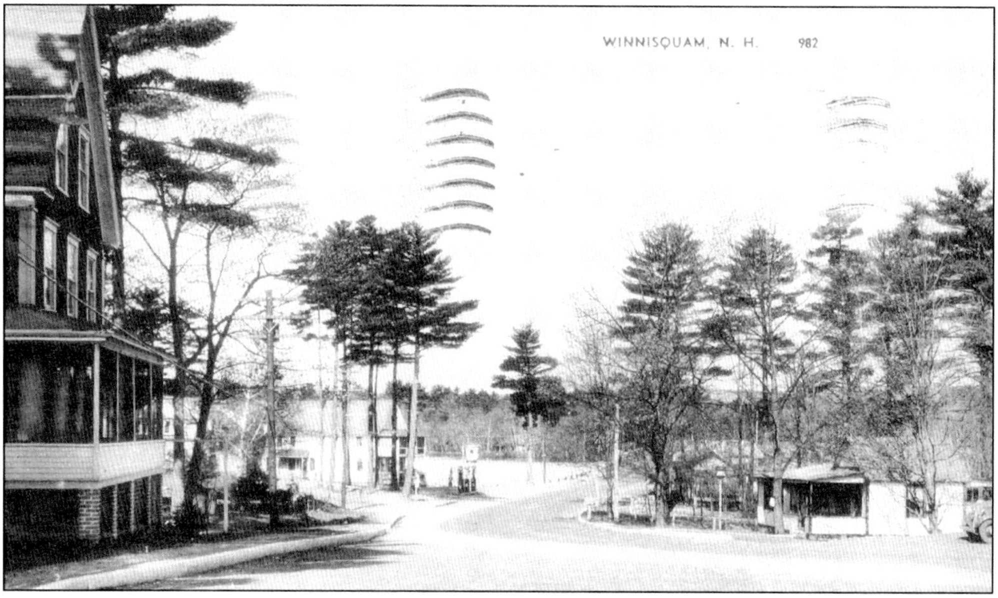

The original bridge was constructed by private enterprise prior to 1840. It was said to have been narrow without railings and that numerous accidents occurred with both horses and people. Both towns located at each end of the bridge claimed no responsibility for the bridge's condition. By law, they were told to replace the bridge with a safer one. This was accomplished between 1840 and 1844. The bridge was close to the water except on the Sanbornton side where a portion rose higher enabling steamboats to pass under. Tilton was created from the southern part of Sanbornton. Both had a considerable amount of controversy over who would get the western end of the bridge and be responsible for its upkeep. This was resolved with Tilton getting title to the bridge although Sanbornton begins immediately west of the bridge. Belmont inherited responsibility for the eastern end in 1859. Belmont and Tilton were responsible for replacing the planks on an annual basis. Both reportedly could not agree on a time to do it; therefore, the bridge was closed twice yearly for maintenance.

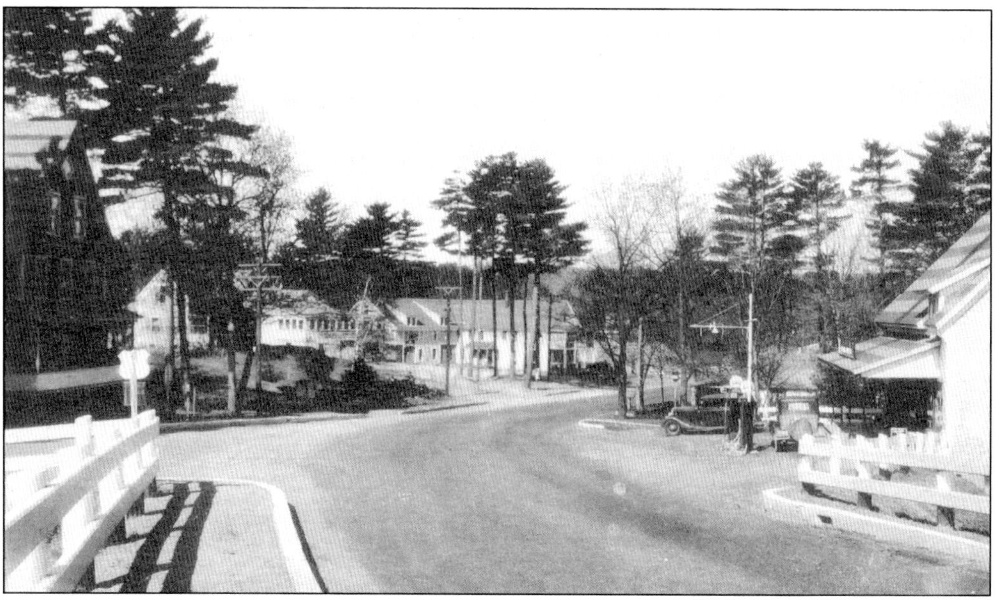

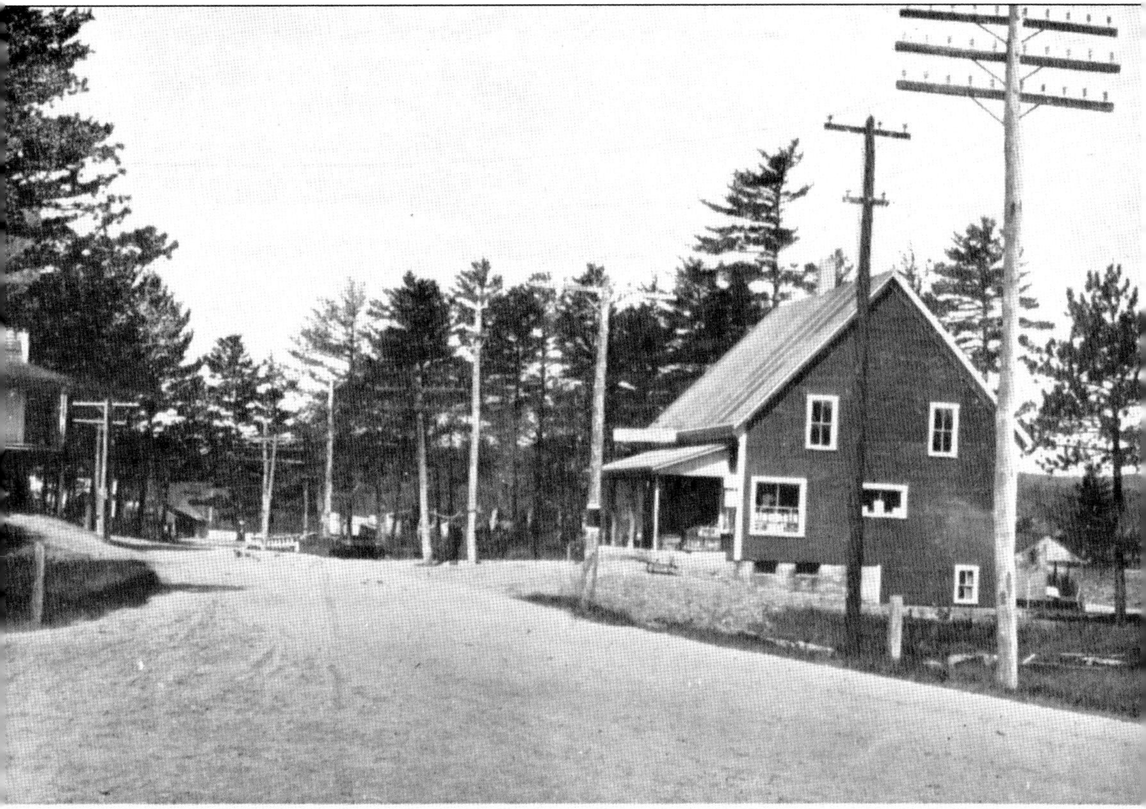

Daniel Webster Highway and General Store of John Morrison, Winnisquam, N. H.

Shown here is John Morrison's post office and general store in Winnisquam on the Sanbornton and Tilton sides of the Mosquito (Winnisquam) Bridge. Lake Winnisquam and the bridge crossing toward Laconia can be seen in the rear of the store. Notice the unpaved street in this early postcard. Previously Morrison's store was on the Belmont side of the bridge, and the store was probably relocated to this site.

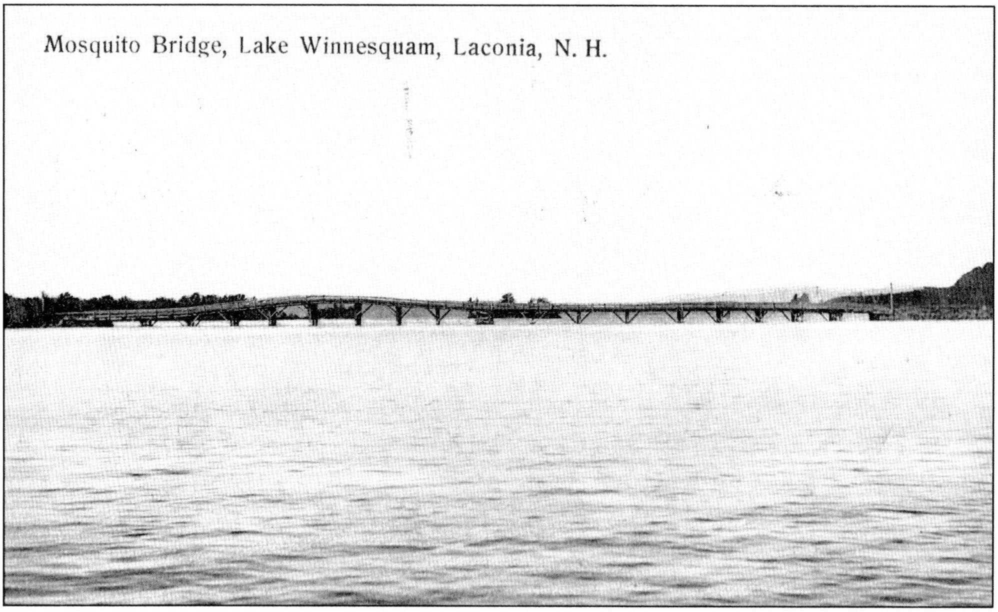

The Mosquito (Bay, New, or Winnisquam) Bridge was first constructed around 1840 by a private enterprise. These images show the second bridge that was constructed between 1840 and 1844. The second structure was wooden, built upon tiles, 36 rods in length, and at an original expense of $2,000.

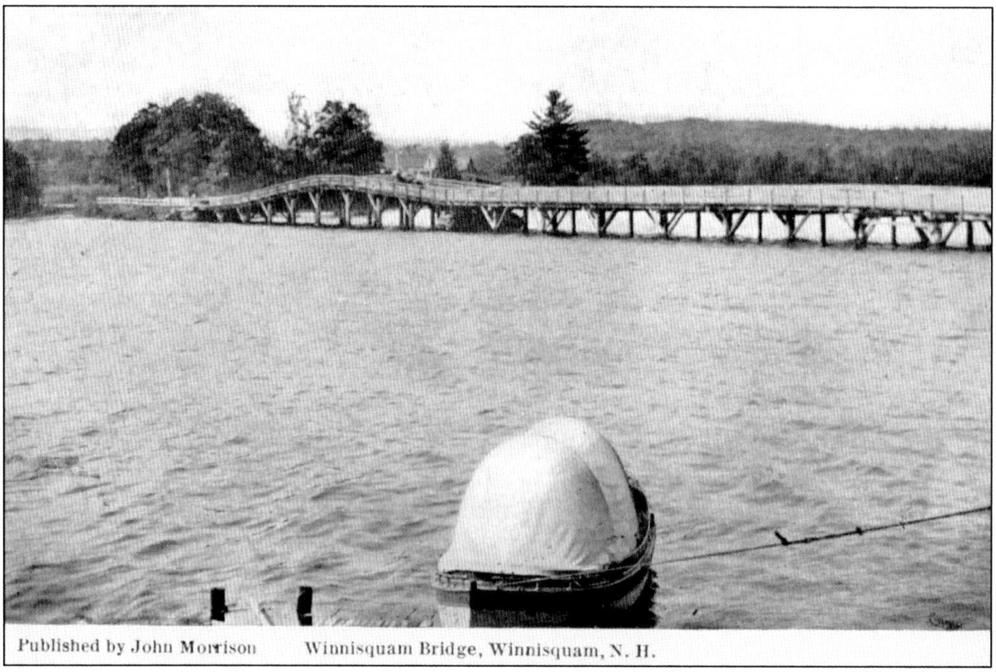

A 1911 newspaper clipping states that Henry Dalton and his wife Sarah lived in East Tilton. Sarah L. Dalton died on June 11, 1911, and was Winnisquam's oldest inhabitant, dying at 87 years. Sixty years before her death, she was the first woman to cross the newly built Winnisquam Bridge. She noticed the hump in the middle, which resembled the back of a mosquito, and called it "Mosquito Bridge." The name has been carried on since.

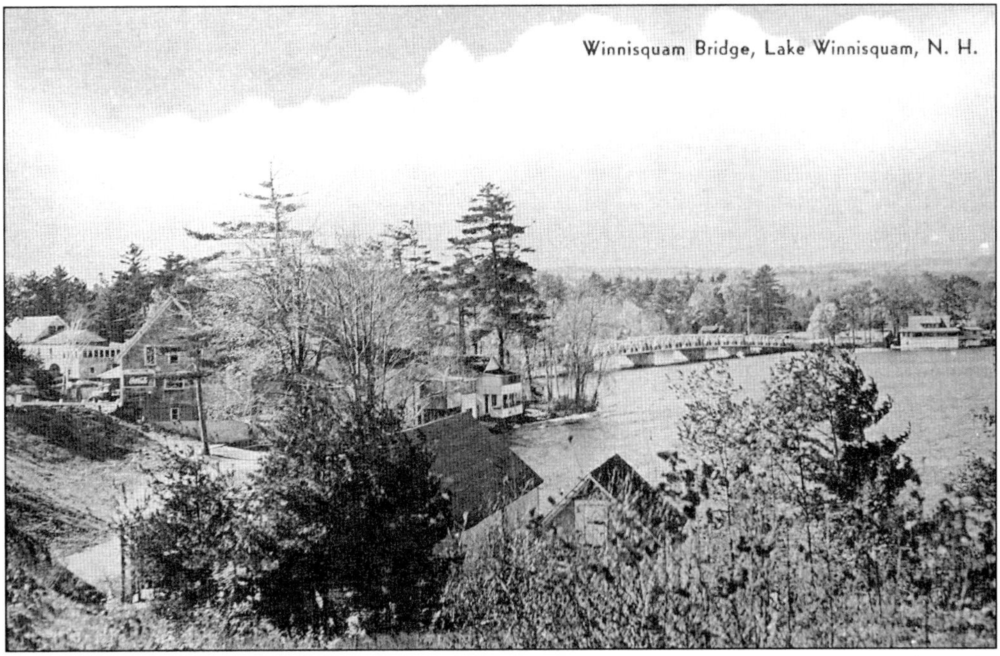

This is an image of the Winnisquam Bridge, also known as the Mosquito Bridge, seen from the shore on the Sanbornton (west) side. Constructed in 1916, this was the first iron structure to exist on the site, the third bridge, and noticeably the hump in the structure, has disappeared. To the right side of each image Sarges' Store can be seen, where for years boats would launch from this area and pull up to this location to get fuel. The store closed in May 2003 after many years of operation. Today the property is currently owned by Winnisquam Marine.

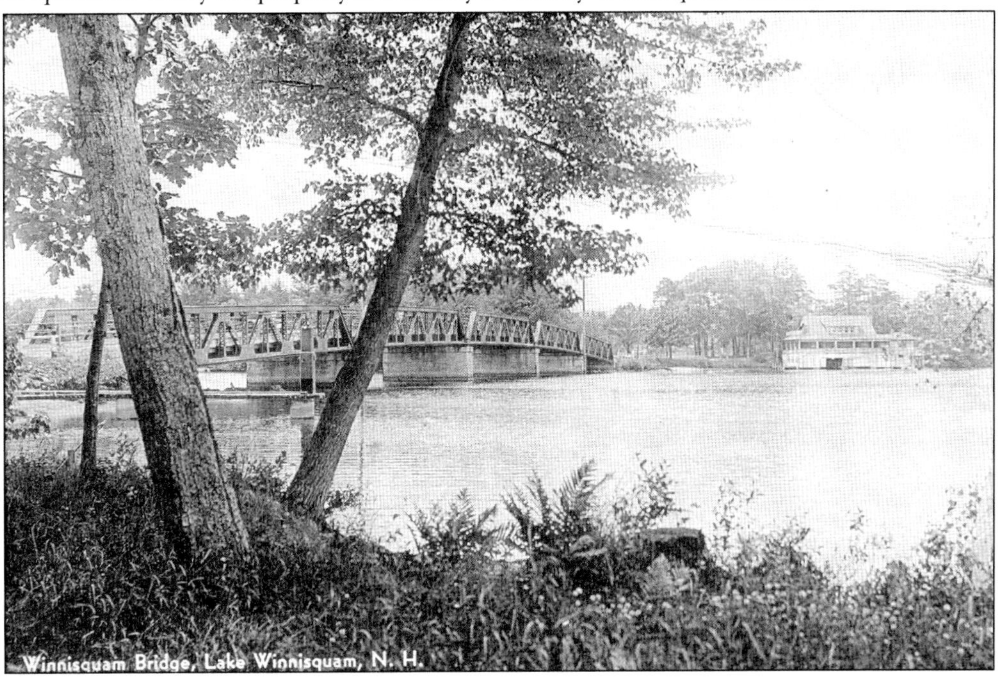

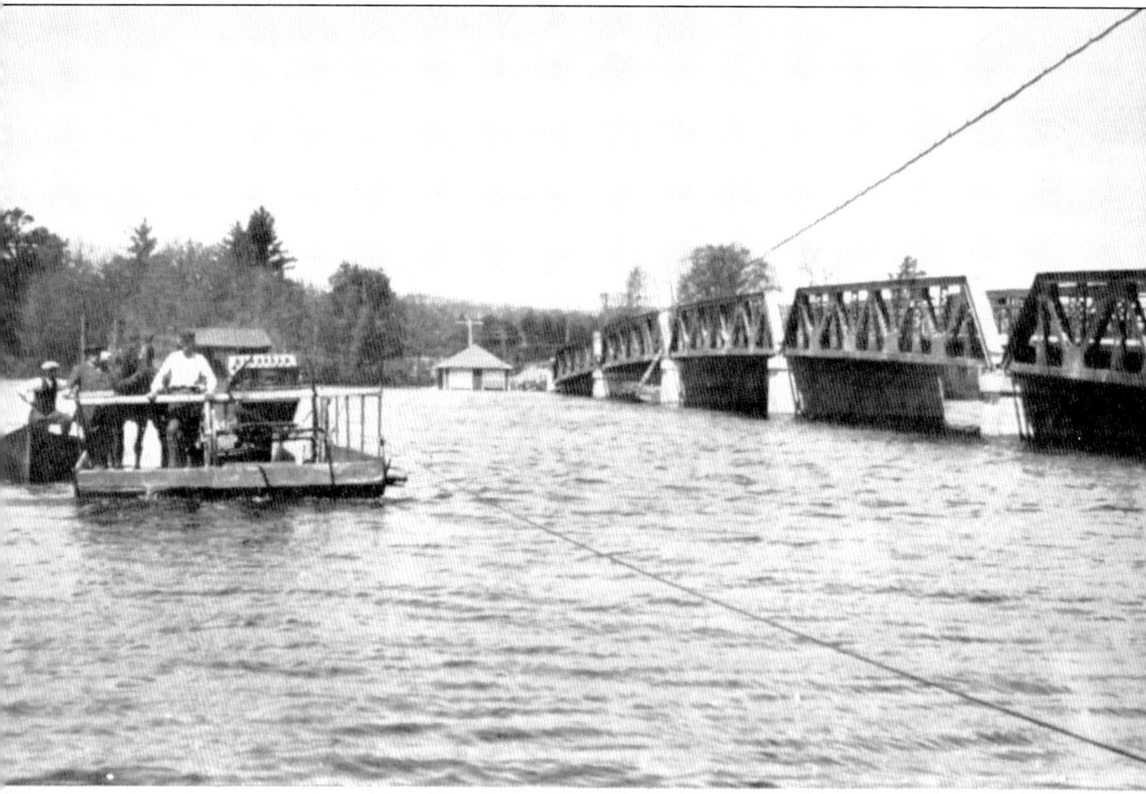

Published by John Morrison The Ferry and Winnisquam Bridge, Winnisquam, N. H.

In the earlier days of the town, there were no bridges across the Winnipesaukee River, so the river had to be crossed by boat. Ferries were run at Mohawk Point, known as Copp's Ferry, and at Union Bridge, known as Gibson's Ferry. Many of the earliest roads constructed led to Copp's Ferry. This postcard shows a ferry possibly being used in the process of constructing the 1916 bridge.

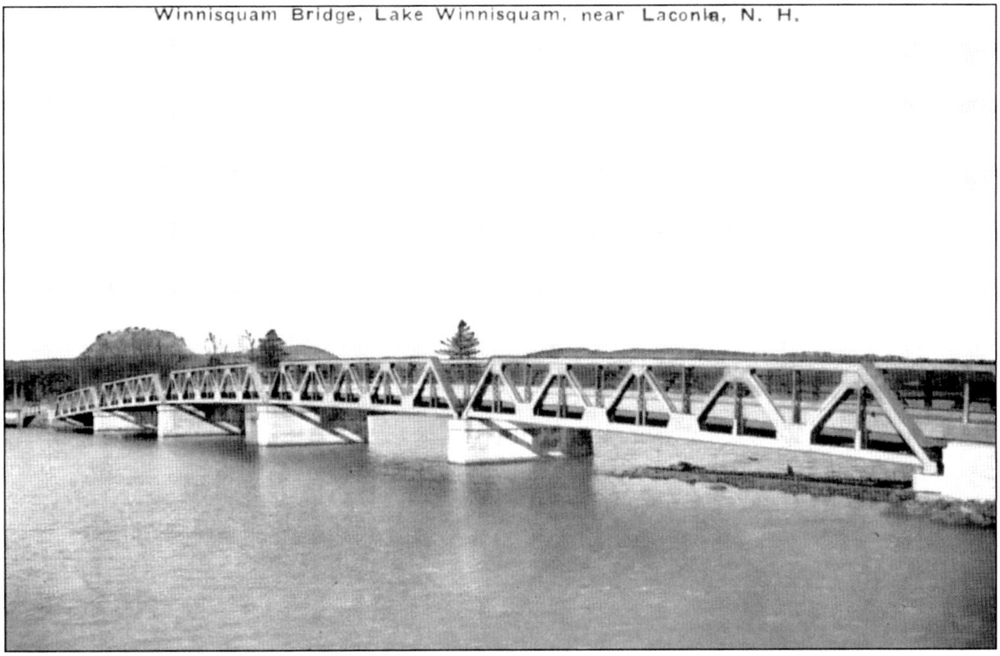

It was reported in 1840 that a series of accidents occurred at the Winnisquam (Bay) Bridge, which had been first built by a private enterprise. It was too narrow, without railing, and otherwise insecure. Several horses were drowned by shying or backing into the bay, and one or two persons had perished during the tragic events.

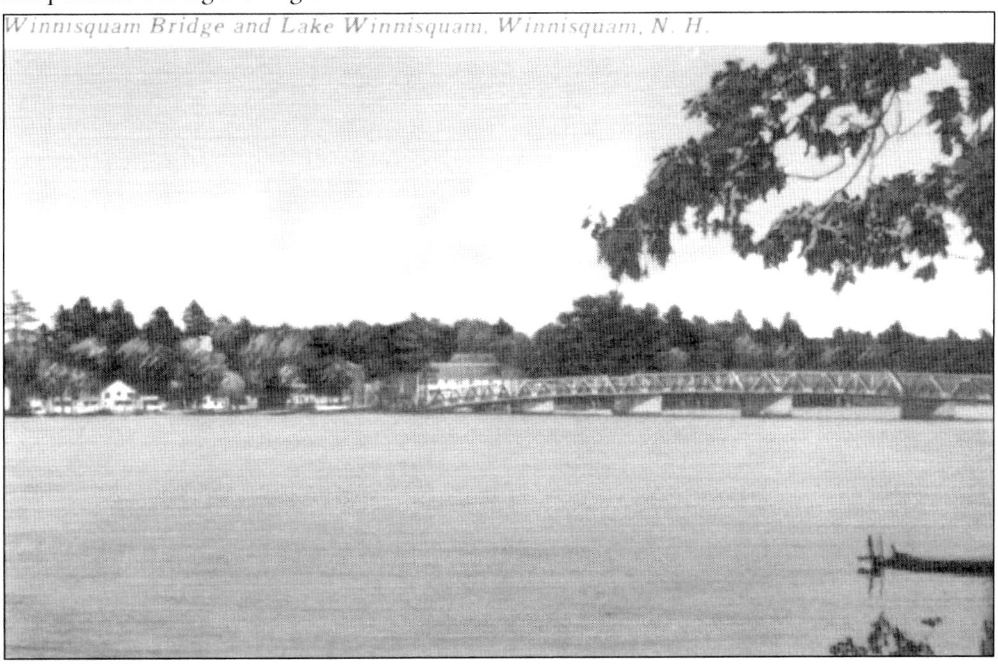

In the early years of the Winnisquam Bridge, it became a notoriously dangerous place for travelers, and the towns surrounding the bridge were denying any responsibility for the unsafe conditions of the bridge. Finally they were obligated by state law to put the bridge in safe condition by rebuilding it.

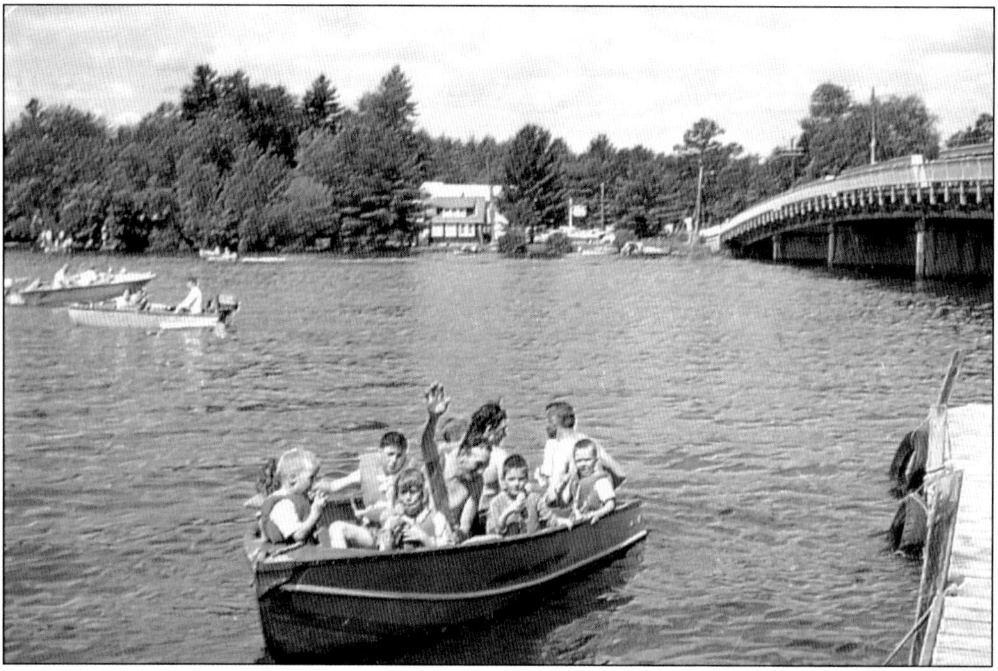

Before the building of the Mosquito Bridge, the area had frequent accidents. Most of the communication between Sanbornton and the Meredith Bridge occurred by boats in the summer months and by crossing ice in the winter months. The freezing up of the bay was quite an important event each year, and often people ventured out on the ice too soon, or before it had sufficiently froze strong enough to be safe.

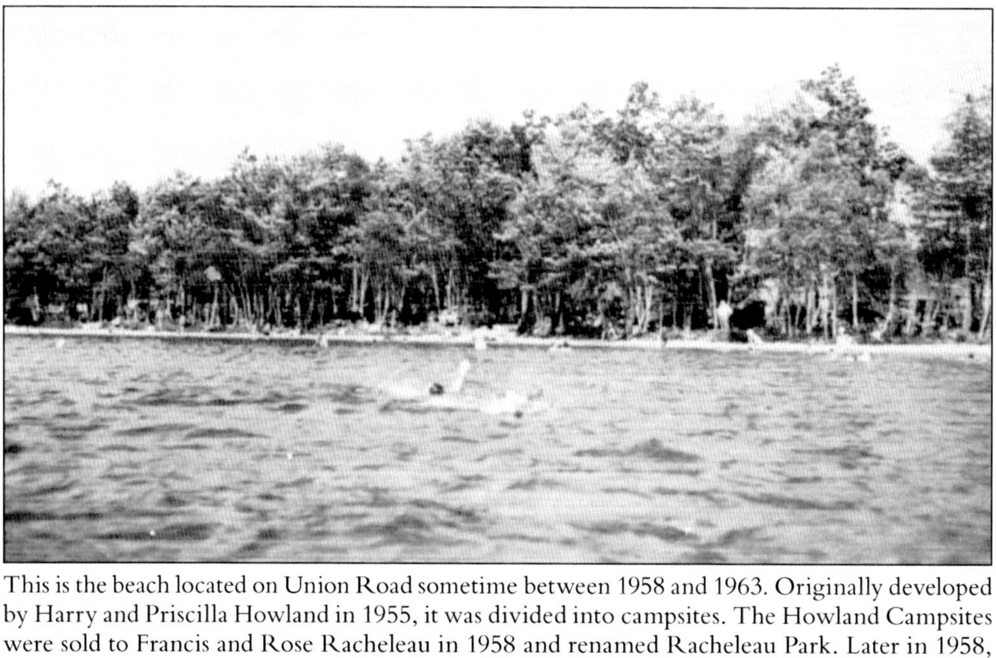

This is the beach located on Union Road sometime between 1958 and 1963. Originally developed by Harry and Priscilla Howland in 1955, it was divided into campsites. The Howland Campsites were sold to Francis and Rose Racheleau in 1958 and renamed Racheleau Park. Later in 1958, Gerald Hickox changed the name to Sandy Beach. Since 1987, the property has been owned by Mallard's Landing, a private association of mobile homes with beach rights.

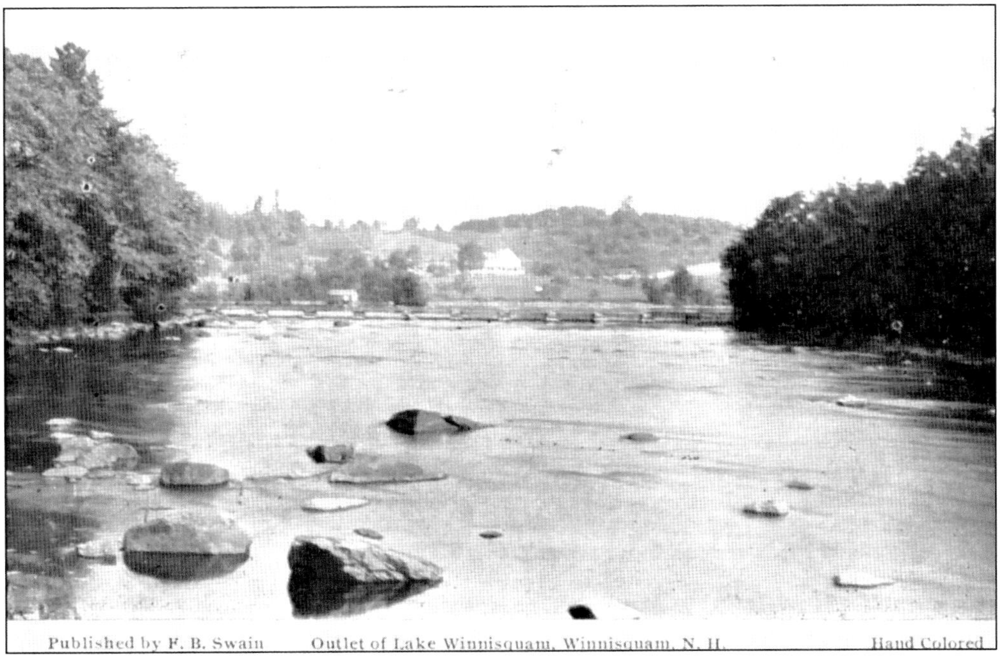

The Winnipesaukee River stretches five miles across Lake Winnisquam leading to the Lochmere Dam at the lake's outlet and a short descent to Silver Lake (formerly known as Little Bay). The river descends at the natural outlet of Silver Lake, on the boundary between Belmont and Tilton. The river passes through the center of Tilton and Northfield, finally descending through a narrow valley into Franklin. Pickerel, shad, perch, trout, and salmon have been caught here.

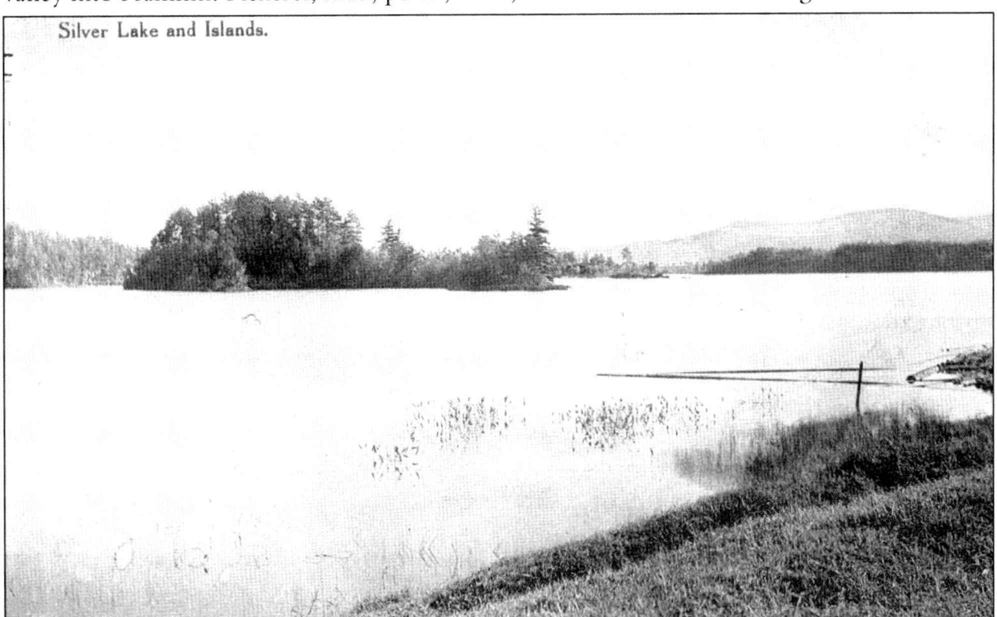

Silver Lake in its early days was known as Little Bay or Lower Bay, and the island once called Atkinson's Island presumably was named after D. C. Atkinson, who built a three-story mansion near the islands in 1809. He graduated from Dartmouth College in 1806 and studied law with the Honorable Daniel Webster. His first law office was opened in the town of Sanbornton.

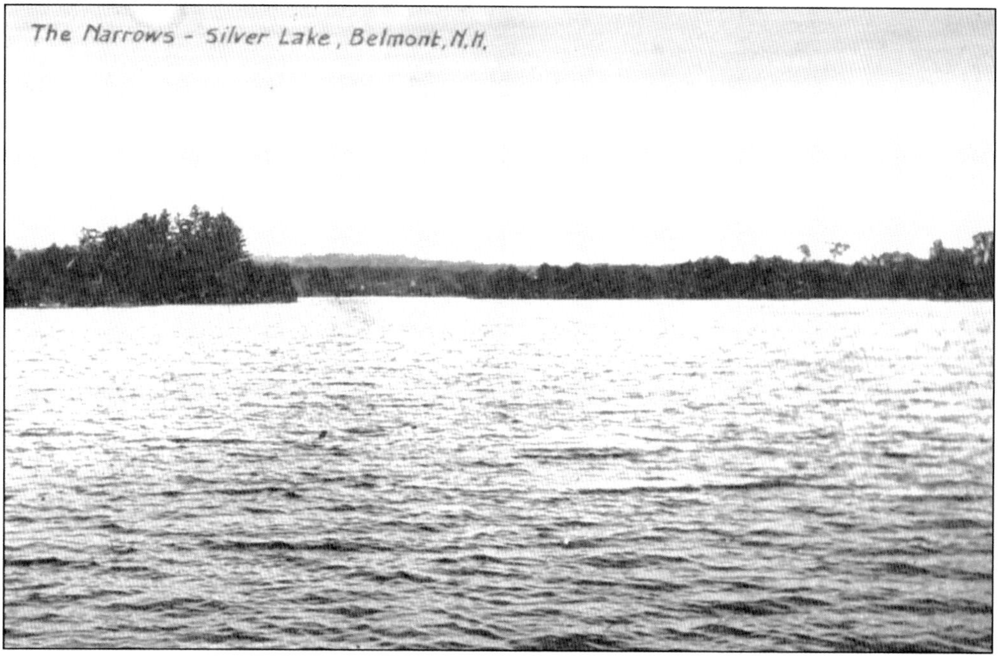

Silver Lake, or Little Bay, in the 1800s was a great resort for fishing pickerel, and one of the largest known to have been caught through the ice was by David T. W. Clark, at the age of nine years in 1859. It weighed six pounds and six ounces.

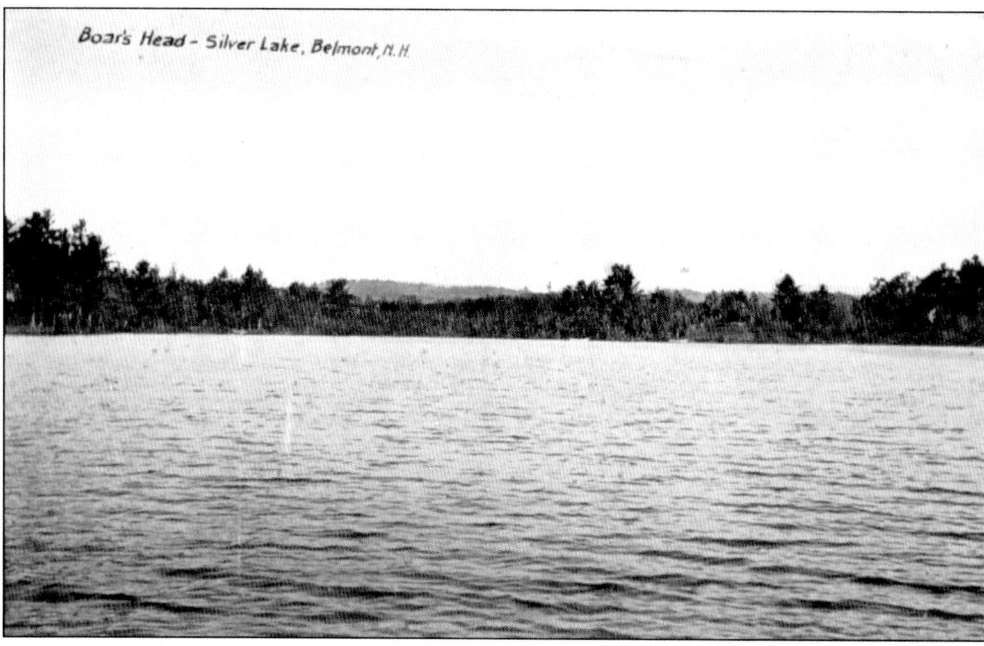

David T. W. Clark was later known to have invented a fishing reel to be used over holes in the ice, which indicated with unfailing accuracy, to one at a distance, when a fish bit the hook. The Clark brothers, David and Alonzo, were known as the head fishermen on the bays, and they kept extremely detailed records of their catch over the years.

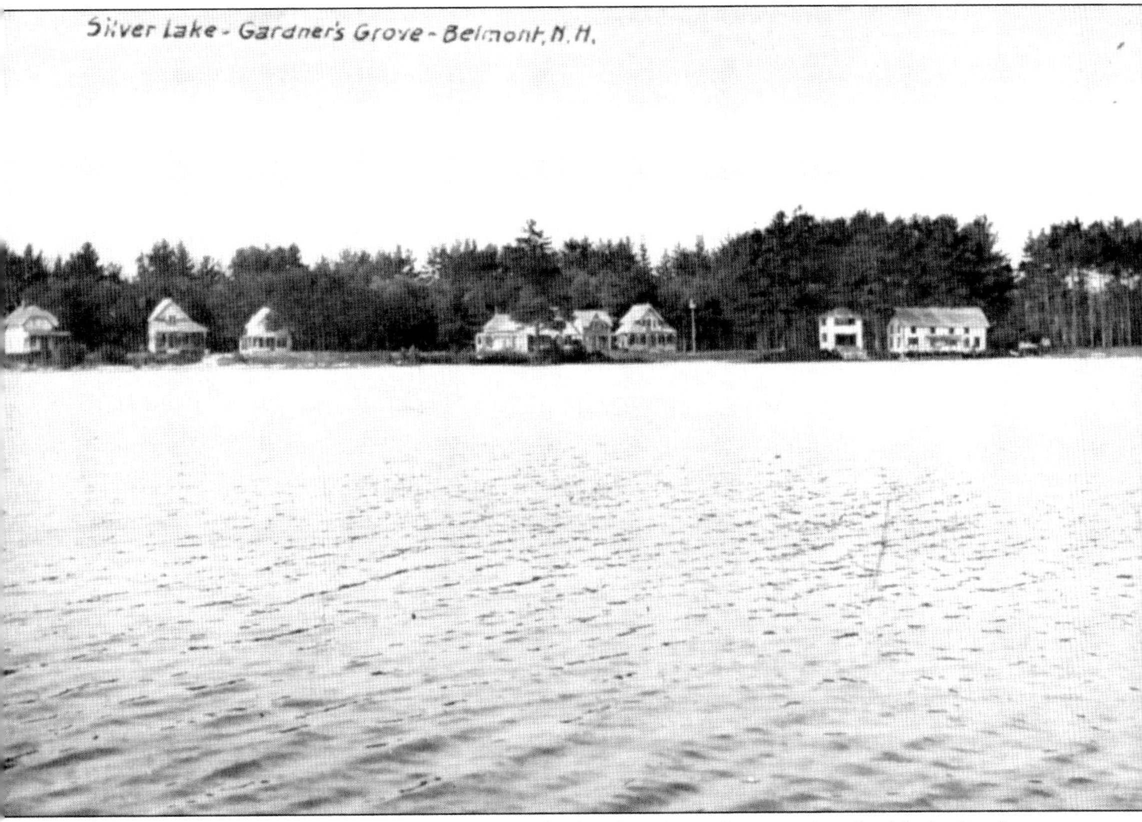

Silver Lake is located just below the canal and hydroelectric station associated with the Lochmere Dam in Belmont. The water level and flow constraints of Silver Lake are a combination of the natural outlet of Silver Lake and the flat marshy expanse at the junction of the Tioga and Winnipesaukee Rivers.

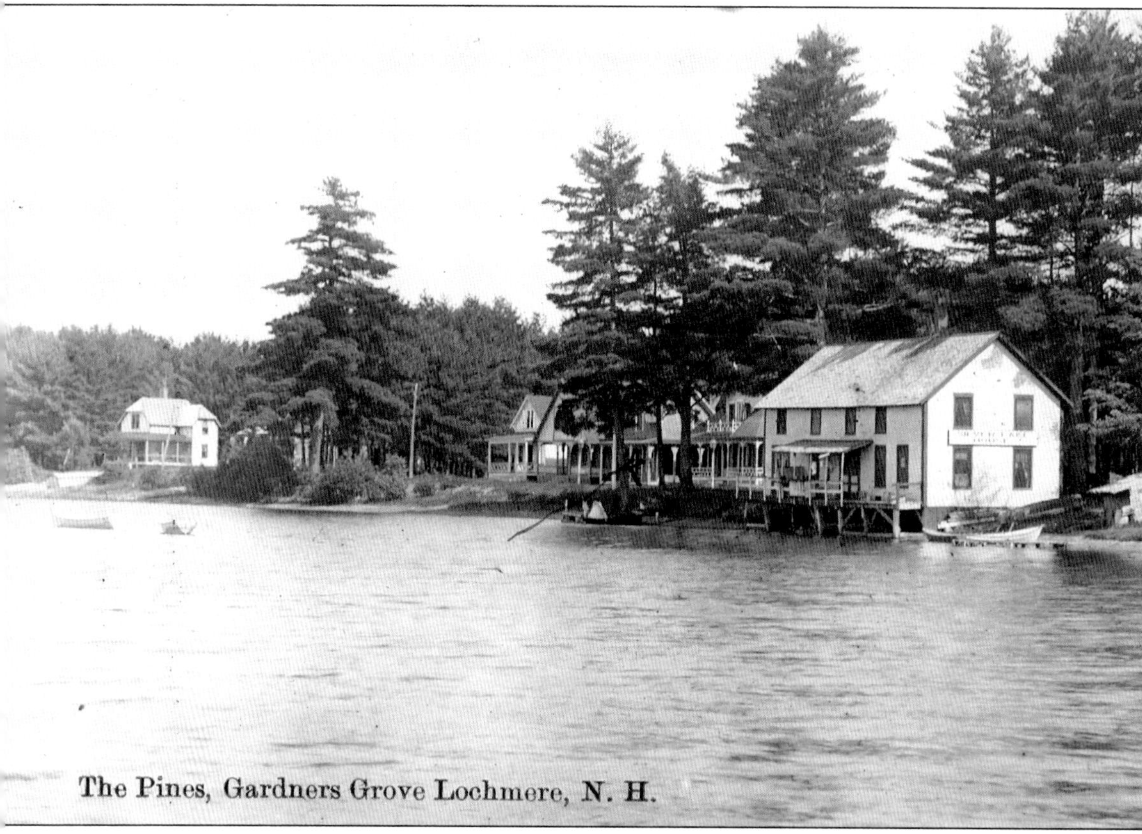

Both the Tioga and Winnipesaukee Rivers act to slow the movement of runoff through Silver Lake. When water flows into this part of the watershed, the level of water increases, either as a result of increased discharge at the Lochmere Dam or the uncontrolled runoff from the Tioga River basin. In order for the additional water flow to pass the level of Silver Lake it must increase.

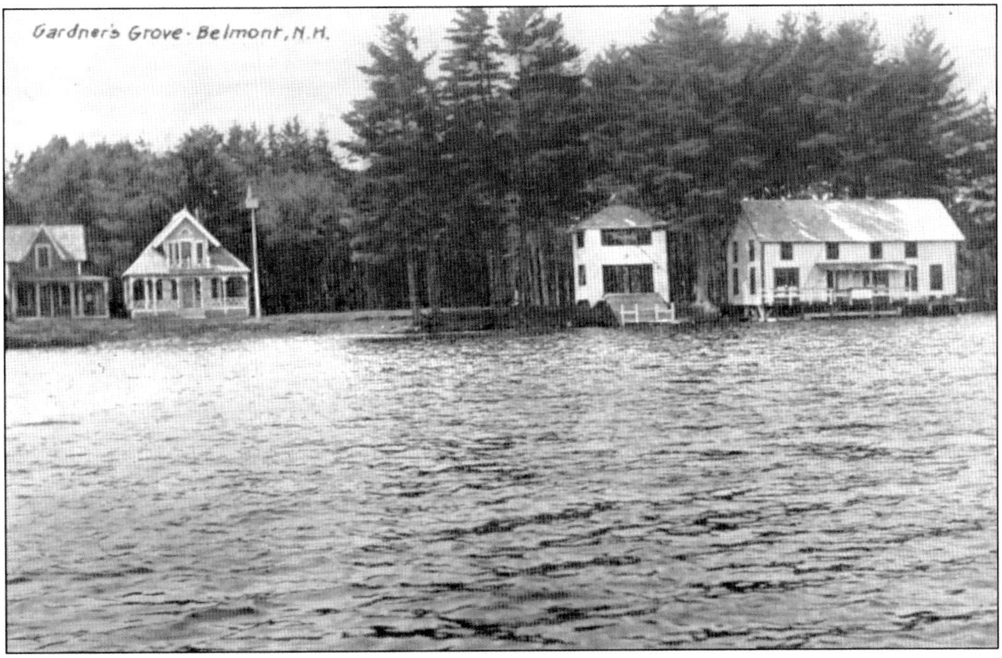

Gardner's Grove, as seen from Silver Lake, was originally called Sawyer's Cove. The buildings to the right show the two-story bandstand and a restaurant known as the Chowder House. This area was used over the years as a vacationing spot. On the left of the postcard, one can see the beginning of the cottage rows that line the banks of the lake even today.

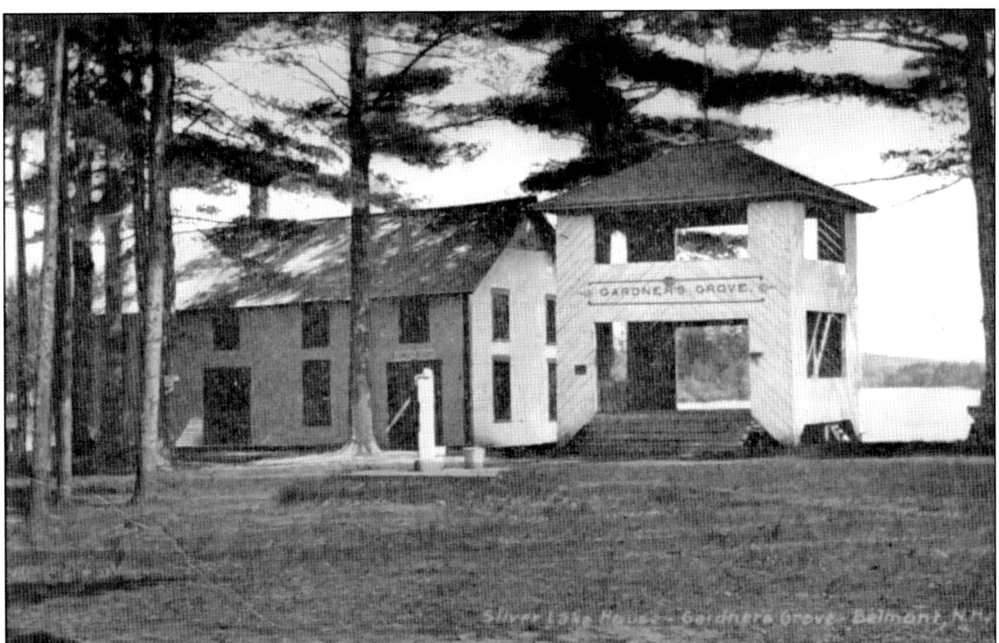

Due to confusion with post office delivery, and with the length of the town's name, in 1869, the citizens of Upper Gilmanton petitioned the legislature to have the name of the town changed to Belmont. The bill passed, and the rechristening of the town was celebrated by having a picnic in Gardner's Grove on July 5, 1869, the day when the act went into effect.

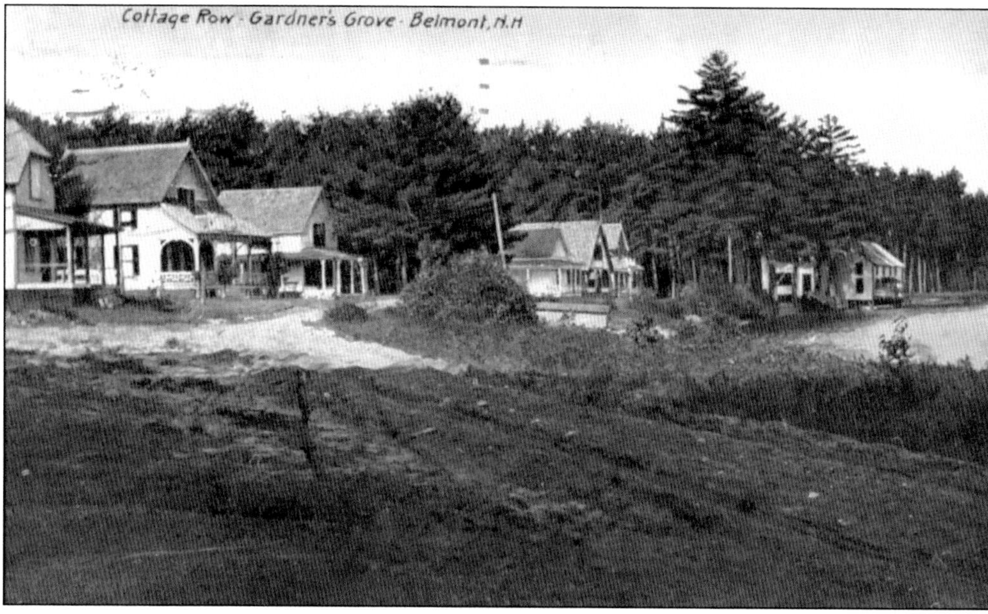

In 1889, the spur rail line to Belmont Village, which crossed the Winnipesaukee River into Belmont near Gardner's Grove, formerly Sawyer's Cove, was completed. This area developed into a summer resort having a considerable number of cottages and, depending on the time period, a bowling alley, roller-skating rink, and eatery.

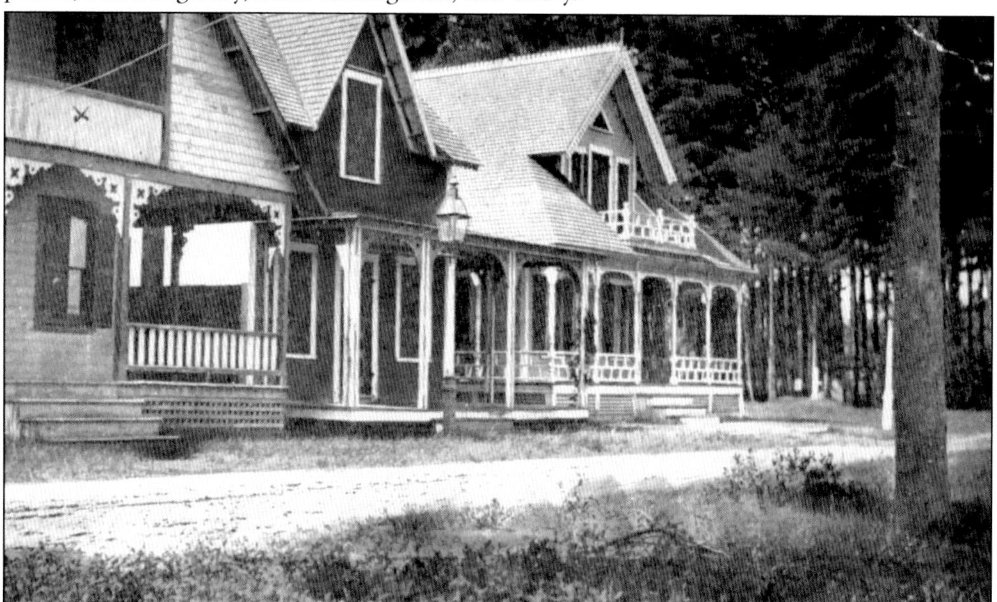

Harry Gardner and Dexter Webster were two neighbors living on Silver Lake Avenue at Gardner's Grove, and neither could bear the other. Webster owned land at the far end of the grove, which he could only get to by crossing Gardner's land. Since he could not obtain permission from Gardner to do so, his only recourse was to use a boat along the shoreline. Both ended their lives violently. Webster was reportedly pushed down the cellar stairs by his housekeeper, and Gardner hung himself on a door casing. Later Gardner's wife hung herself on a bedpost, and their son Fred hung himself in Webster's barn.

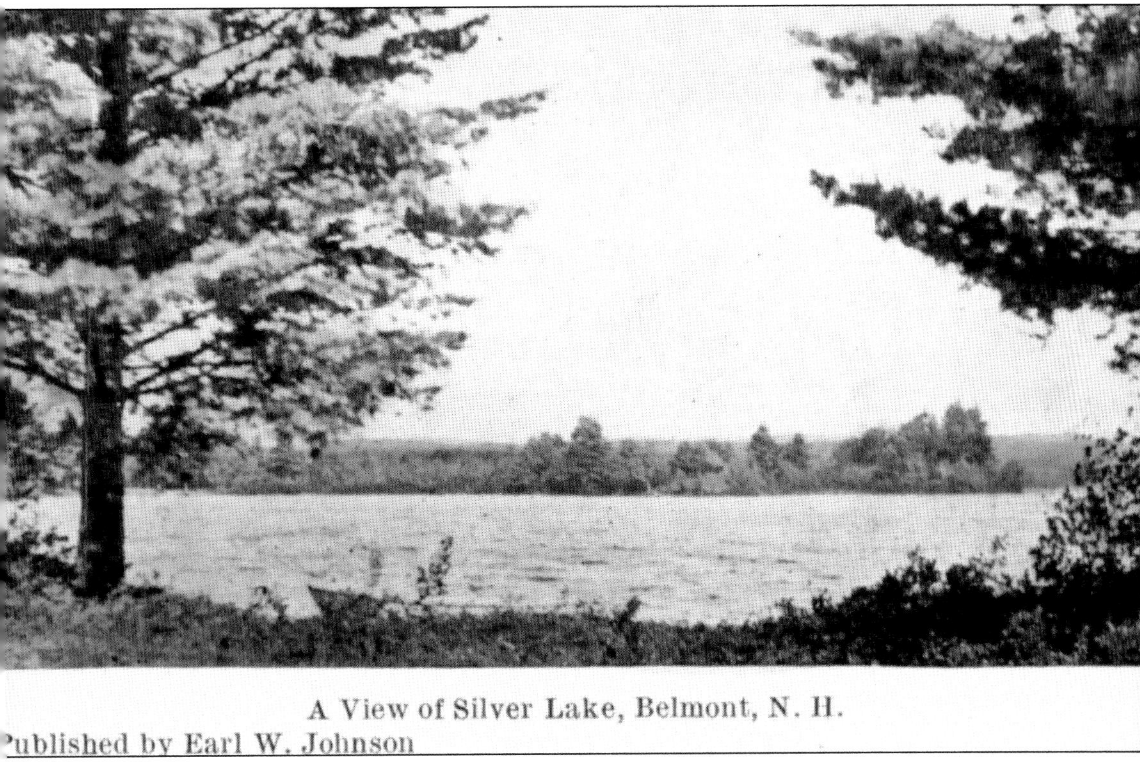

Silver Lake's elevation is a function of the amount of water entering and leaving the lake, as the lake has an uncontrolled natural outlet. The lake's outlet is located at the State Route 140 bridge crossing near the lines of Tilton and Belmont. The Lochmere Dam powerhouse discharges directly into Silver Lake; under certain meteorological conditions, the level of the lake increases and does on occasion flood homes surrounding Silver Lake.

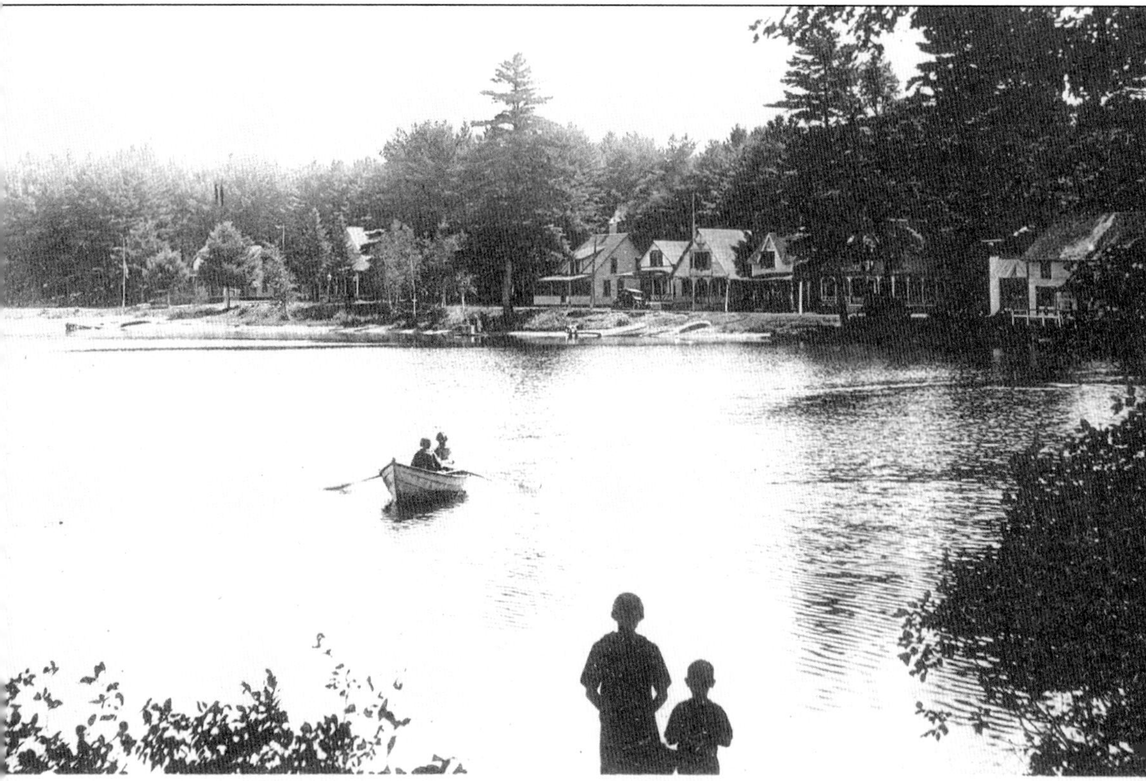

GARDNER'S GROVE, SILVER LAKE, LOCHMERE, N. H.

Silver Lake has no ability to pass additional water flow at the outlet of the lake beyond the capacity of its natural channel. The Lochmere Dam is the only controllable discharge into Silver Lake. This discharge is usually determined by conditions at the Lakeport Dam. In addition, the Tioga River drainage area alone can produce a fairly significant amount of runoff during the spring freshet.

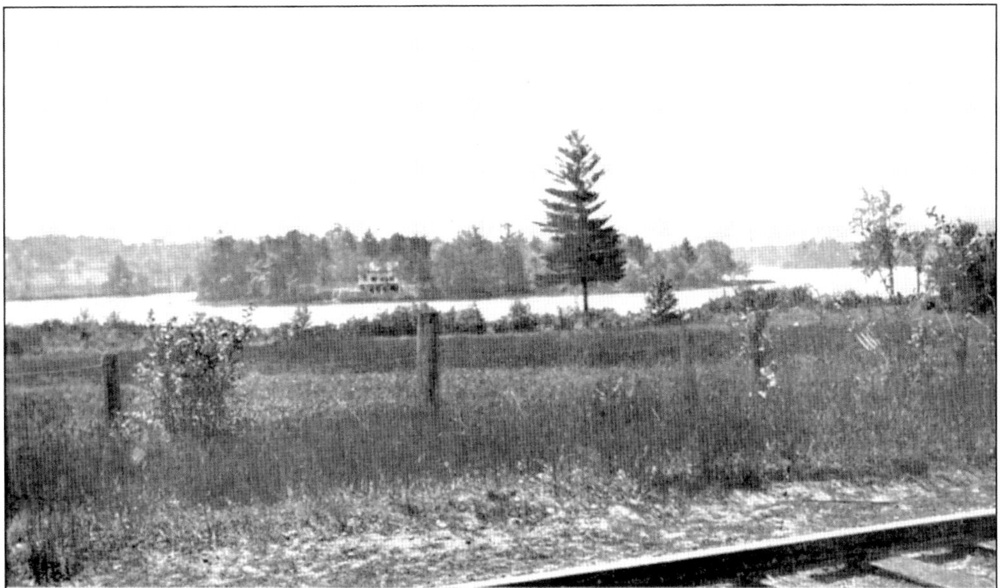

Published by E. W. Johnson View of Silver Lake from East Tilton, Belmont, N. H.

Silver Lake, under certain conditions, requires additional discharge from the Lochmere Dam; generally the Tioga River is usually approaching peak flows, which contributes to the elevation of lake levels and to the flooding in and around Silver Lake. Operational decisions related to managing the lake's level involves both Lakeport and Lochmere Dams. The New Hampshire Department of Environmental Services strives to reduce the potential damages due to flooding around Silver Lake.

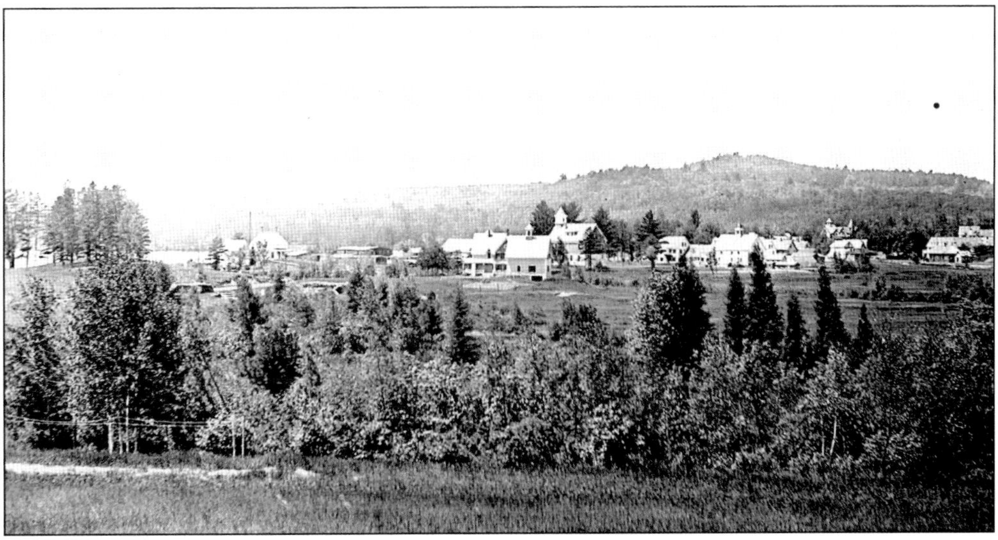

When storage room exists in Lakes Winnipesaukee or Winnisquam, using a combination of the storage may result in a reduction of peak water levels on Silver Lake. Lake Winnisquam, however, has over 50 square miles of additional drainage area contributing to Silver Lake, making flood storage minimal. There is no annual drawdown, but when flows at the Lochmere Dam are reduced every second year, and Lake Winnisquam does not experience a temporary two-week drawdown, the level of Silver Lake is reduced to about 1.2 feet below its normal summer operating level.

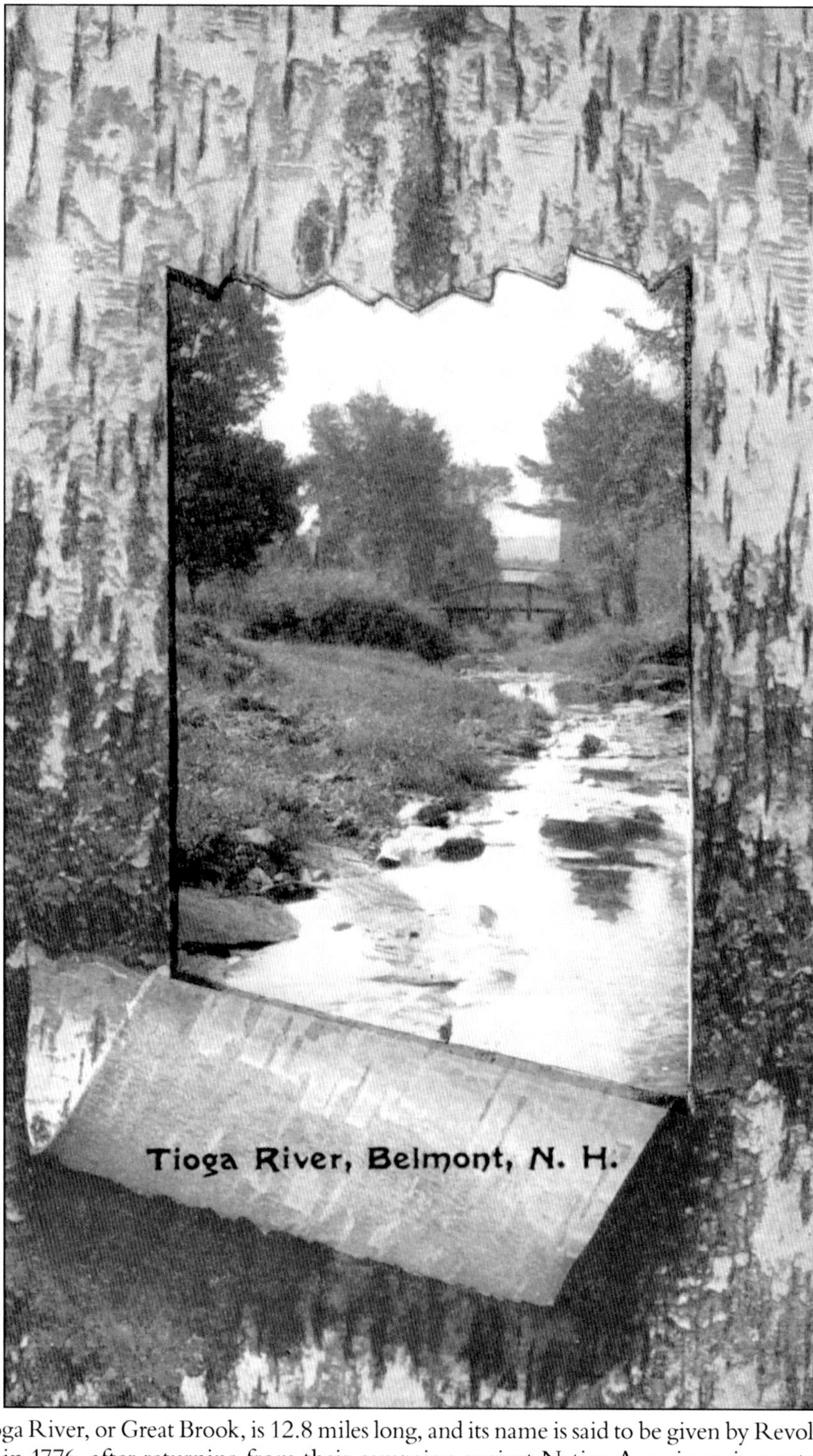

The Tioga River, or Great Brook, is 12.8 miles long, and its name is said to be given by Revolutionary soldiers in 1776, after returning from their campaign against Native Americans in western New York, because it resembled a place near their encampment called Tioga. This river has been a part of the town's primary source of power for the many mills on its banks over the decades.

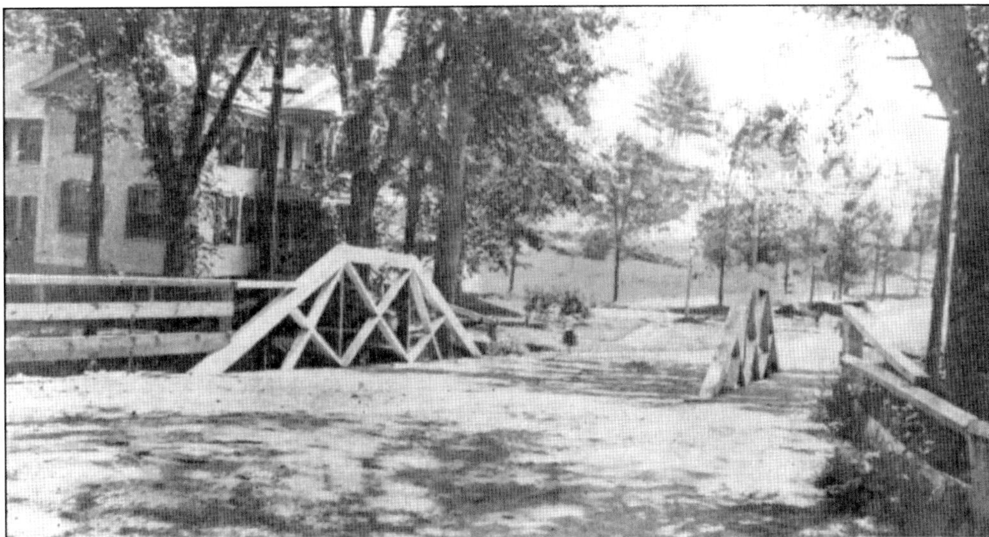

North Church Street Bridge, Belmont, N. H.
Published by Earl W. Johnson

The North Church Street Bridge is above the Tioga River and was constructed in the late 1700s. It was first constructed of wood, originally having wooden planks and a sidewalk. This structure was replaced in 1913 by an iron bridge, built by the United Construction Company at a cost of $415.87. Seen in the background is Brown's Hotel, later known as Currier's Hotel, which still stands today. North Church Street Bridge (below) can be seen from the river with the Fellows Dam in the background, which was the original site of the Fellows Grist Mill. Parts of Church Street were constructed around 1793.

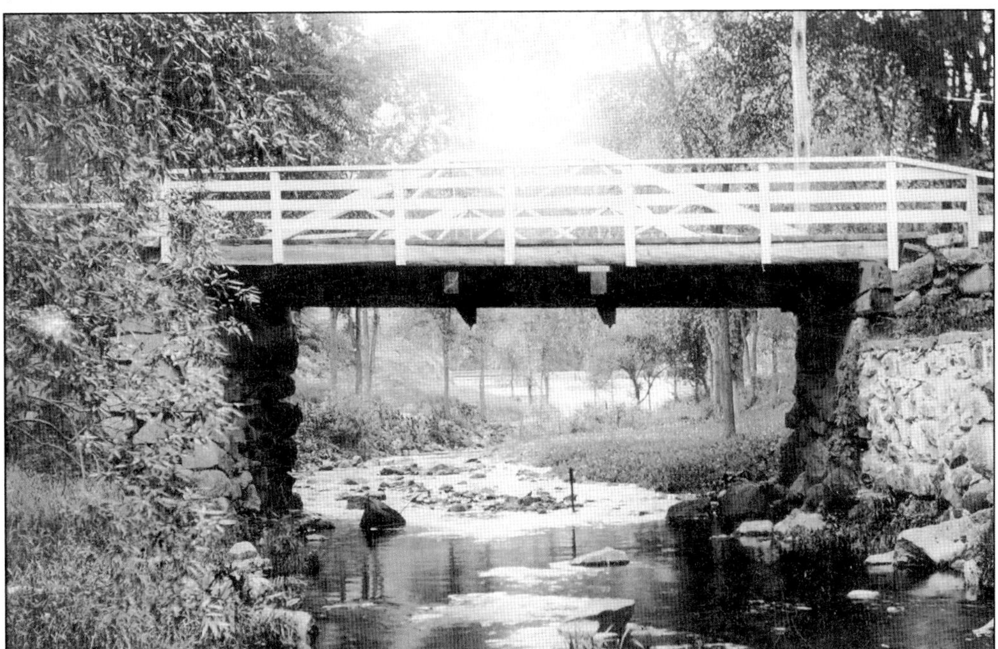

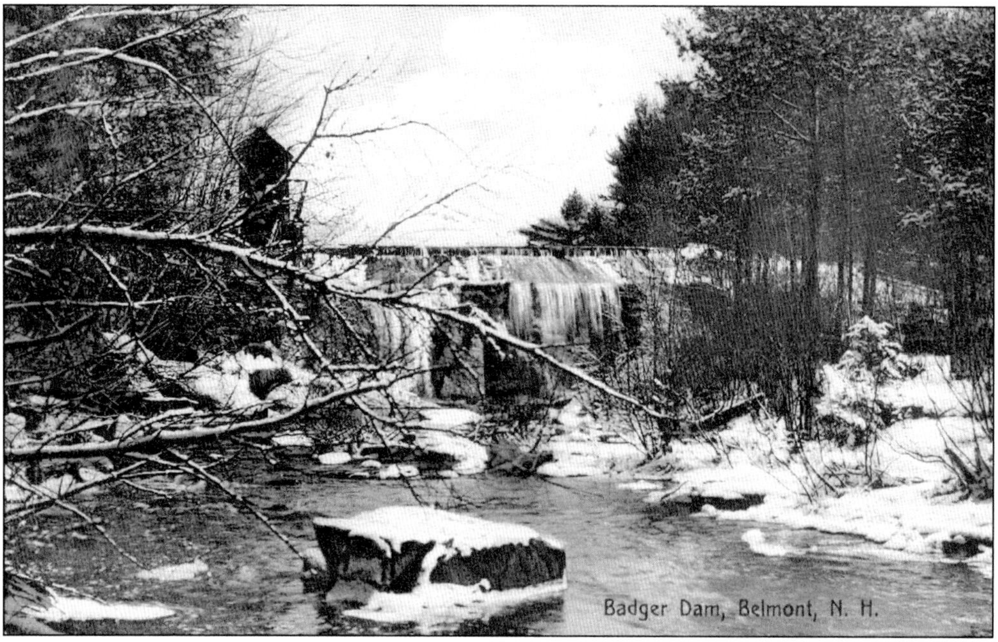

In 1854, Capt. William Badger bought the mill privilege at "Brookfield," about a mile above Belmont Village. He built a dam of stone and wood and used this reservoir of about 15 acres for the benefits of the mills below. Over the years, this dam has been used as a hydroelectric plant, skating rink, boating area, and wildlife habitat. The dam was breached on December 5, 2003.

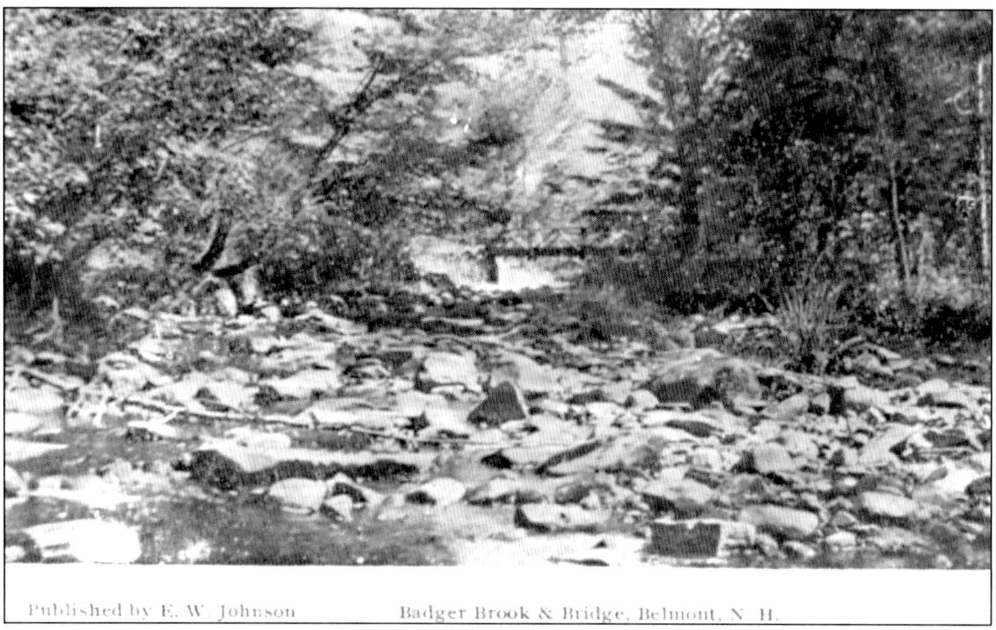

Badger Brook flows from Badger Dam in Belmont. In the rear of this 1918 postcard, Badger Bridge can be seen. This bridge was located on Laconia Road (State Route 106 South) on the left before turning onto North Main Street.

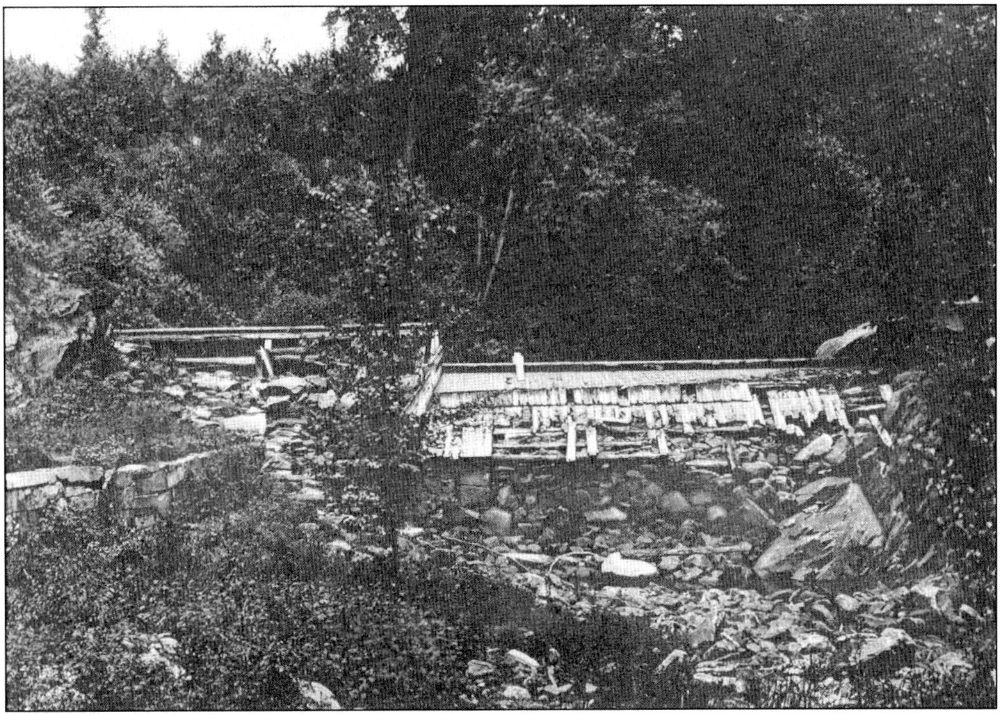

In 1794, Joseph Fellows Sr., a native of Sandown, purchased the site at the rapids in the Great Brook (Tioga River) and constructed the first saw- and gristmill, which he operated until his death in 1817. The village of Belmont was constructed around the nucleus, which Fellows started at the north end of the settlement. At this time and for years after, it has been known as the Fellows Dam.

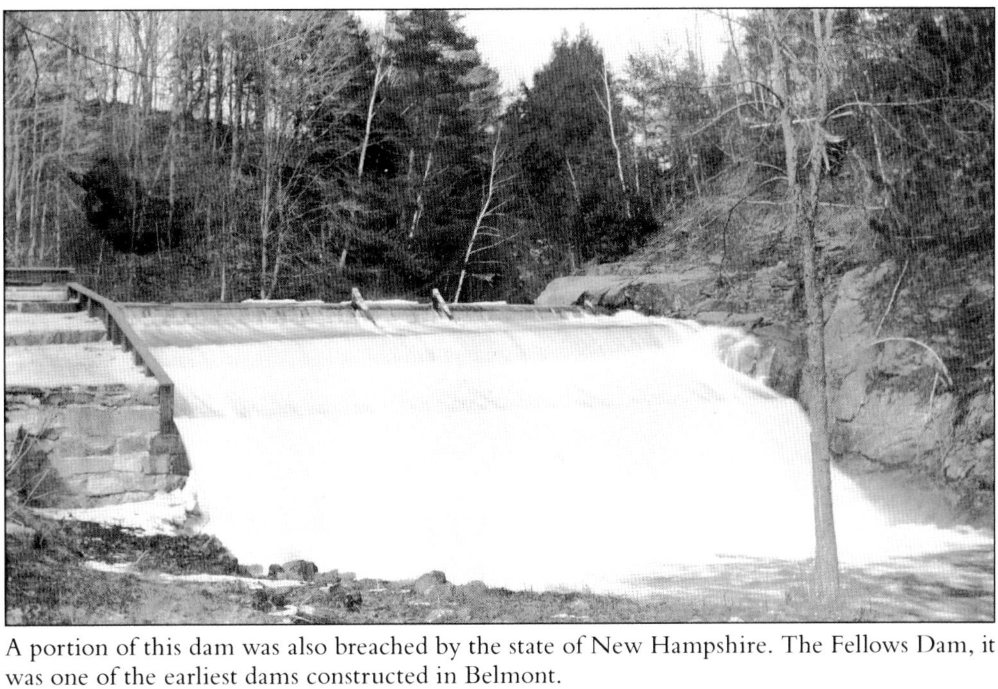

A portion of this dam was also breached by the state of New Hampshire. The Fellows Dam, it was one of the earliest dams constructed in Belmont.

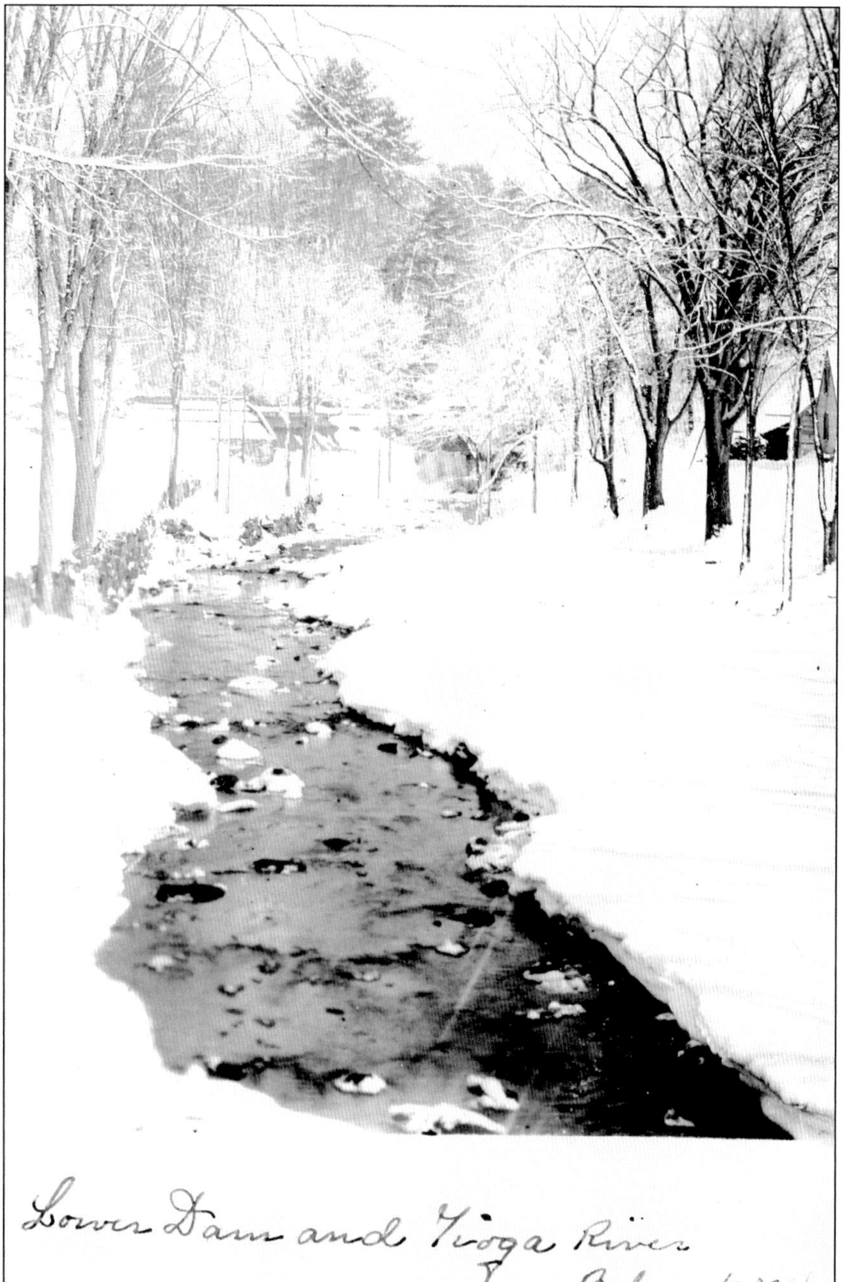

Fellows Dam, located at the upper end of Belmont Village, was purchased by Joseph Fellows Sr. in 1798 from Ephraim Morrill Jr. The deed in part describes the millpond, indicating that Morrill had already built a mill on the site. Morrill had purchased the entire 100-acre lot, of which this was a part, in 1788. He thereafter sold off several parcels at the northern end of the village and in the Church Hill area. Fellows either built, rebuilt, or continued to operate the gristmill on the site until his death in 1817, at which time the property passed to his son Samuel and eventually was sold to William Badger in 1825. Around 1839, Badger rebuilt the dam, raising it by five feet. This is substantially the same dam as remains today, although it has been breached.

Prior to the construction of Depot Street, all travel to Tilton or to the Jamestown section of Belmont was by way of Dearborn Street. Before the construction of the Belmont Railroad, the nearest railroad connection was on the main line in East Tilton. Travelers from Belmont could make the trip by way of the Gilmanton and Union Bridge stagecoach.

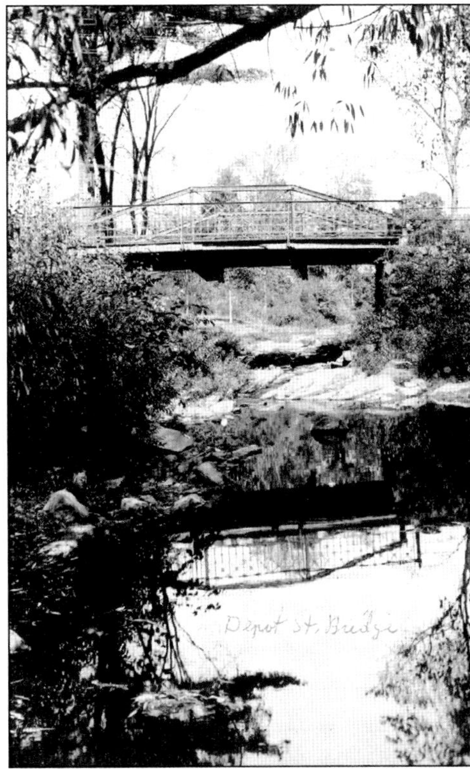

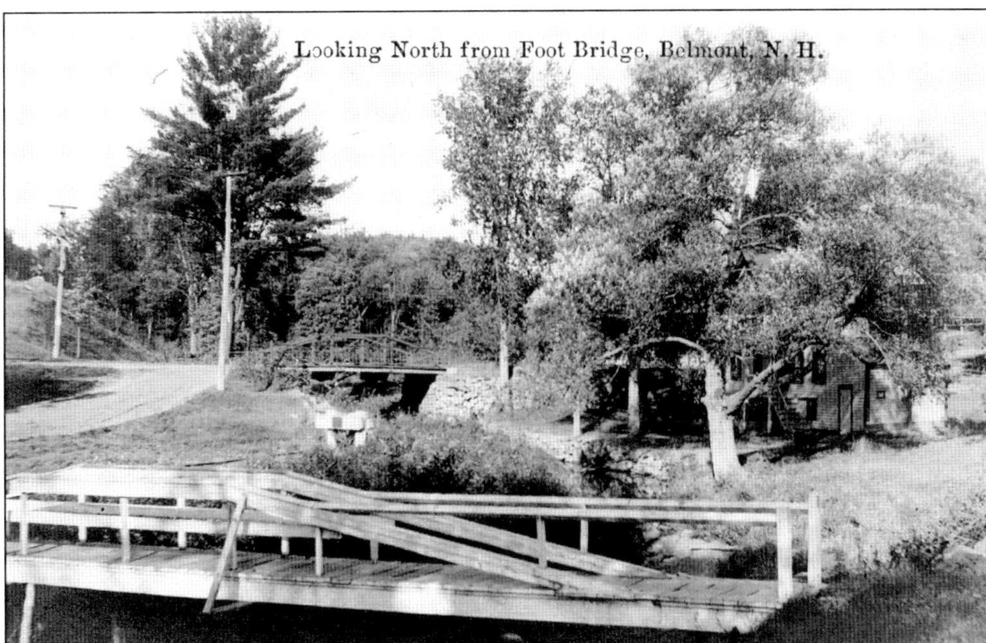

Located between the Belmont Mill and the Belmont Railroad station off Depot Street, this footbridge was a significant shortcut from the station and from Depot Street to the mill. Since most employees of the mill traveled by foot, it was undoubtedly appreciated by many. The bridge foundation on the mill side of the bridge still exists as well as the steps up the hill.

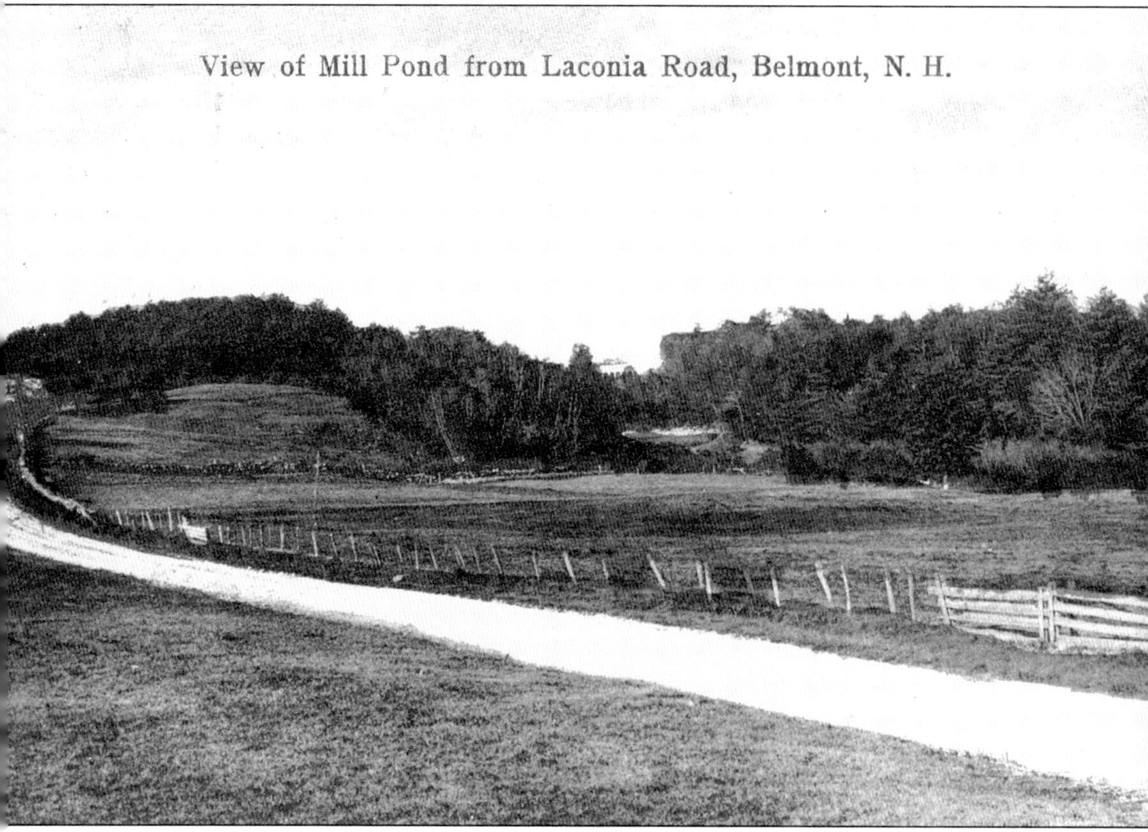

In 1833, a new dam and pond were constructed at the site of the original Fellows sawmill dam. The dam was constructed from fill with the western portion being of plank. From this dam a canal crossed Main Street at the approximate location of Spring Street and joined the brook to the rear of the houses. The combined flow of water accumulated in a small pond where Belmont Village Store is today, continuing to the mill as a source of power. Later it was used as a backup system for the town's water supply.

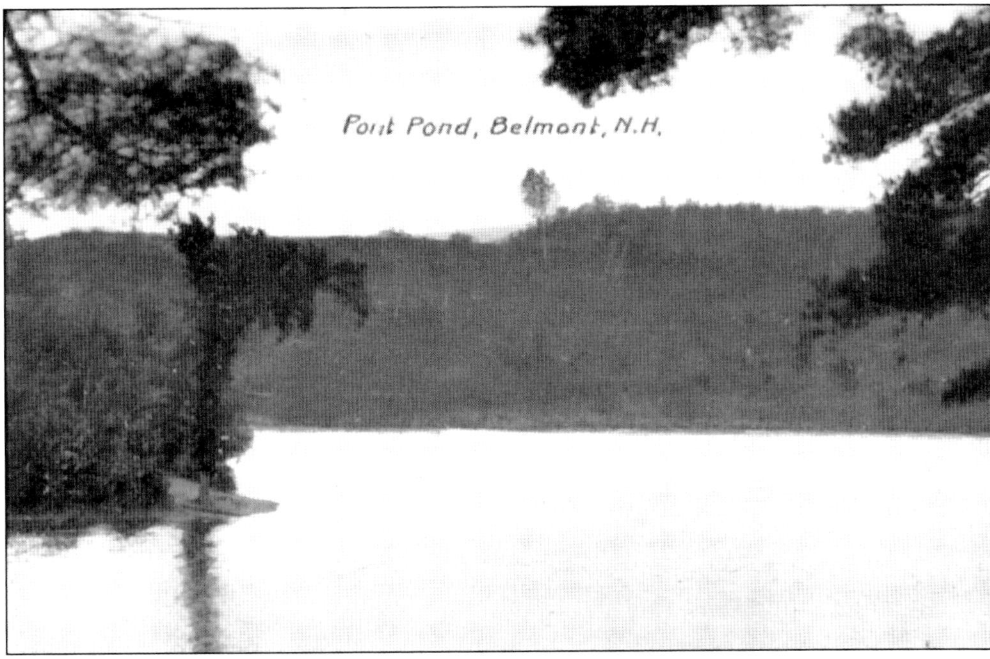

Pout Pond on Shaker Road sits on the aqueduct that supplies the town's water system. In 1893, the town purchased the Belmont Aqueduct Company for $9,000. Included were 20 hydrants, 500 feet of hose, a hose carriage, and firefighting tools. The water system originally consisted of three wells holding 20,000 gallons each, and the reservoir was constructed on Gilmanton Road with a capacity of holding 115,000 gallons of water. A windmill at the top of the hill was constructed to produce power, pumping water from an artesian well near the reservoir. A backup system tying into the mill allowed water to go through the penstock that connected to the millpond above the village, thus setting the force pumps at work, filling the reservoir in a half day's time, and insuring water in any given situation. Water was conducted to houses through wooden (log) pipes that were banned together with iron.

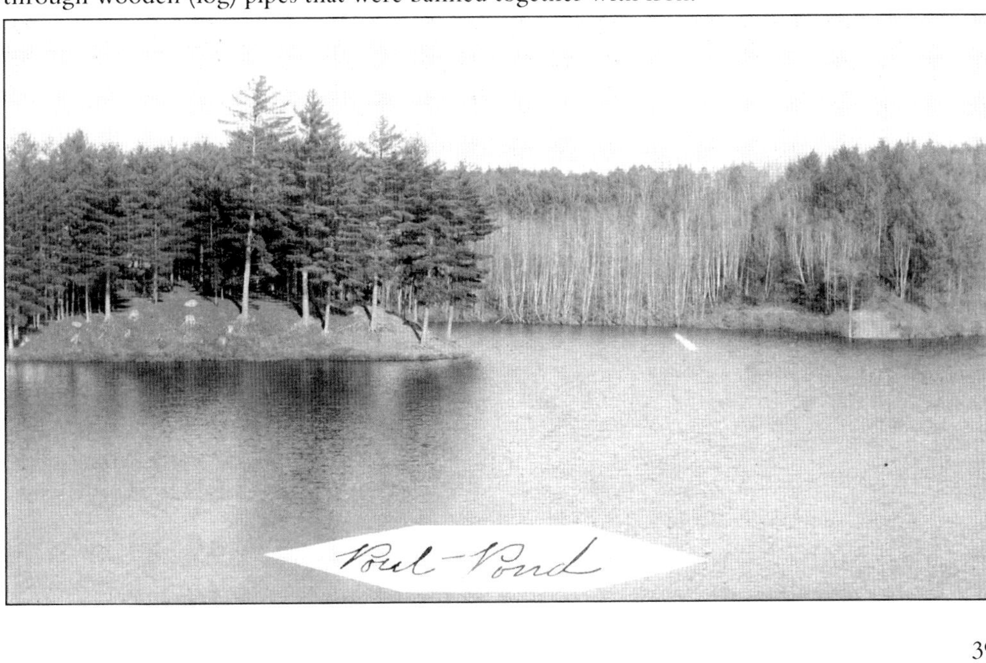

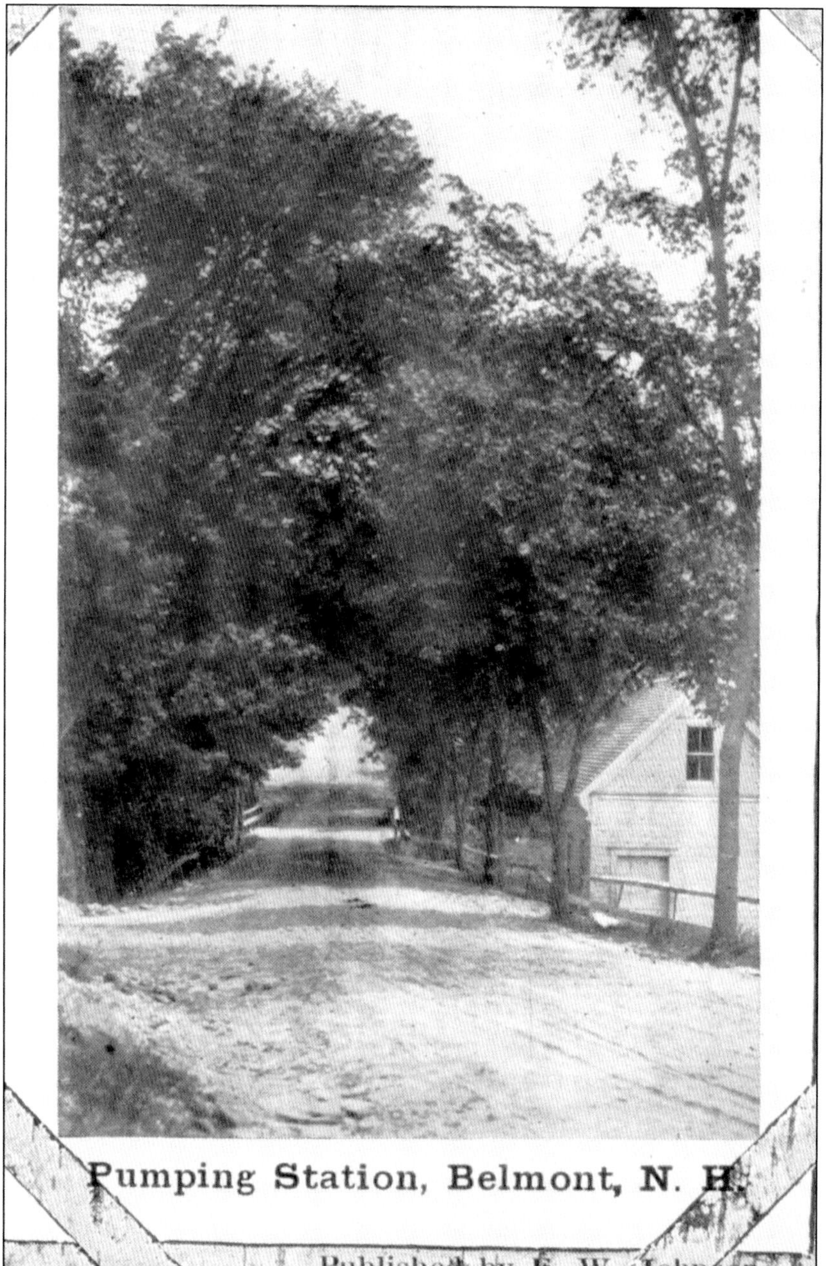

This pumping station was located on Shaker Road on the left, after the bridge (shown above). It would pump surface water to the reservoir where it would then be treated with chlorine. In the early 1900s, the largest expenditure of Belmont Water Department was for wood. This was used to fire the boiler of this pumping station. In 1937, the use of surface water was discontinued, a pump house constructed, and a well dug at Pout Pond to supply groundwater to the system. In the early 1950s, the distribution system was completely renewed and expanded. In the 1970s, a problem with a considerable amount of sand being pumped into the pumps caused the capacity of the pumps to weaken. Therefore, the third pump house construction occurred, and another well was dug 700 feet southwest of the second site, at and near Pout Pond.

Two

Mills

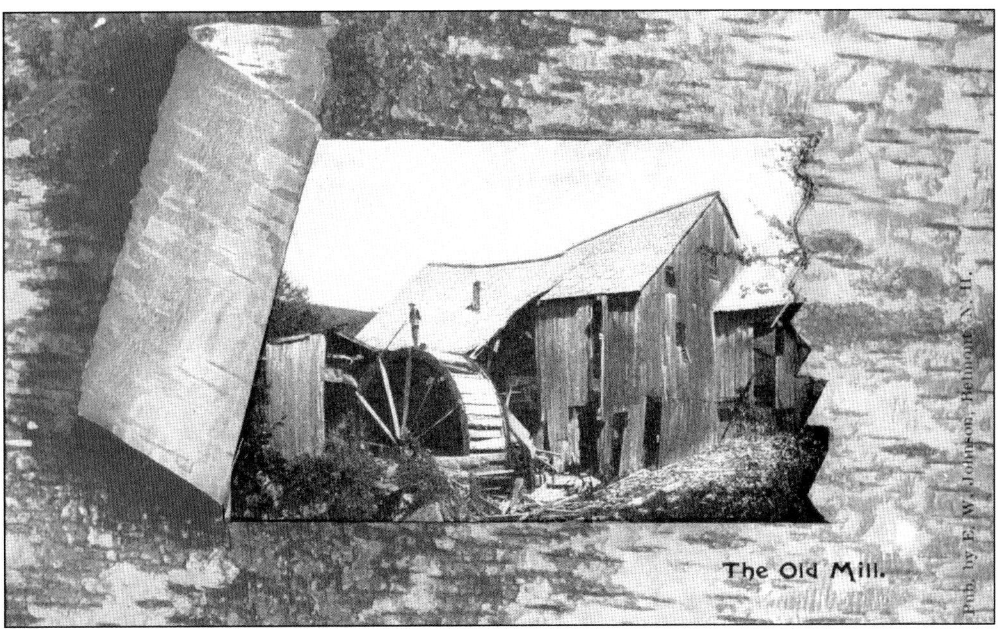

This postcard is believed to be the original Fellows sawmill constructed in the 1790s. The image clearly shows the mill in great disrepair and on the verge of collapse. The site appears to lend itself to an undershot wheel with water flowing under the wheel such as seen here in the picture.

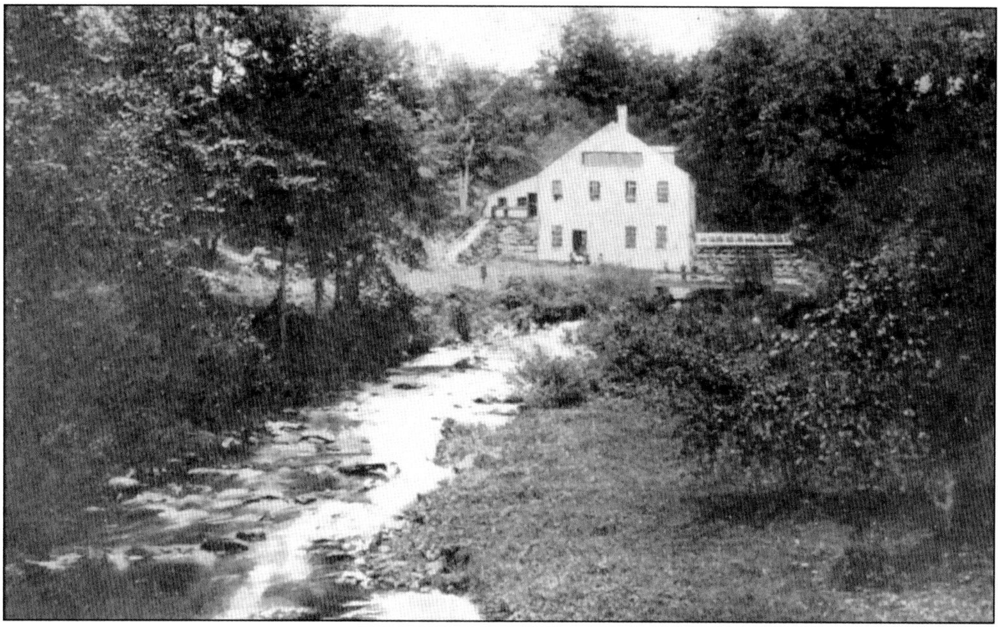

The saw- and gristmill at the Upper, or Fellows, Dam was built after a previous structure was washed out in the freshet of 1852. In 1872, shingle-making machinery was added, and from 1876 until the structure burned on May 7, 1885, it was used for the manufacture of cases for the hosiery mill by the Gilmanton Mills Company, which enlarged and altered the building for the use at that time.

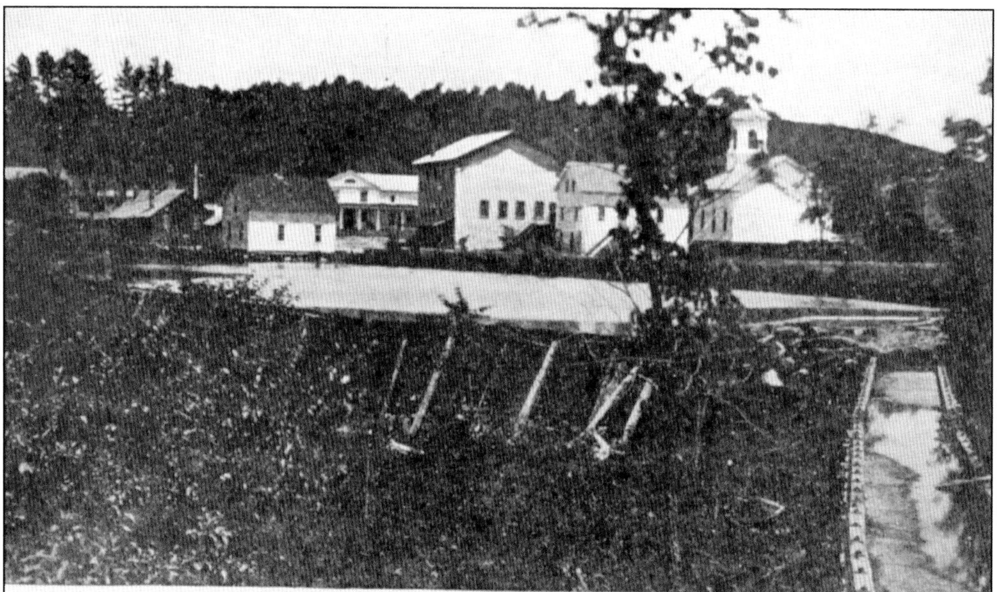

Published by E. W. Johnson Upper End in 1875, Belmont, N. H.

Shown here in 1875 is the historic millpond site that the Gilmanton Village Manufacturing Company built so the water could be directed through a covered canal across Main Street and to the mill. During the 1890s, the dam was removed and a penstock was constructed from the Fellows Dam to the mill. The remains of the steel penstock, which replaced the original wooden one, are still visible today.

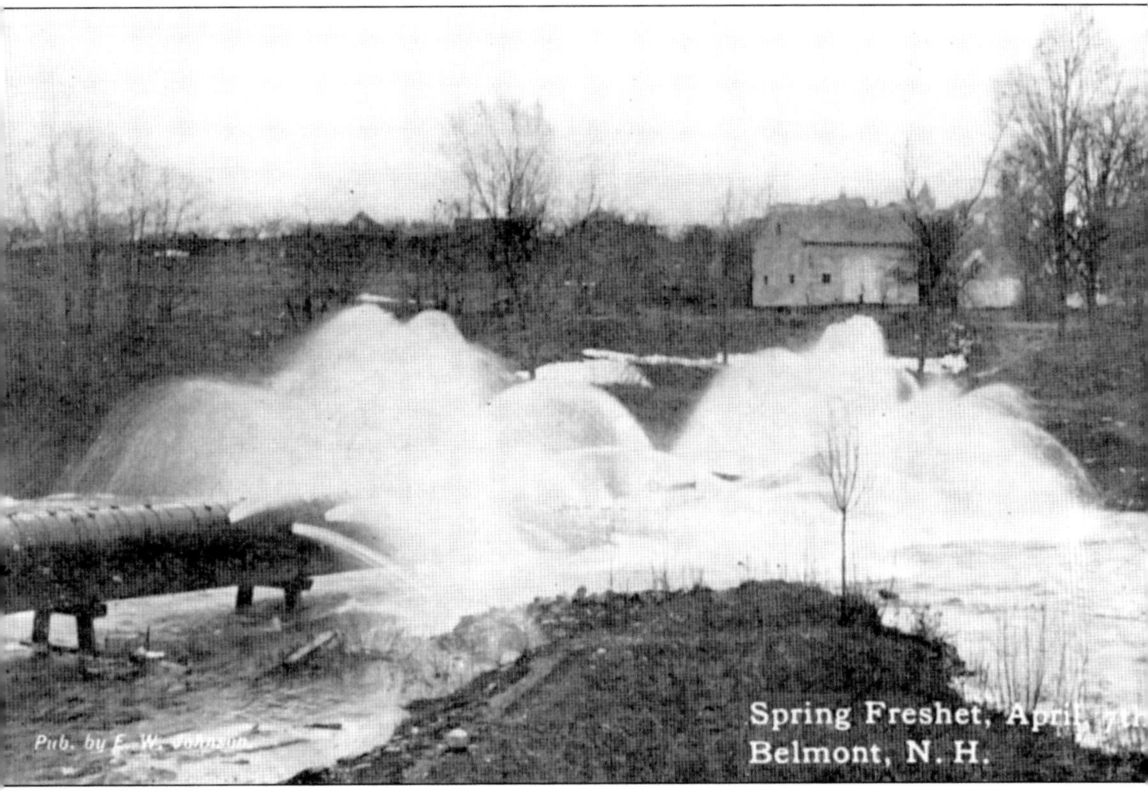

The old wooden penstock, shown here on April 7, 1901, had sprung a few springtime leaks. In the foreground are the remains of the dam, which had originally held back the Great Brook (Tioga River). This waterway was used to operate the mills.

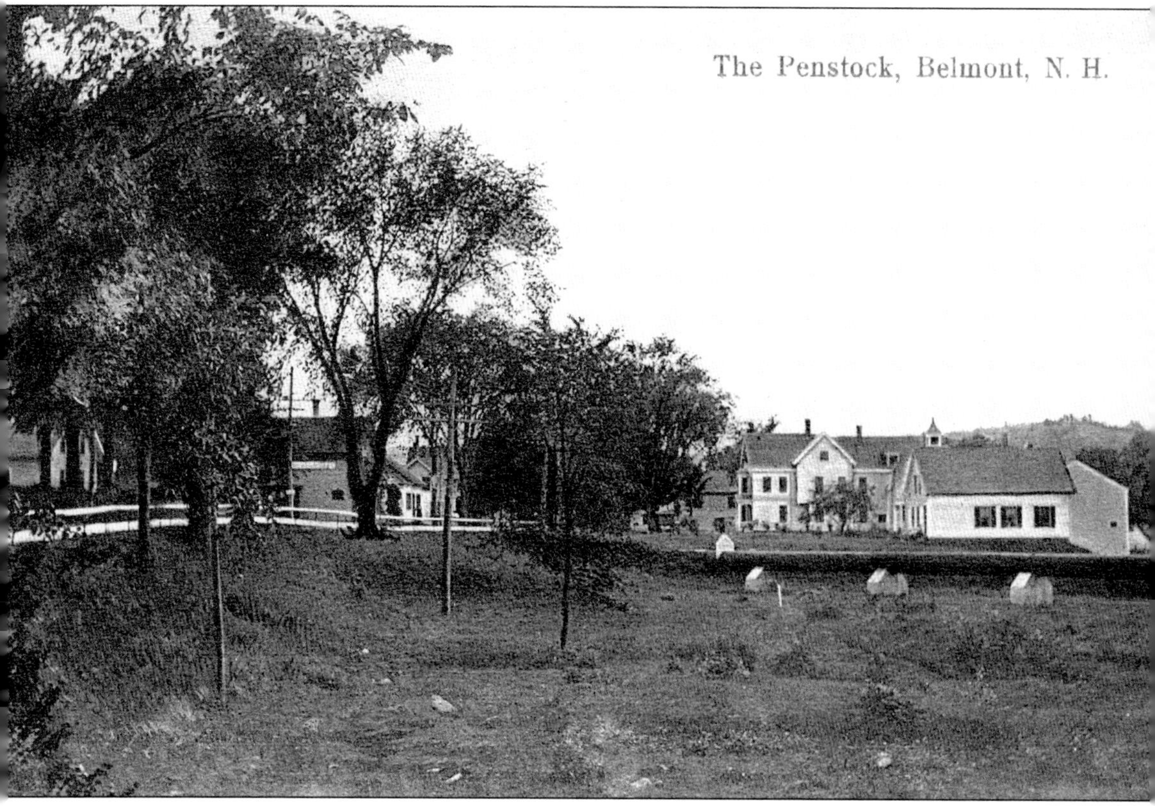

In 1876, Fellows Dam was purchased by the Gilmanton Mills Company. It operated the dam until it burned. A wooden penstock held together by steel bands was built and extended from where the lower dam sits to the mill on Mill Street through an open canal. The postcard above, from around 1910, shows the penstock and Main Street where water was conducted through this pipe until 1955 when the Fenwick Hosiery Company purchased the mill property and discontinued usage of waterpower.

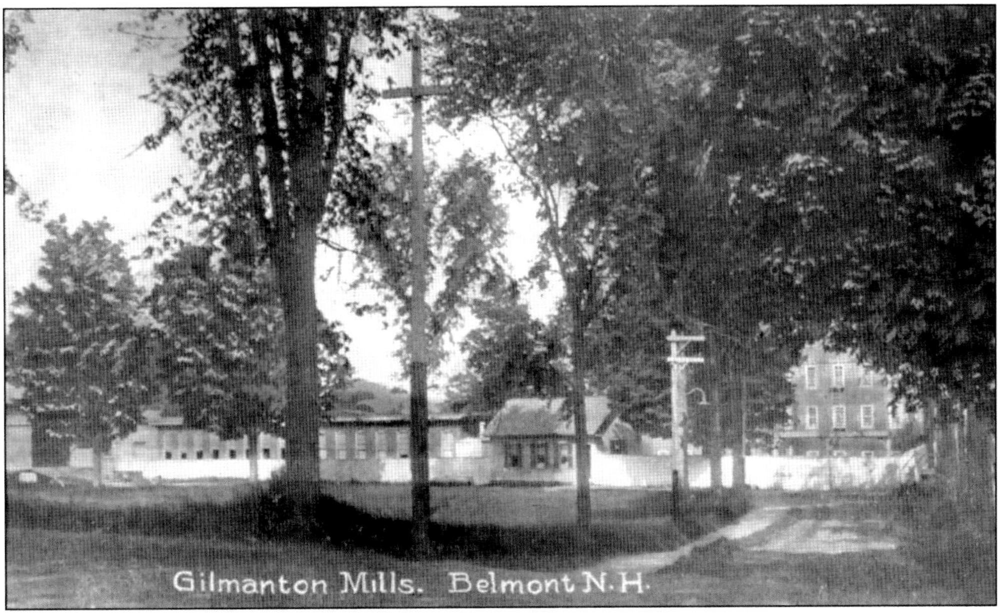

In 1832, Gov. William Badger built a brick factory for the manufacture of cotton cloth, and a company was organized at Badger's Mills called the Gilmanton Village Manufacturing Company. Samuel Cate was appointed agent. This company bought the sawmill, house, and lands previously owned by Joseph Fellows Jr. They also purchased land on the east side of the river, including the falls by the dam that was built with a canal on the east side, thereby consolidating both falls and confining the waterpower to one place. This company sold out to the Union Manufacturing Company in 1836. Jonathan Clarke resigned his position in the 1840s, and William Badger was named in his place. The company later operated as the Tioga Manufacturing Company until sold to Moses Sargent Sr. in 1865.

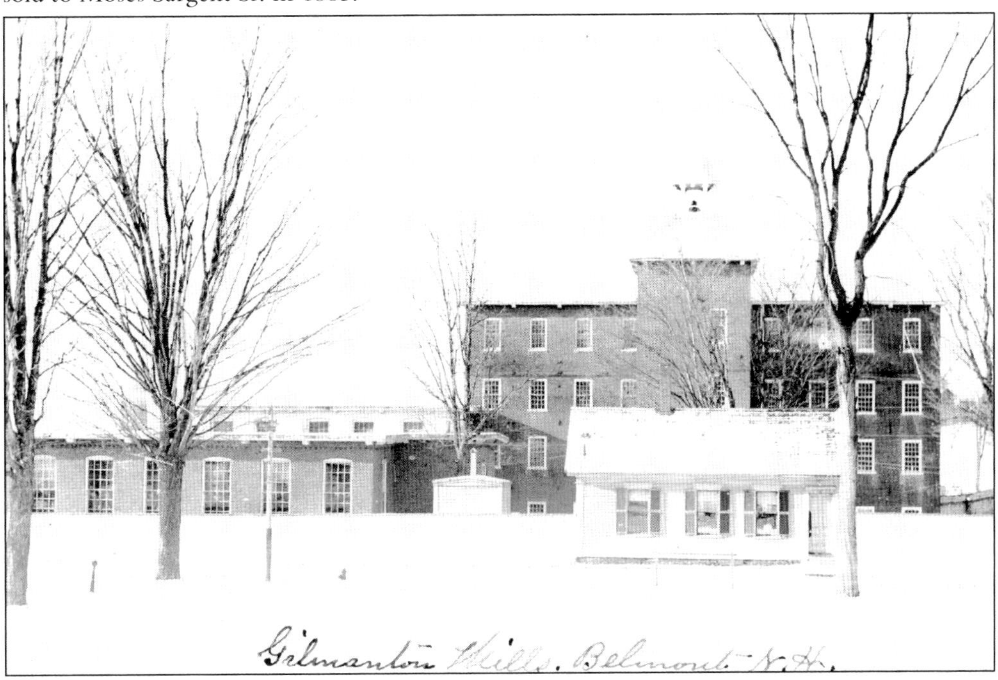

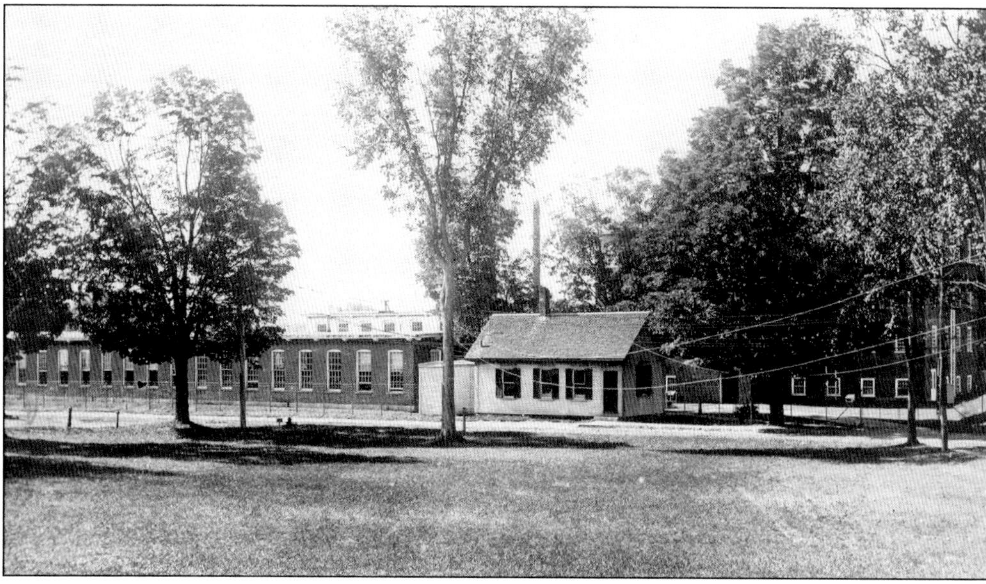

Moses Sargent Sr. of Lake Village and his two sons improved the property, converting it to a hosiery factory. The Sargents sold the business to Amos A. Lawrence of Boston in 1870. He employed Moses Sargent Jr., an educated and practical manufacturer, as superintendent. Sargent worked at the mill for more than 40 years. In 1872, the Gilmanton Mills Company began constructing mill houses to the left of the property for the use of its employees. This street had been known as Lawrence Street for many years, although it is now called Mill Street. A female operative at the mill could easily earn $2 a week, and many schoolteachers at the time had left their professions to take advantage of the monetary benefits. The mill also installed a library for the use of its employees; at this time there were approximately 200 employees working at the mill. In 1875, the establishment was chartered with a capital of $100,000. Since Lawrence took control of the property, the village improved in size, wealth, and appearance with its active employees being the life of Belmont.

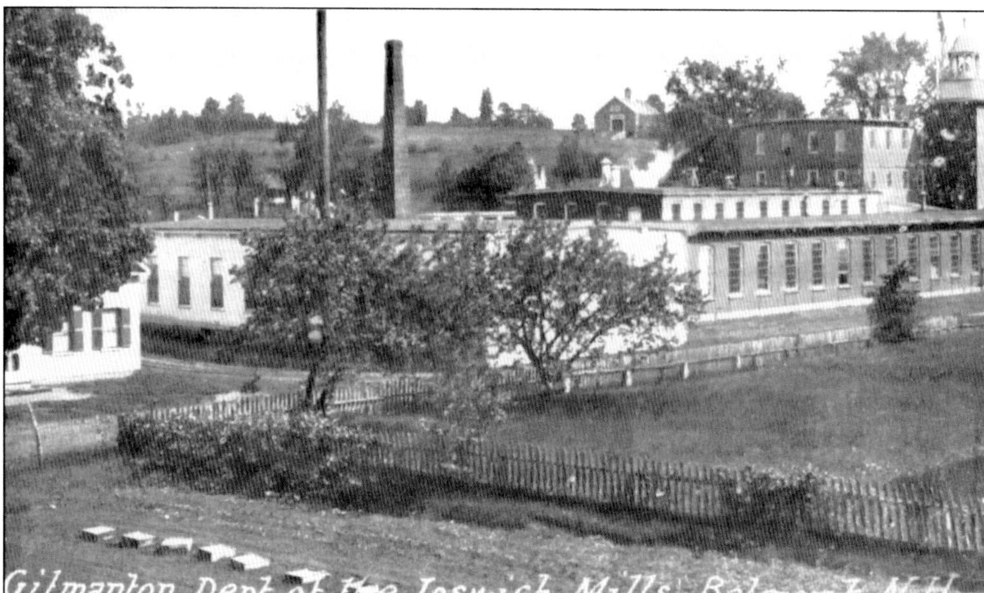

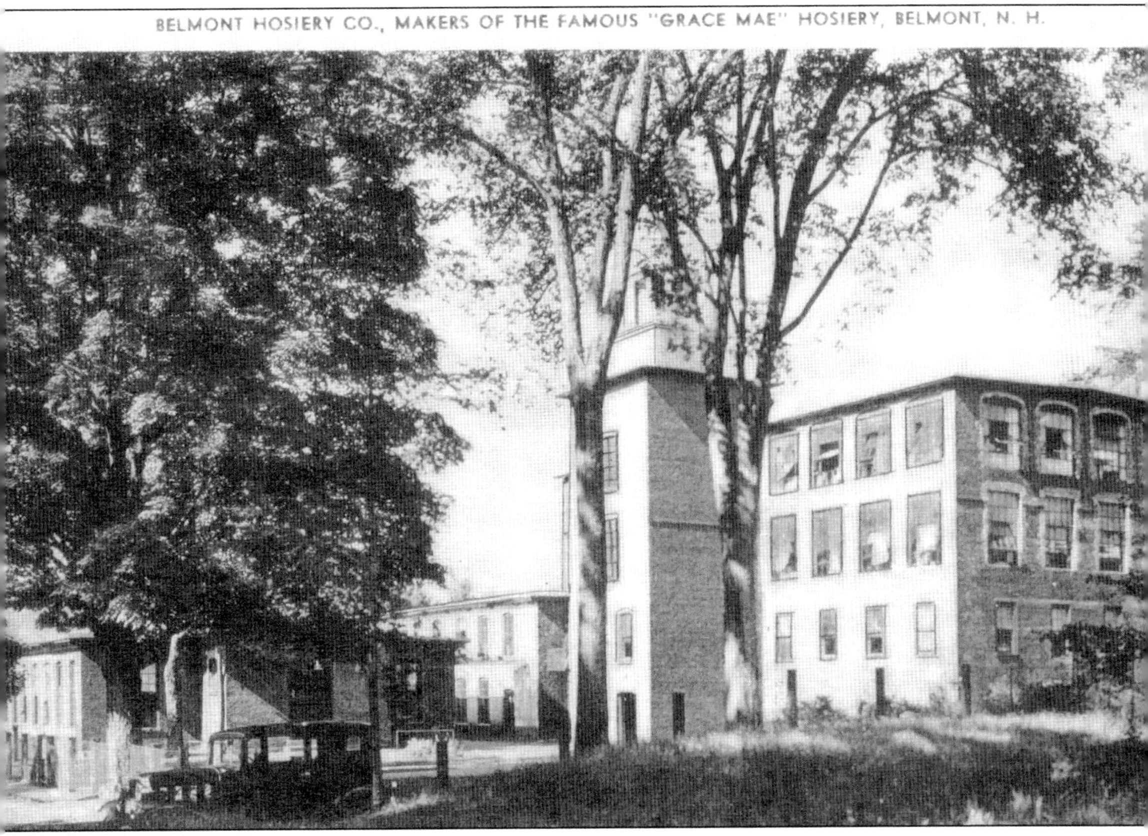

By about 1900, the manufacturing complex had grown to include not only the main mill, which had been raised from the original three stories and attic to a full four stories, but also a variety of support structures, including a picker house and finishing room. In 1909, the Gilmanton Mills Company sold the property to Ipswich Mills. In 1921, after a period of decline for Ipswich Mills, George and Walter Duffy purchased the mill complex and incorporated the firm known as Belmont Hosiery Company. Allen M. Agle took over as superintendent. With the death of his brother, Walter continued to operate the complex until 1955 when he too passed. The following year, the complex was sold at auction, and the Fenwick Hosiery Company was the successful bidder. The fortunes of Belmont would be linked to the mill from 1833 to 1970, when the last textile operation closed. On August 14, 1992, the building was severely damaged by fire, bringing to a close manufacturing activity in Belmont Village spanning over a period of 160 years. Today the mill lives on through restoration efforts.

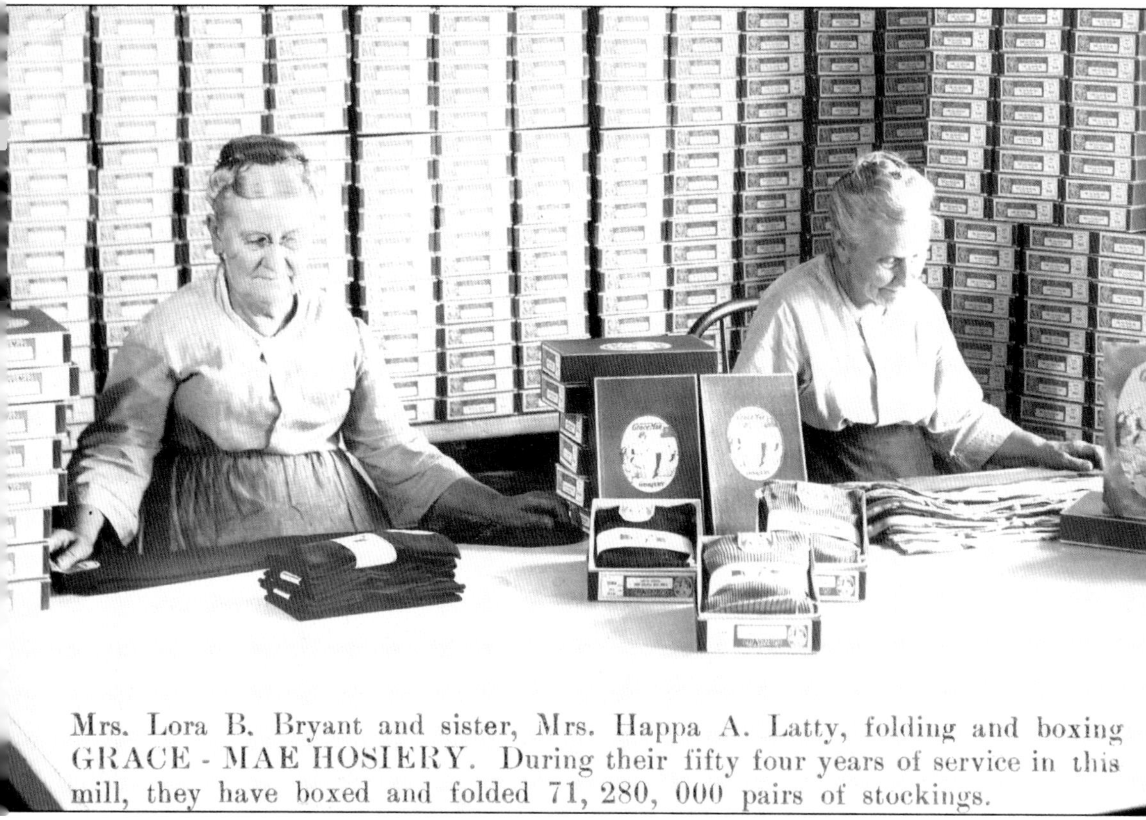

Shown here are two employees, Lora B. Bryant and Happa A. Latty, of the Belmont Hosiery Company.

Three

RAILROADS

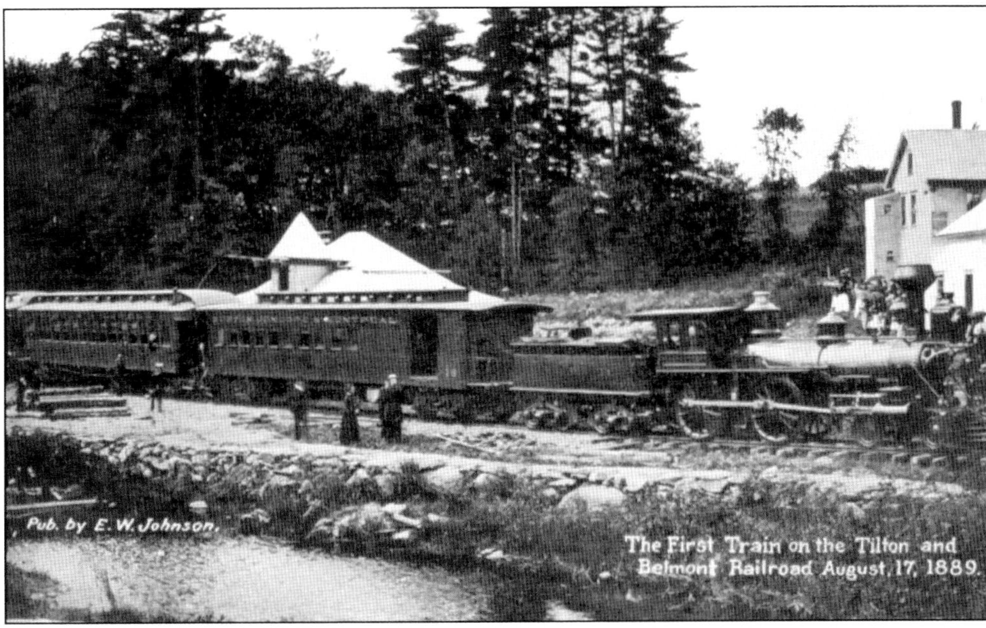

The natives turned out in force to welcome the very first train into Belmont on August 17, 1889. Reflecting the confused state of railroad affairs at the time, this historic occasion is commemorated by a train powered by the *Governor Gilmore* of the Concord Railroad with equipment from both the Boston and Lowell and the Boston, Concord, and Montreal Railroads. This first train was occupied by railroad dignitaries, including presidents and directors of various railroads as well as most of the state's political figures, among them five men who had been or would afterward be governors of the state. It was reported that free meals were served to all on that day. Without a doubt, this was the most momentous occasion Belmont has ever experienced before or since. Charles E. Tilton, a resident of the town of Tilton, which bears his name, was extremely instrumental in the construction of the railroad. He brought a cannon to the event, and it was set on the lawn at the corner of Depot Street (State Route 140 West) and Main Street and fired to commemorate the occasion.

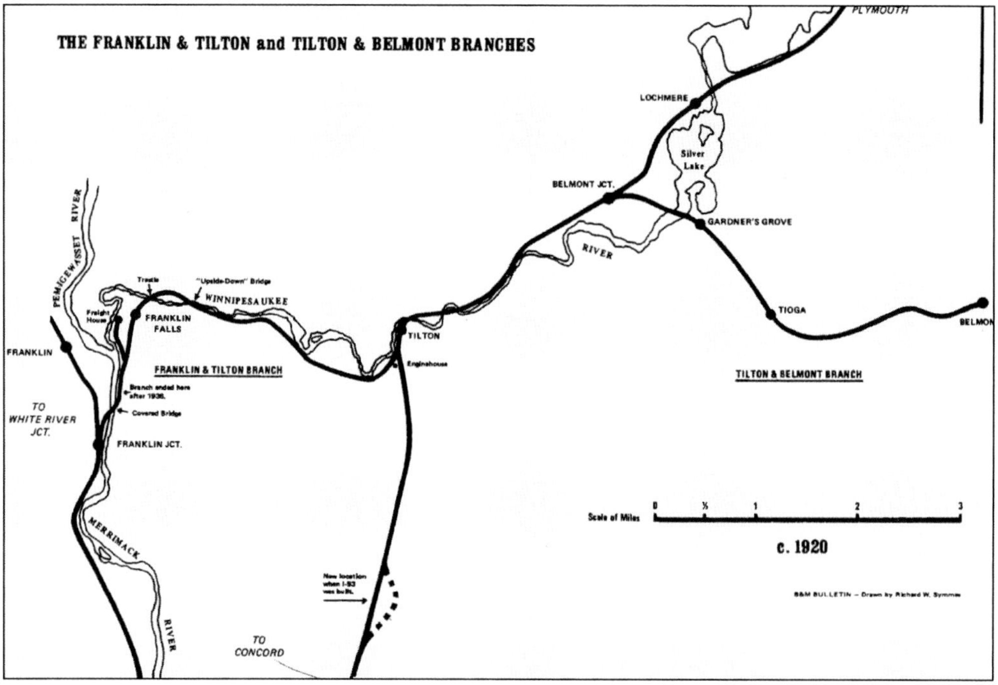

The map above shows the path that the Tilton and Belmont branch of the Boston and Maine Railroad (B&M) took from 1889 through 1929. During this time, it was much faster to travel to the station to catch a train than it was to ride in a wagon being pulled by horses to a destination.

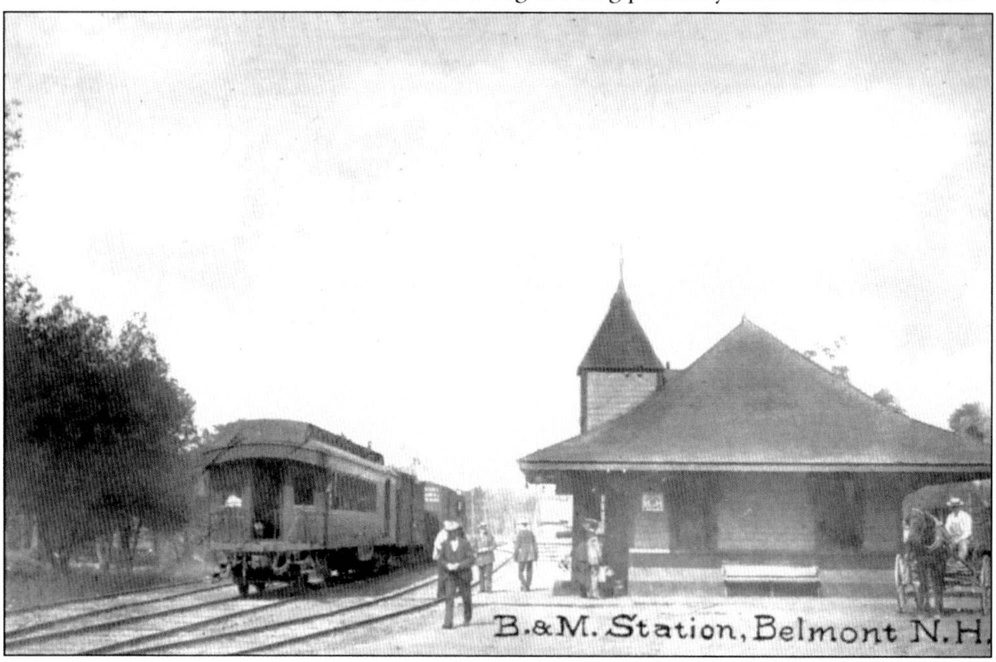

Seen here is the rear of the passenger station of the B&M. Before completion of this line, the Union Bridge depot (East Tilton) was the closest connection to Factory Village and was used extensively for shipping by the mill. Many depended on the rail to get them from one place to another.

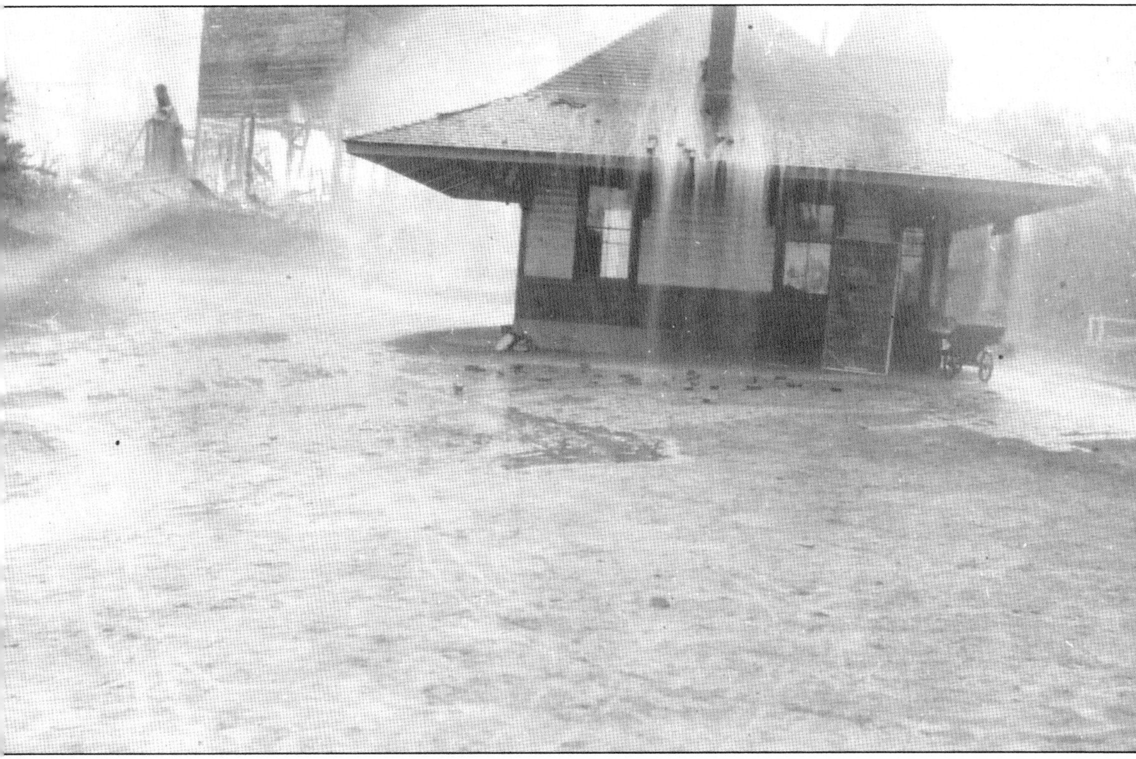

In 1894, John Dearborn constructed a large grain elevator and gristmill near the depot. The gristmill was powered by a steam boiler, which was used for grinding the grain and also could be used to unload grain from the freight cars. This structure burned in 1913 and was not rebuilt.

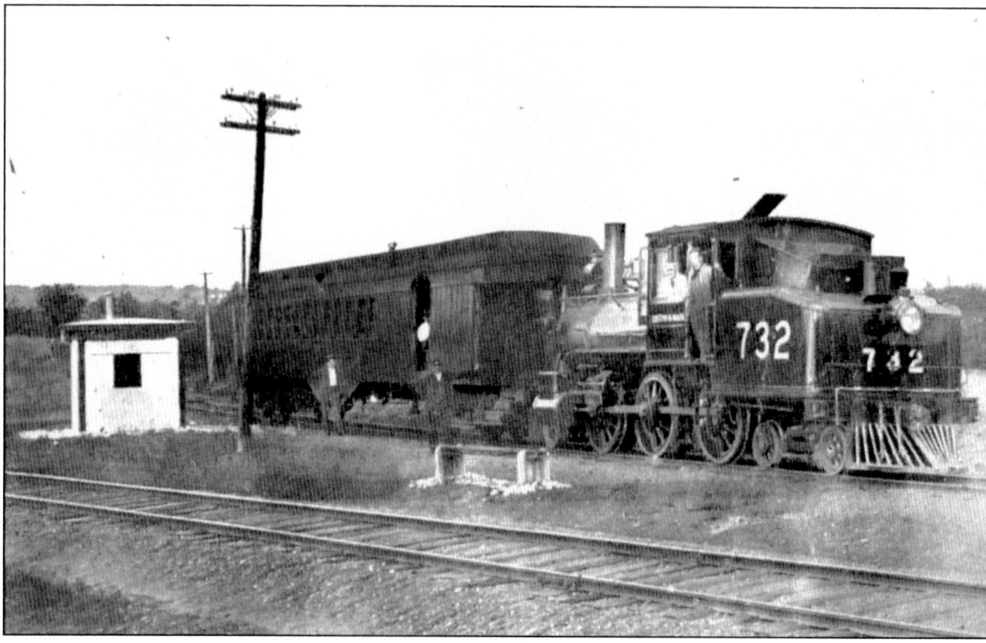

The No. 732 train ran from Tilton to Belmont a total of seven miles. Here at the Belmont Junction, it connects with the White Mountain Division's main line. Engine No. 732 was formerly J. W. Johnson No. 32 of the Concord Railroad, having the same name and number as it did in 1895. This train became Bill No. 732 in 1911 and after became known as No. 46. It was scrapped in 1918. This engine was built by a Rhode Island company in 1891 and weighed 67 tons.

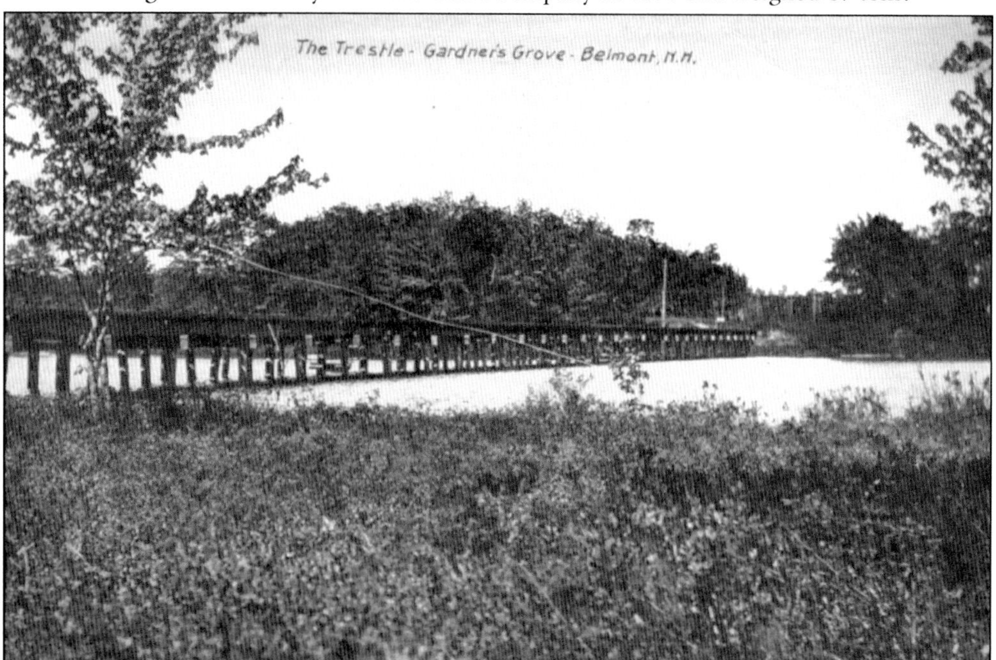

Shown here is the Tilton and Belmont Railroad trestle crossing part of Silver Lake at Gardner's Grove in the 1900s. This would have been the route taken to the Winnisquam and Laconia train stations, after passing through Gardner's Grove.

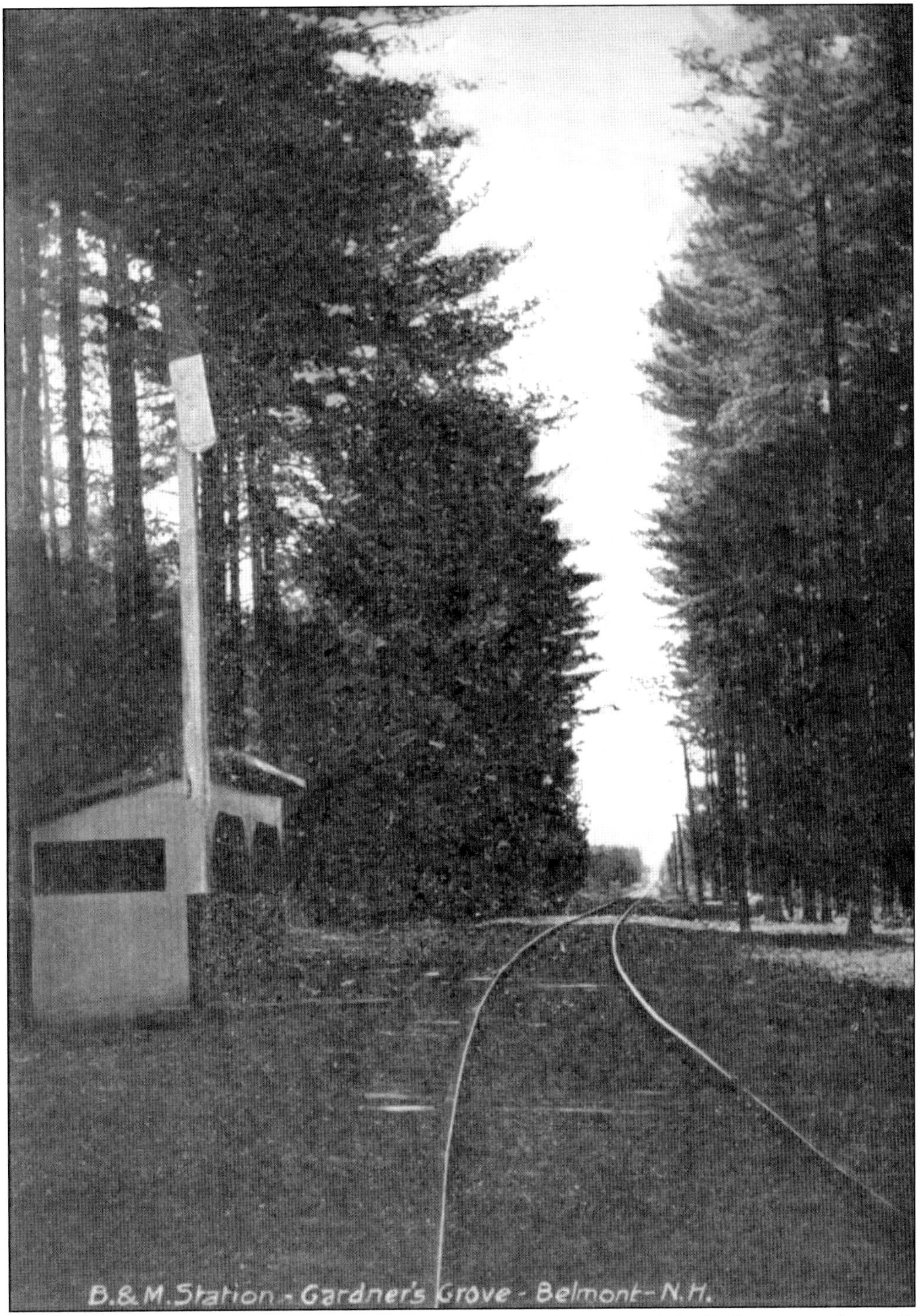

The B&M station was located at Gardner's Grove in Belmont. Originally known as Sawyer's Cove, this is where the town's rechristening celebration was held on July 5, 1869 (changing the name from Upper Gilmanton to Belmont). Gardner's Grove was an extremely busy vacationing spot for many tourists during the late 1800s and early 1900s.

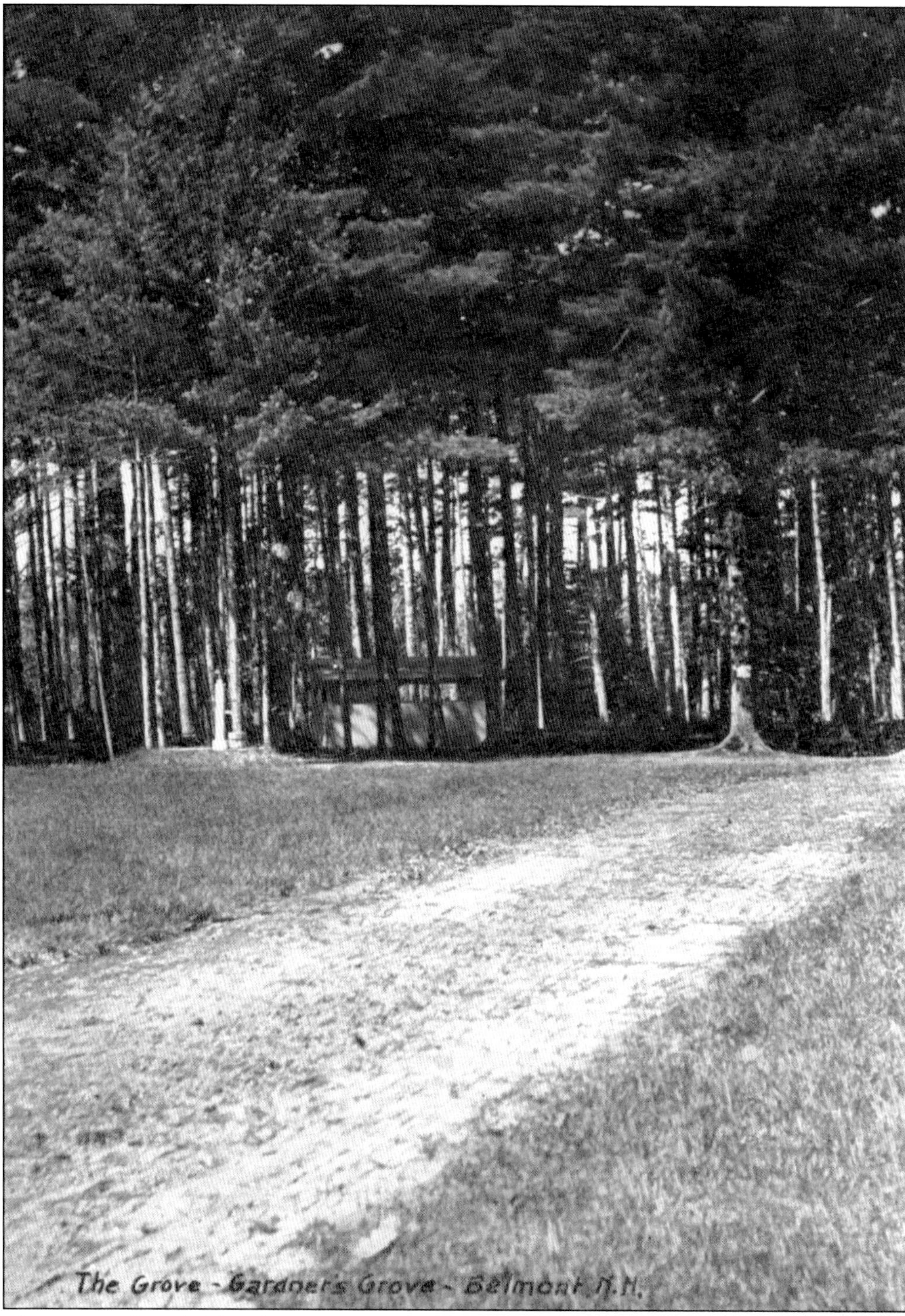

The grove is about halfway between Tilton and Belmont and near the line of the branch railroad of the B&M. It was one of the latest offshoots from the main line of the Concord and Montreal Railroad. As the name implies, the branch connected the towns of Tilton and Belmont and was about 7 miles in length.

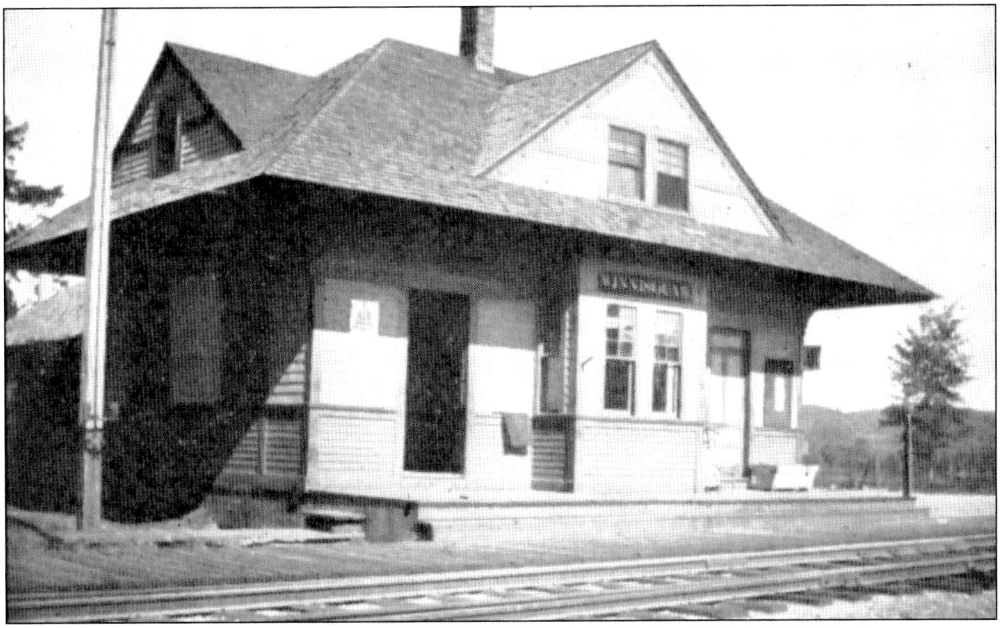

This B&M station was located on the left before crossing the Winnisquam Bridge into Sanbornton. It burned in the mid-1980s. At one time, State Route 3 crossed the railroad on an overpass bridge, but this was replaced with the present grade crossing in the mid-1970s. New protection crossing lights were installed in December 1999.

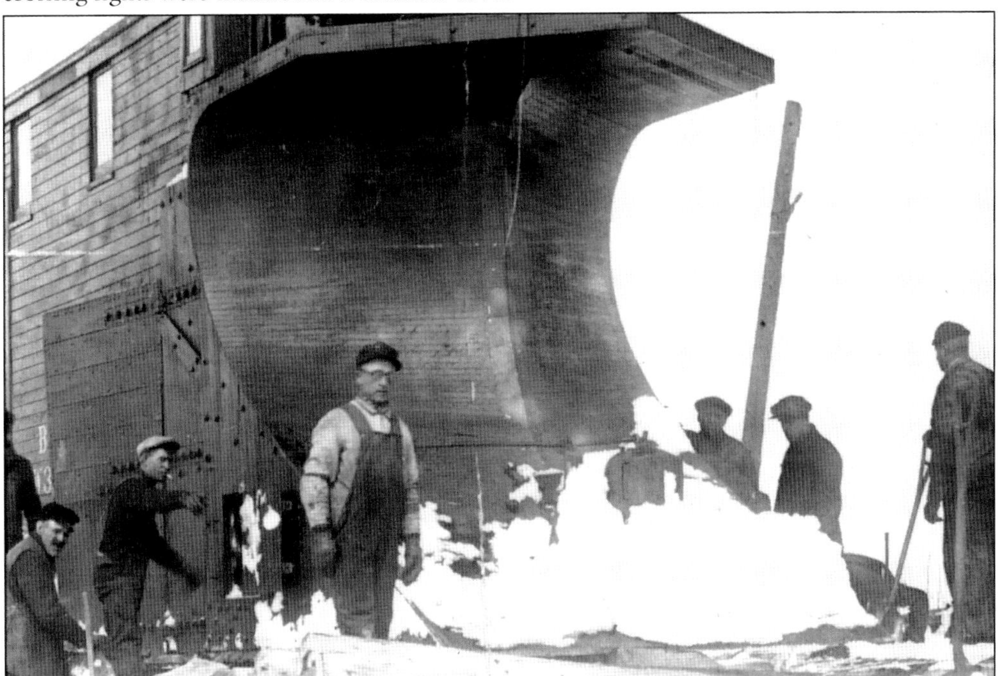

Snow removal operations on the Tilton and Belmont branch in 1926 are seen in the reprinted photograph above. On March 9, 1926, the Mongul 1481 derailed near Gardner's Grove while removing snow from the rails. This event managed to attract the attention of some of the locals living in or around Gardner's Grove at the time.

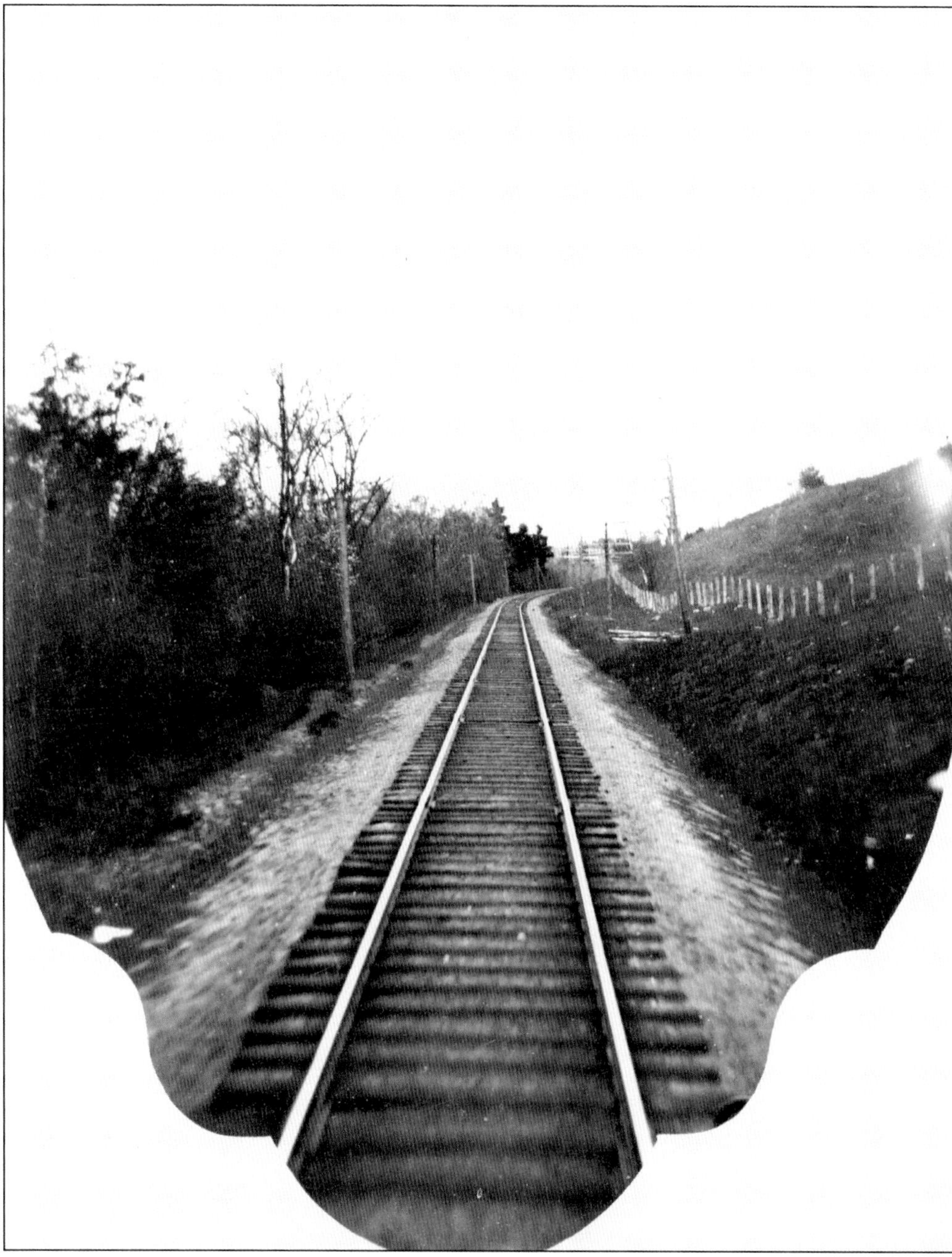

Seen above is the B&M line running through the back of the Hancock property located on Shaker Road in Belmont around 1913. Travelers of the rail would often sit and chat while riding the rail and observing the tremendous views of the countryside. It was not uncommon that nearly 60 to 100 people would unload at a time at a stop.

Four

VILLAGE DISTRICT

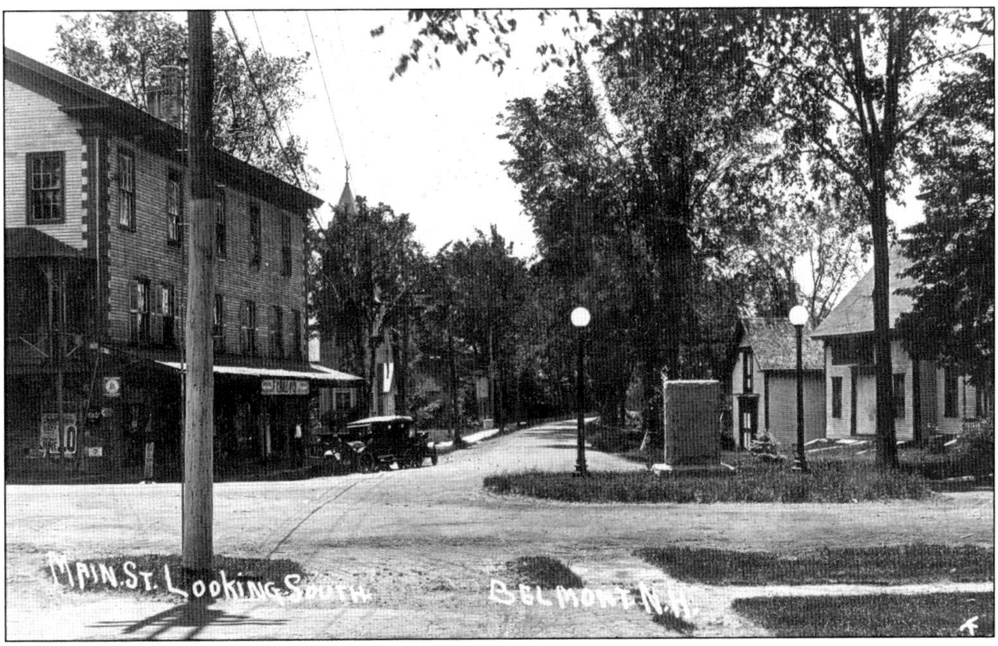

The image above shows how the Main Street business district at the upper end of Main Street (now Monument Square) once looked. The building to the left was built by George W. Riley in 1874. The monument was erected to honor those soldiers who fought for the country and was donated by Moses Sargent Jr. in 1919, costing him $5,000. The dedication of the monument reads as follows, "Dedicated to the men and women of Belmont who served in the Wars of this Country and in memory of the following who made the supreme sacrifice Herbert A. Prescott WWI, Phillip O. Swain WWII, Ernest B. Piper WWII, Steven C. Santy Vietnam, Arthur M. Hackett WWII, Harliegh C. Brown WWII, Leo J. Rolfe Korean, and John J. Moynihan Air Force." Each Memorial Day, the American Legion has a parade to honor those who died for the country, the parade marches to the monument where a ceremony is held in remembrance, guns are fired, and a bouquet of flowers is tossed over the Church Street Bridge.

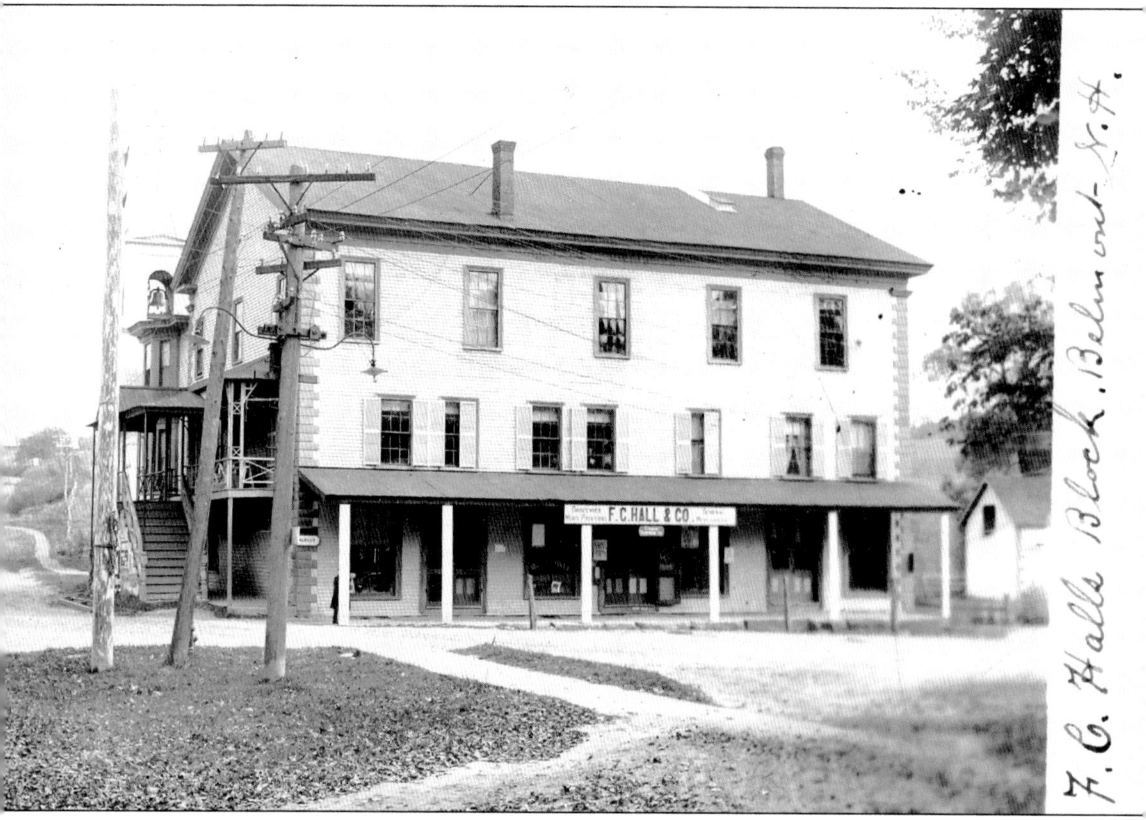

In 1874, George W. Riley constructed a three-story building, which housed on the main floor a store and post office, on the second floor apartments, and on the third floor a large hall, which was used for years for most of the social and political functions of the town. It became known as Riley's Block and was later known as (Reuben) Hoyt's, then as (Hazen) Grant's, and lastly as (Fred) Hall's Block. The building was torn down in 1927.

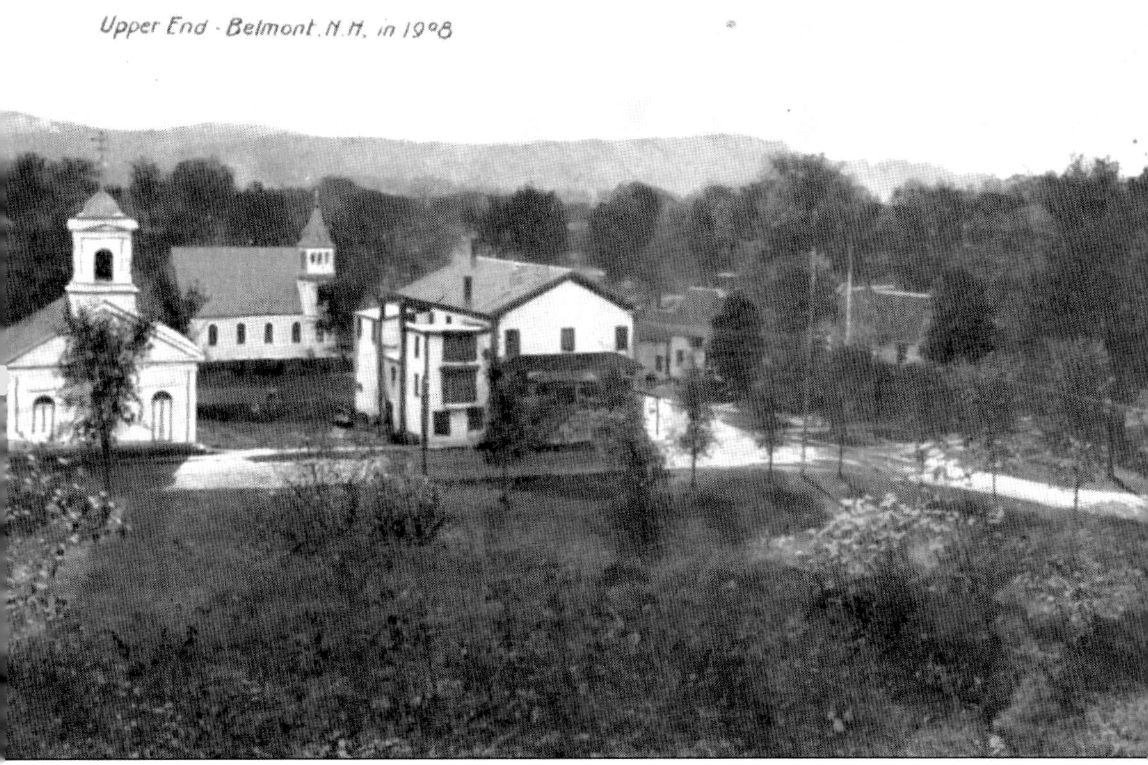

Pictured here is the upper end of North Main Street in 1908. In the center of the postcard is Hall's Hall, to the rear of this building is St. Joseph's Church, and on the left of the image is South Church (Christian Baptist Church), which was constructed in 1840. In 1867, the church burned and was rebuilt the next year. This structure was then torn down in 1925 after years of disuse.

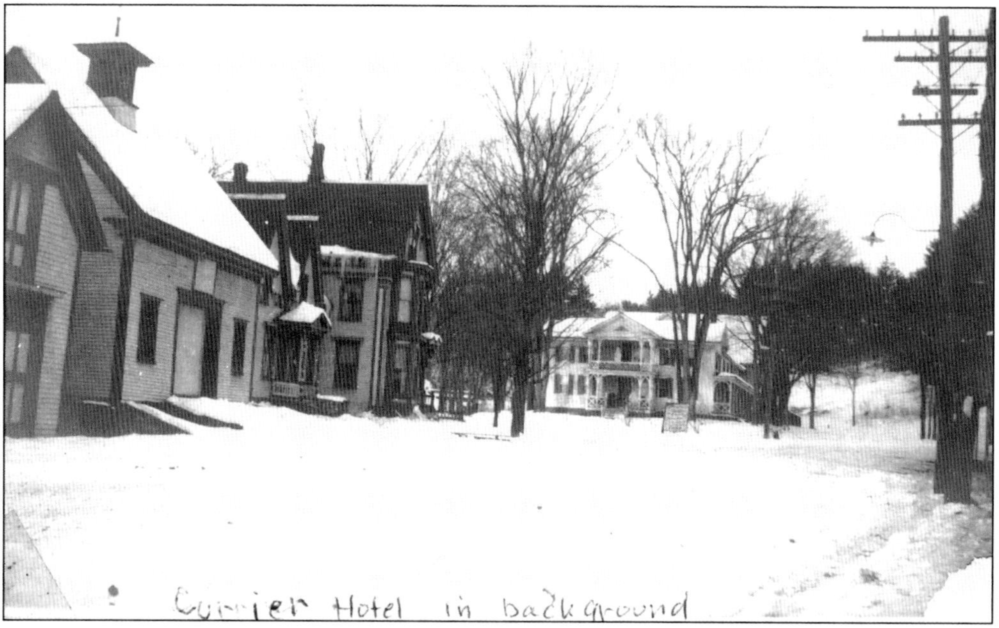

The image above shows the upper end of North Main Street prior to the monument construction in 1919. Hall's Hall is on right of the image (not seen). In the rear of the postcard is Currier's Hotel. On the right, the residence of Reuben Hoyt is seen, also called the carriage house, and on September 20, 1920, fifteen World War I veterans gathered here and organized the Charles Kilborn Post No. 58 American Legion; later it became the site of All Peoples Church of Belmont.

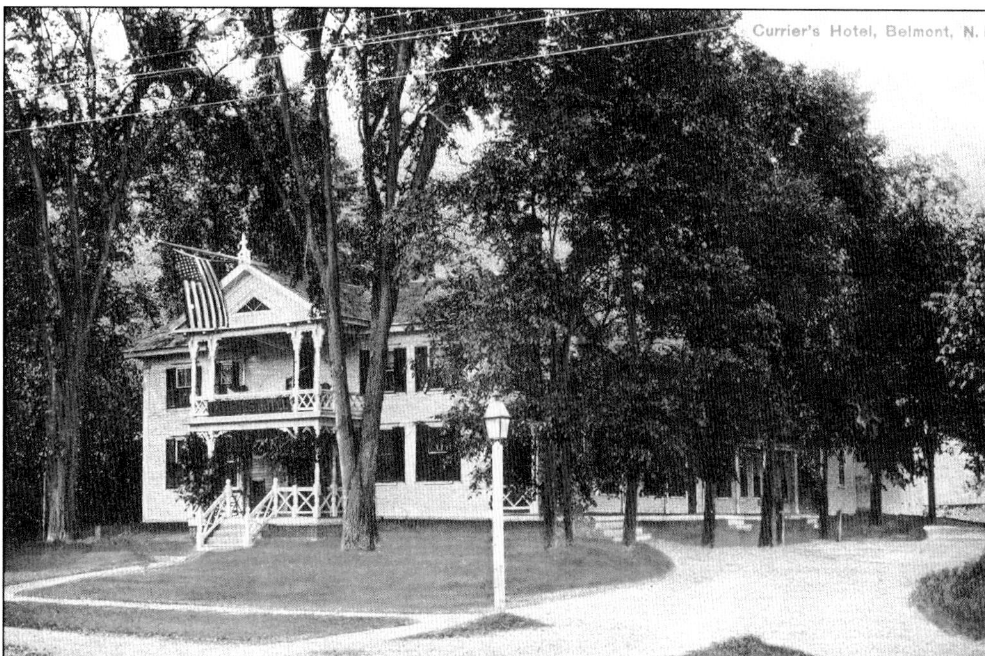

This building was built by Ira Mooney in 1859. Mooney conducted the hotel at this location for 12 years. Later it became known as Brown's Hotel and lastly Currier's Hotel. This building still stands today at the bottom of Church Street on the left.

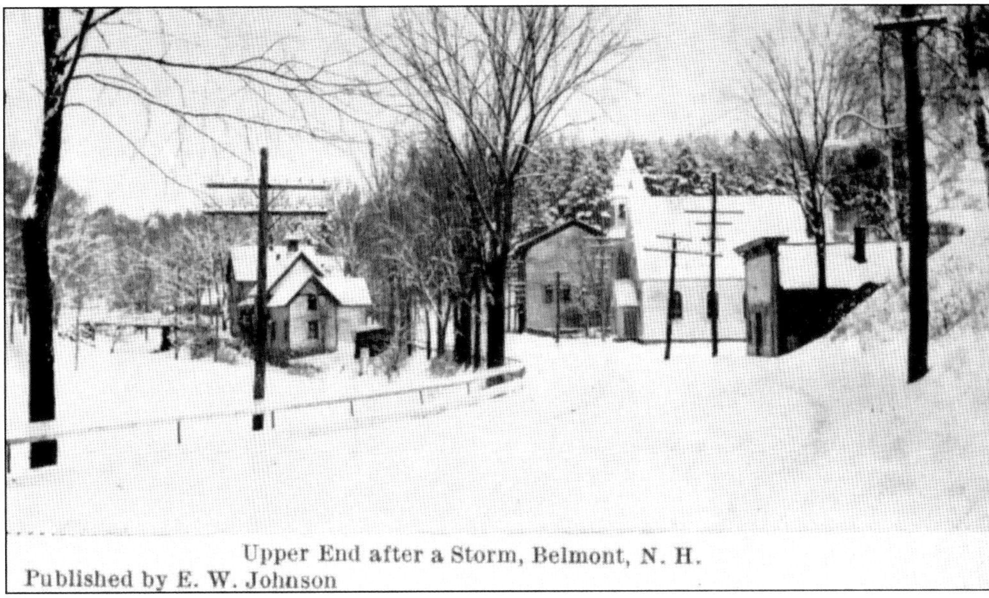

Main Street, looking north in the winter, is pictured here. The image shows St. Joseph's Church second on the right; the first structure on the right no longer exists and is now the location of Main Street today. Also seen are Hall's Hall, third on the right, and Belmont House, first on the left.

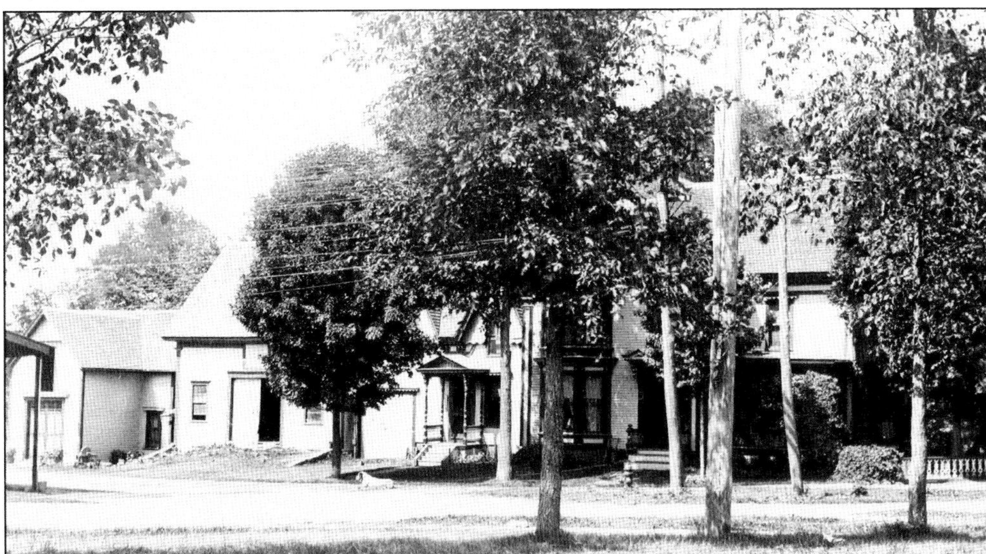

This building was constructed in the 1880s. In 1920, 15 World War I veterans gather in the old carriage house and organized the Charles Kilborn Post No. 58 American Legion. First post commander was Walter C. Harris. The post was named after Charles Cutting Kilborn, who died at Camp Yaphank, Long Island, New York, on October 5, 1918, just four weeks to the day after he left home. Kilborn, a native of Belmont, spent nearly all his life at his family's farm off Bean Hill Road in Belmont (formerly Kilborn, or Perry, Farm). All Peoples Church was organized in this building in 1950. The building was purchased and a portion converted into a place of worship. Later it was torn down, and a new building was erected. Today an apartment building is located here.

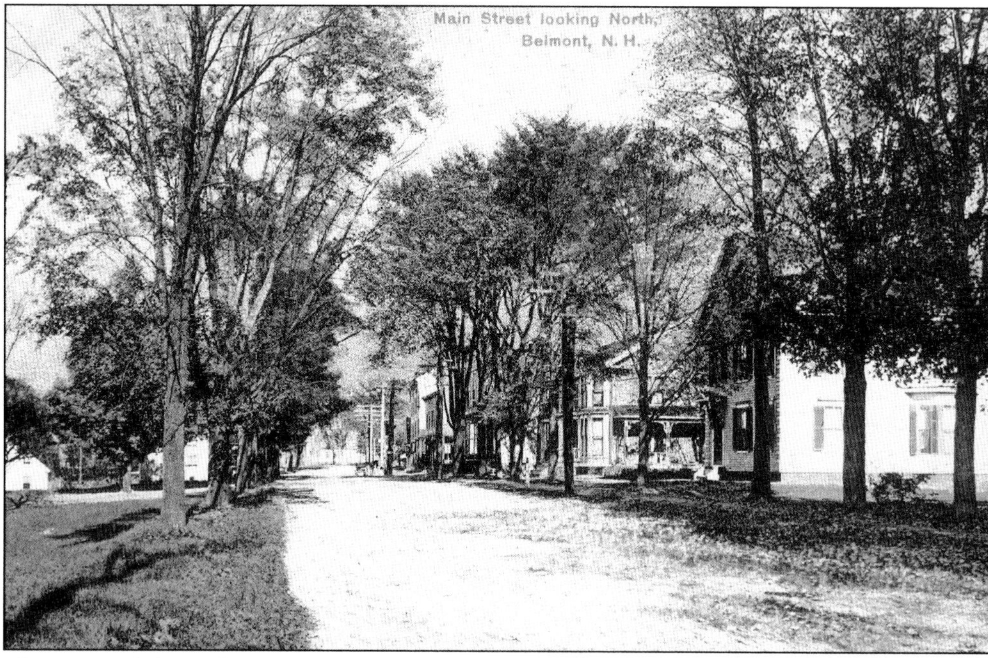

The postcard above shows Main Street prior to the construction of the Northway Bank, which was originally known as Citizen's Bank. Later name changes include Citizen's National Bank, First Deposit National Bank, and Providian Bank, all branches of a Tilton bank. These banks have all been a part of the Belmont community since the 1960s. It is said that prior to the 1960s, a tennis court was present at this location, and the property was the common area owned by the mill.

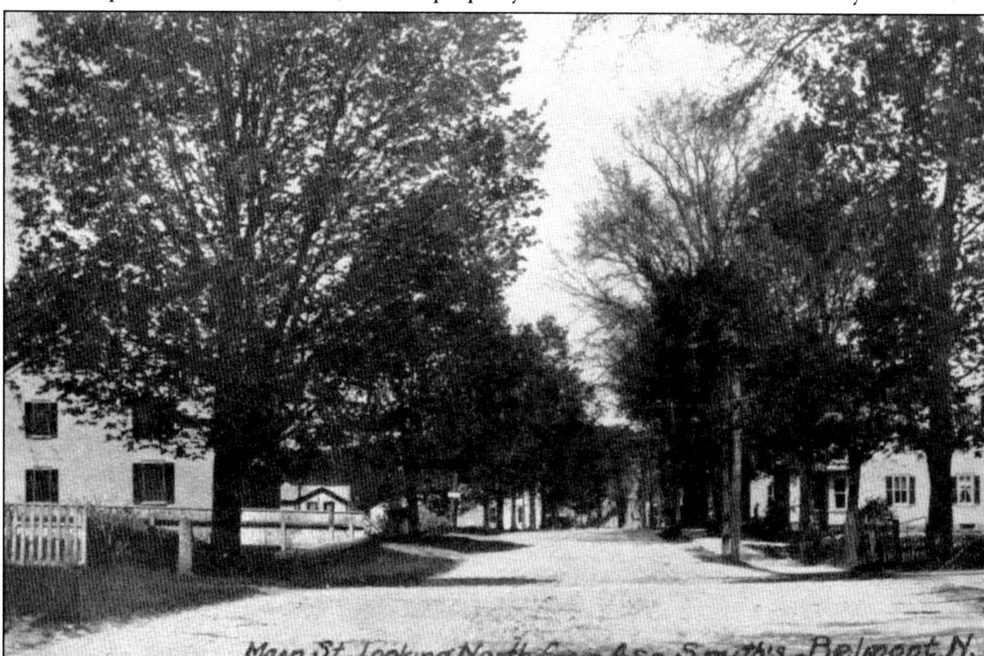

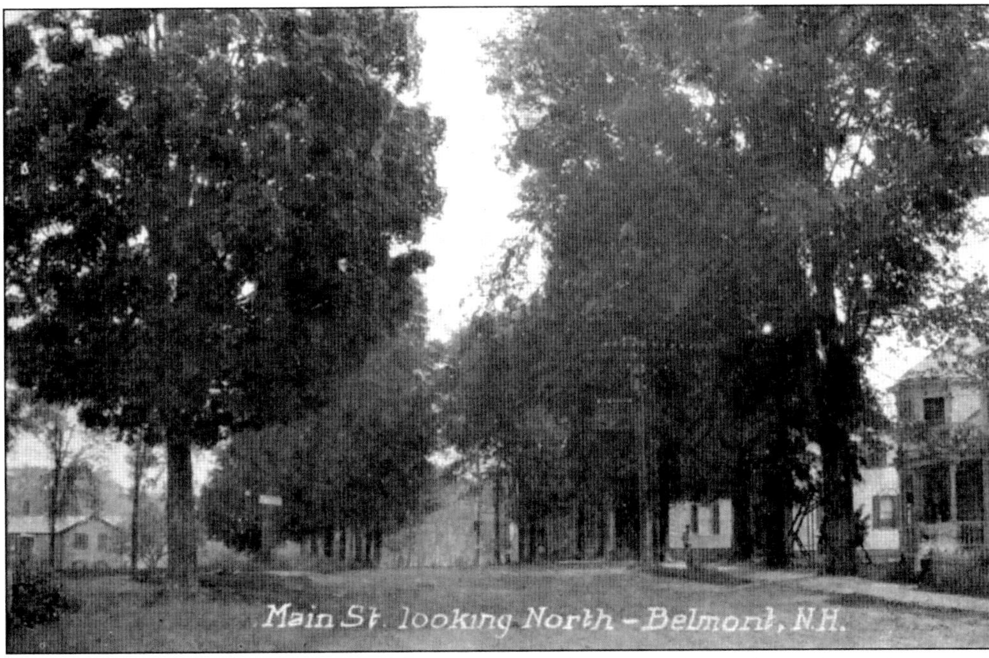

The postcard above is looking north from today's Belmont Hardware Store. Note the street is unpaved. To the left of the image is the location of the former millpond. People standing on the right are in front of the Moses Smith house, where Belmont Hardware now sits. Moses Smith sold carriages and horses from his barn. The view below shows Main Street looking north at the junction of Center Street and Main Street. The house in the background on the left stood where the present municipal parking lot is today, next to the Belmont Public Library. To the immediate left is the mill common area, which was once occupied by tennis courts, now the home of Northway Bank.

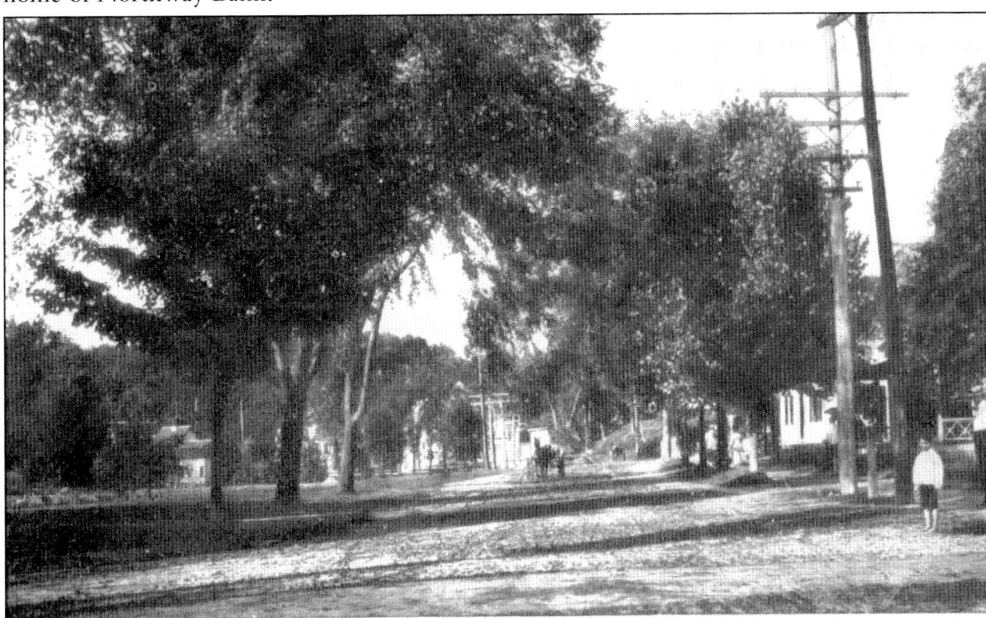

Published by E. W. Johnson Main Street, looking North, Belmont, N. H.

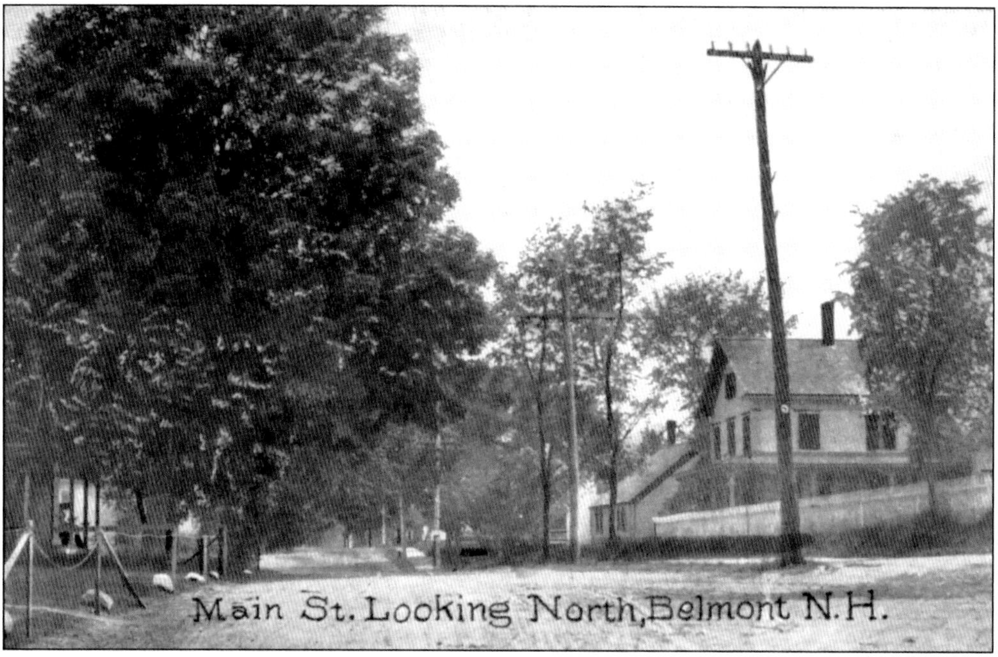

Seen above, around 1900, is a view looking north from the corner of Concord Street and Shaker Road. The second building on the right is the original Badger homestead at the end of School and Main Streets. Below is a winter scene looking south on Main Street in 1915. The empty location on the right side of the postcard is where Northway Bank stands today. These roads were more than likely rolled during the winter months with a snow roller being pulled by teams of horses.

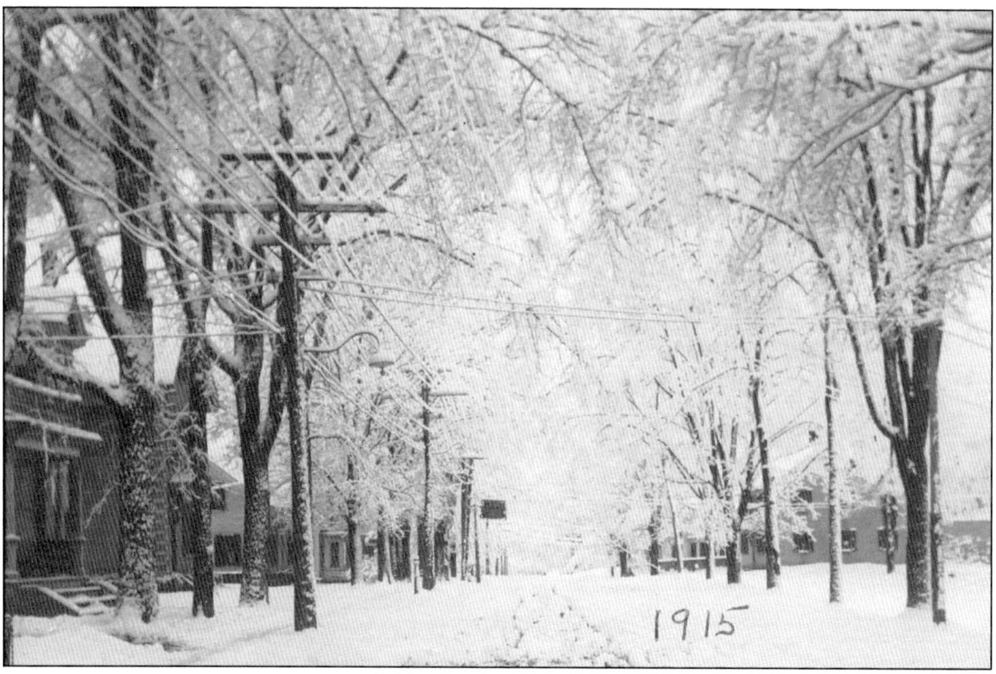

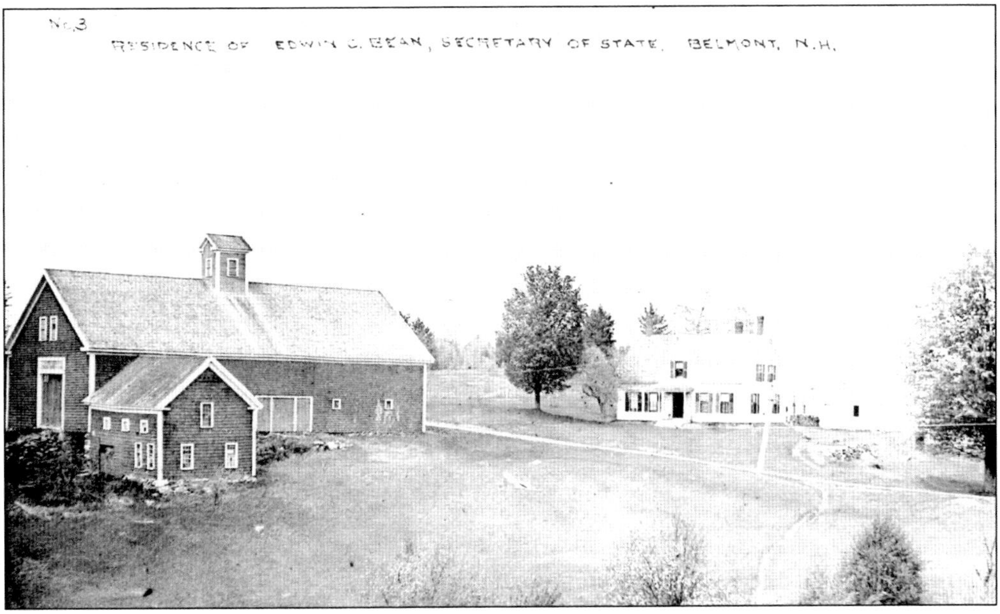

The Edwin C. Bean residence is located on Dearborn Street. Today the barn no longer exists. The house sits at the corner of Dearborn Street and Glenridge Road. Bean documented the coming of the railroad and raised $100 from interested citizens to pay for the charter before it had lapsed, which was approved by legislature in August 1883. Bean was prominent in local affairs, serving as the speaker of the New Hampshire House of Representatives in 1915 and secretary of state from 1915 to 1923.

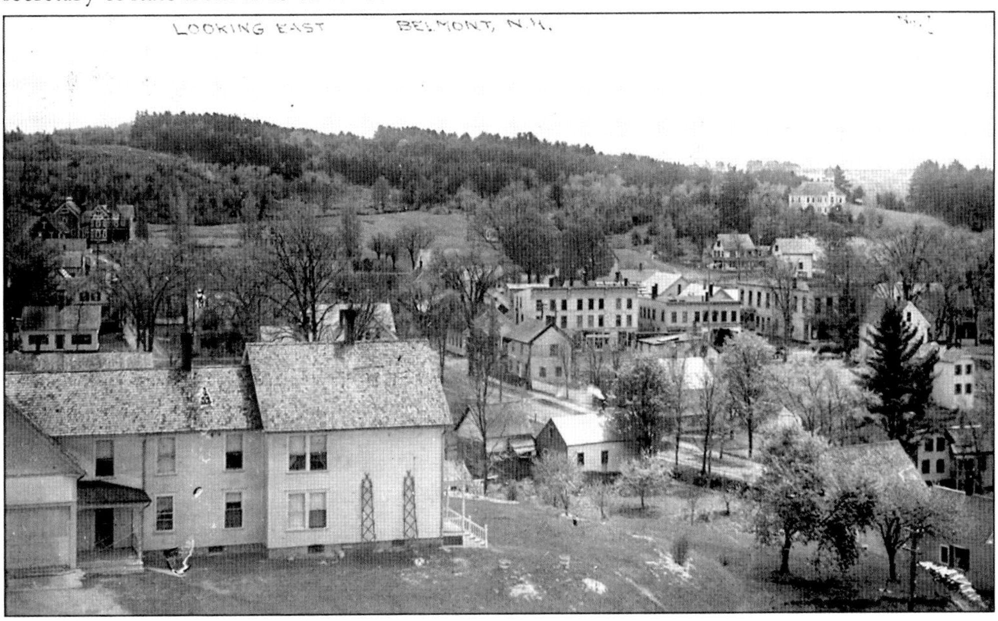

This 1915 postcard is a wonderful view of the village district from on top of the Johnson House located on Johnson Street, which was constructed in the 1890s. Shown here are Johnson's Block, built in 1891 by Frank K. Johnson, and Bryant's Block, built in 1894 by Edwin H. Bryant. Bryant's Block was later known to be community hall and is the site of today's town hall. Also, Gale School, constructed in 1894, can be seen to the far rear on the right.

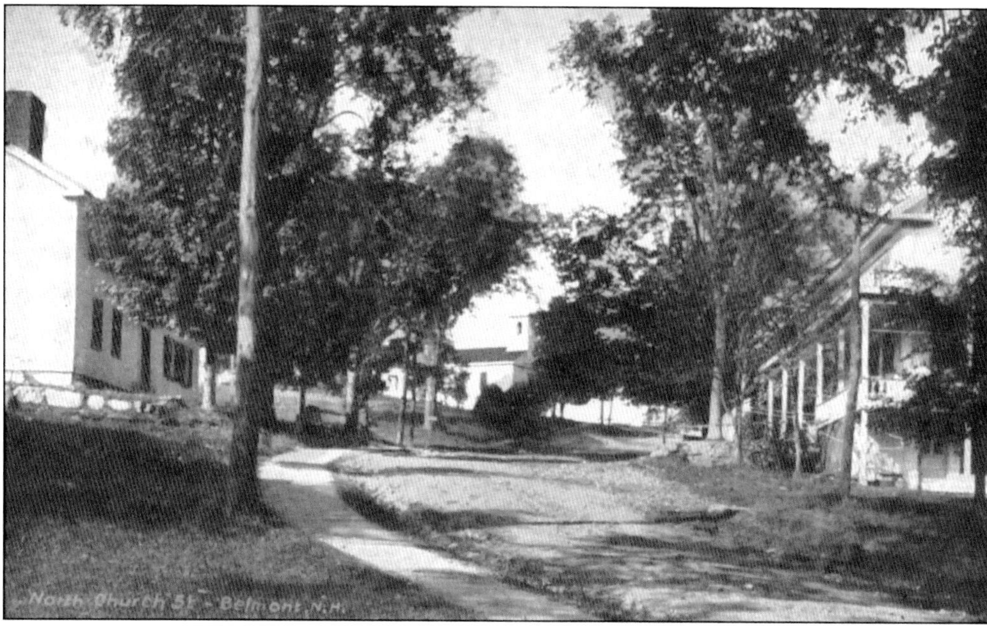

Shown here is North Church Street. Cate's Tavern, built in 1818, can be seen on the left and Belmont House on the right. Belmont House was constructed by Ira Mooney in 1871. Church Street at one time was known to locals as Tavern Hill. Samuel Cate had originally owned and operated the tavern, then later his widow until she married James S. Hill, when it then became known as Hill's Tavern. The building on the right burned, and a new apartment building was constructed in its place.

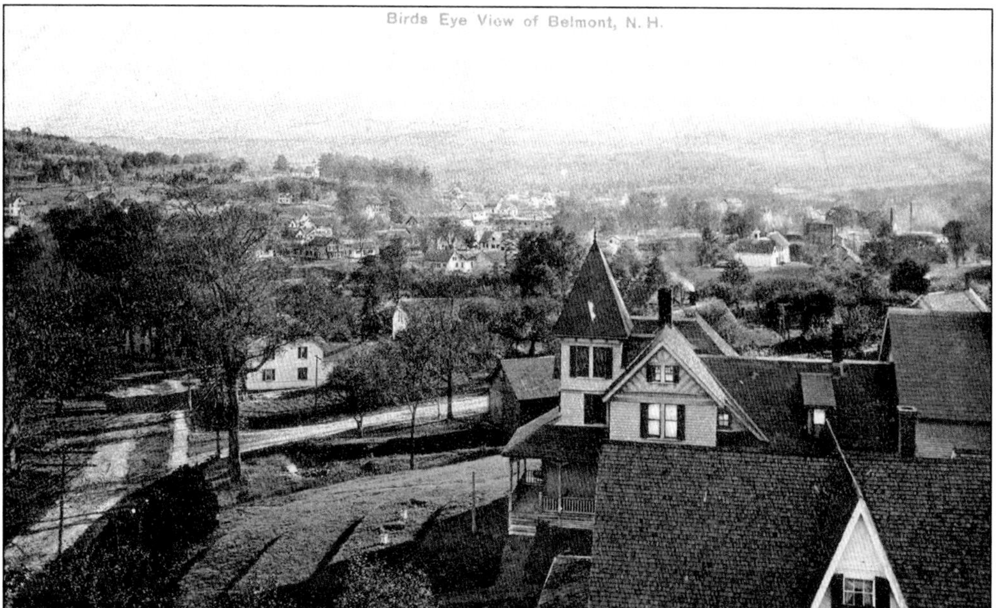

This spectacular view was taken from the top of the Baptist church belfry. At the right top corner, the mill stacks are seen. At the bottom left, Church Street starts its descent turning right onto Dearborn Street, which at this time is a mere cart path down the hill into the village. Cate's Tavern can be seen to the left of Dearborn Street.

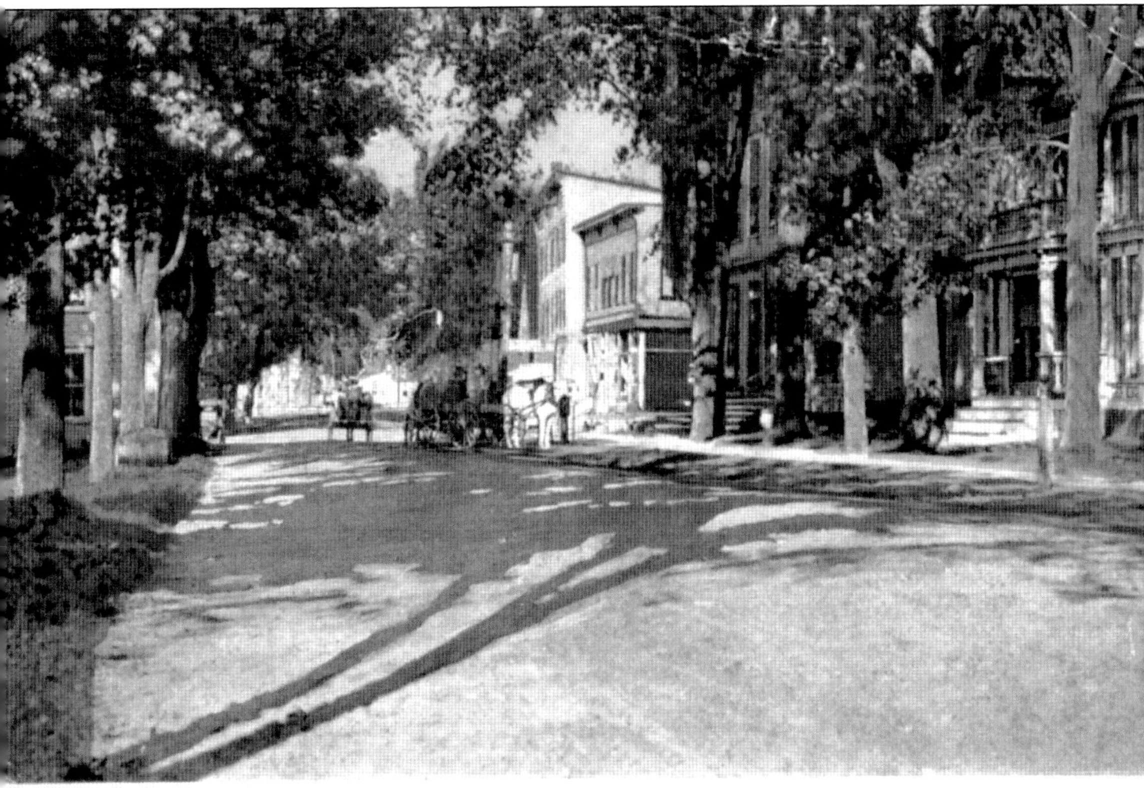

MAIN STREET, BELMONT, N. H.

Main Street is seen here before it was paved. Horses are seen in the background in front of the Johnson's Block. To the left, the watering trough can be seen just before the "Old Hose House." The Hose House was later moved to Fuller Street. The building also housed the library and selectmen's office on the second floor. The watering trough still sits in front of the library and is used as a planter today.

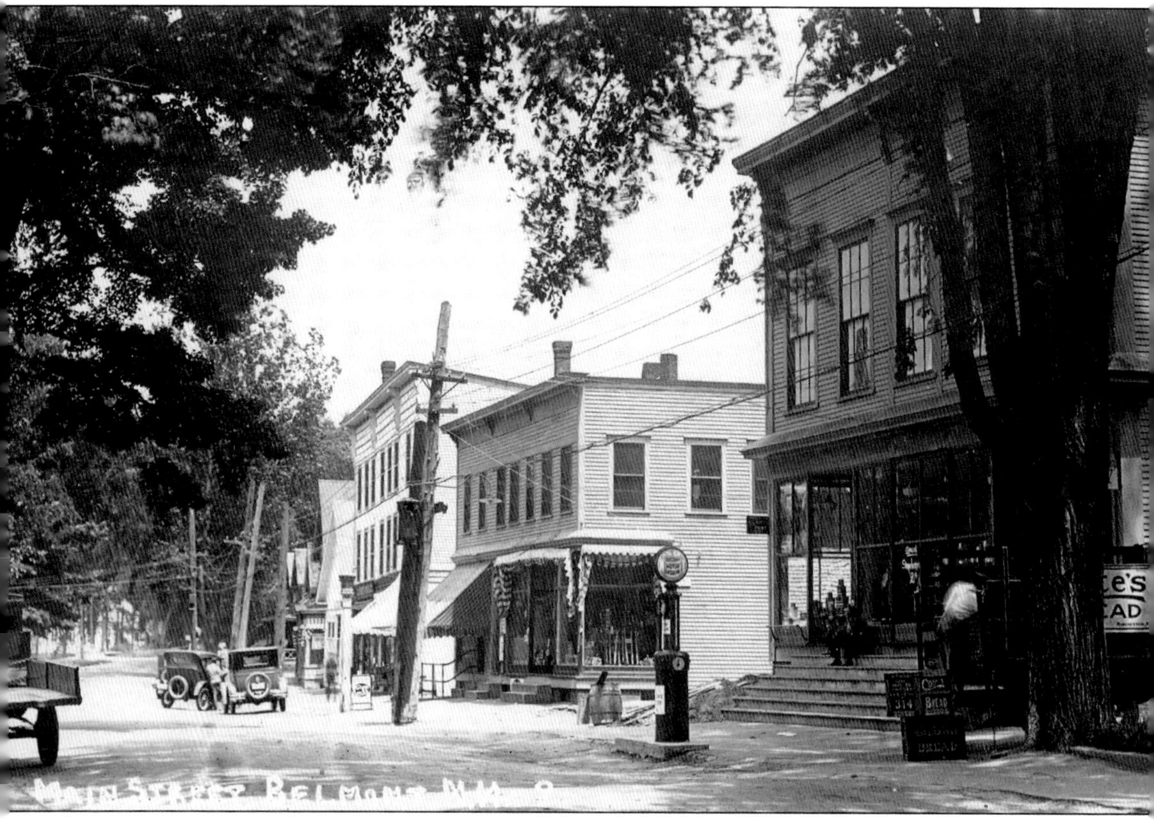

This postcard from the 1920s is a reflection of the times. The gas pumps are seen on the right in front of Bryant's Block. Later it was known as community hall, and today it is town hall. Notice the stairs in the front of the building, which were later moved to the rear of the building.

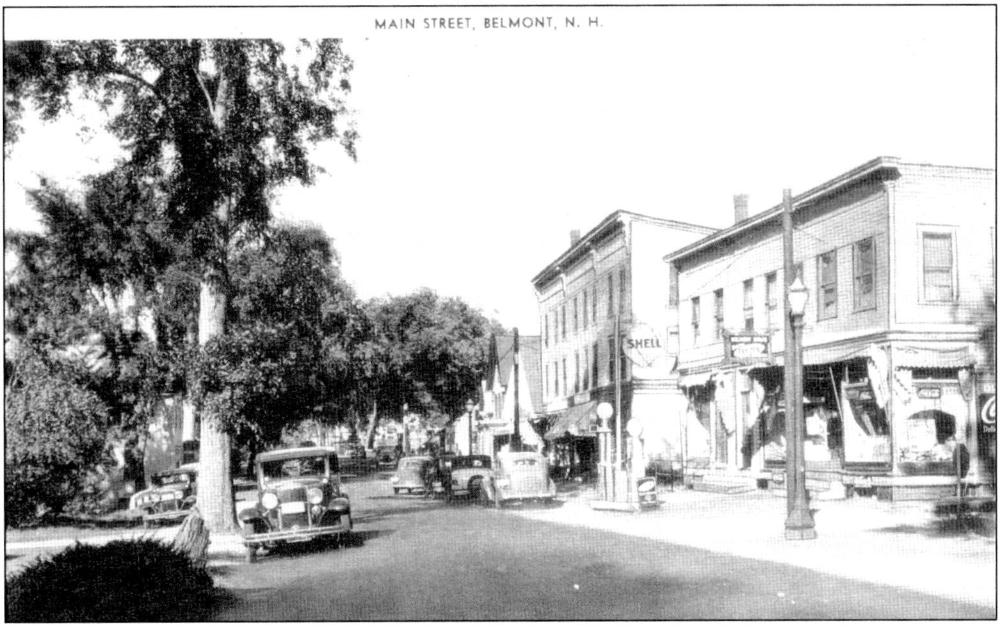

Pictured here is Main Street in 1937. Before the installation of electric streetlights (around 1900), the village was lit by kerosene streetlamps. Each evening, the lamplighter walked the village streets with a ladder, lighting the lamps. This duty was done for years by Bill Chaplin. The first electric lights in the village were installed in the houses of John Lyford and Moses Sargent Sr. The power was supplied by a generator at Judkins Pond (Pout Pond) on Cutler's Brook.

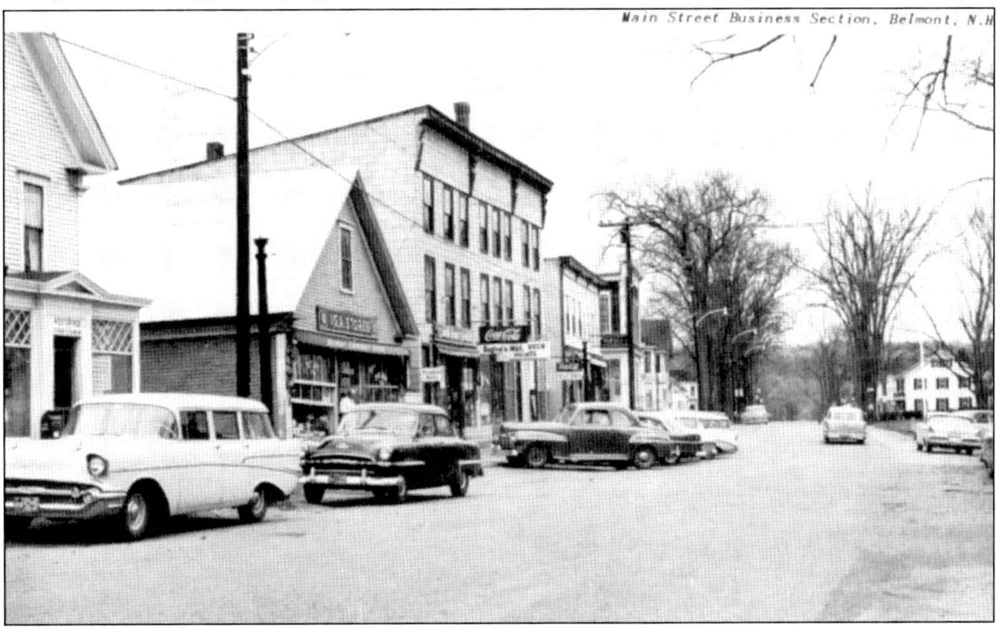

This is the Main Street business section in 1961, showing the old village schoolhouse, which was moved to this location. At this time, it housed the IGA grocery store. The building was demolished to make way for gas pumps, which were operated by the Belmont Village Store until they were removed for additional parking. Originally the schoolhouse building sat at the junction of Church Street and Laconia Road before the construction of the Gale School in 1894.

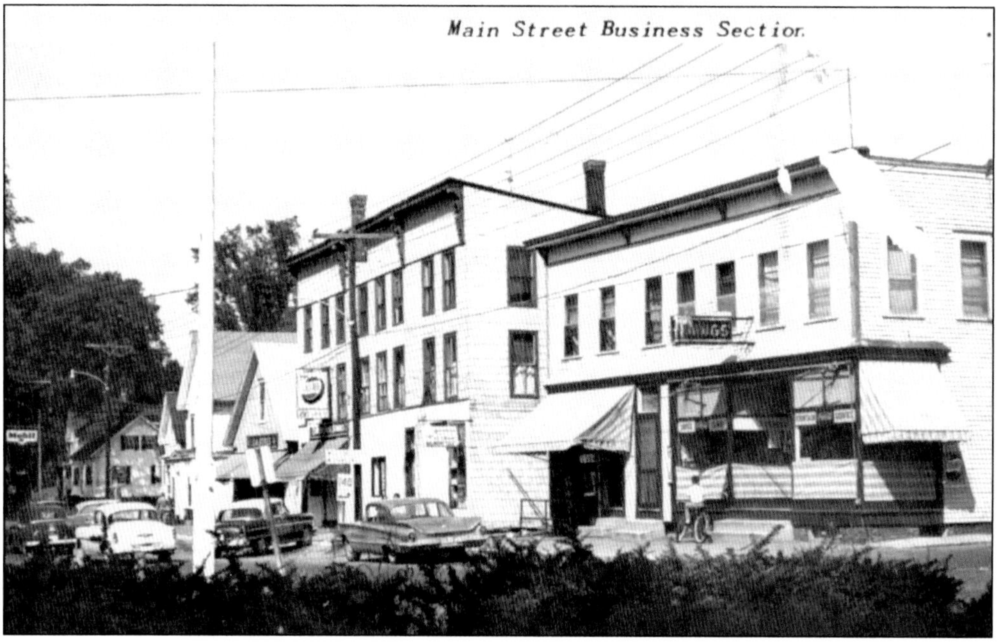

The Main Street business section is shown here. Notice the building (old schoolhouse and former IGA store) where the Belmont Village Store's parking lot is today and where gas pumps once were before being removed. One of the first-known vehicles in town was owned by William Barrett. Barrett had a 1907 Maxwell, and in order to have gasoline, it was purchased by the barrel. Barrett soon found himself measuring out gasoline by the gallon to those who needed the vital product for their automobiles.

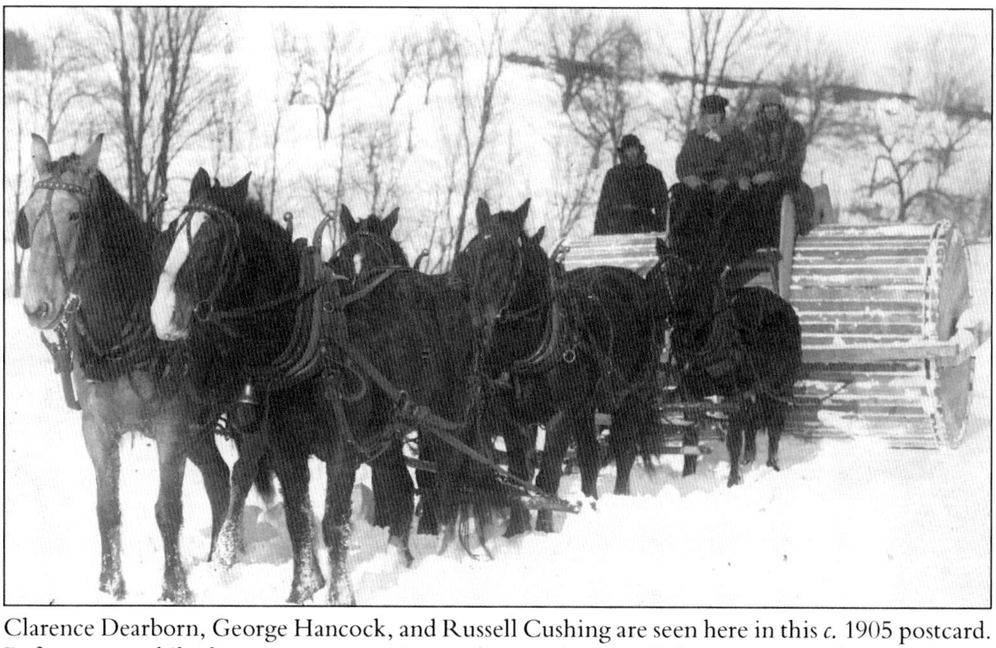

Clarence Dearborn, George Hancock, and Russell Cushing are seen here in this *c.* 1905 postcard. Before automobiles became common, it was the practice to roll the snow into a hard surface so that horses and sleighs could travel during winter months. This worked fine until there was a thaw and the surface gave way.

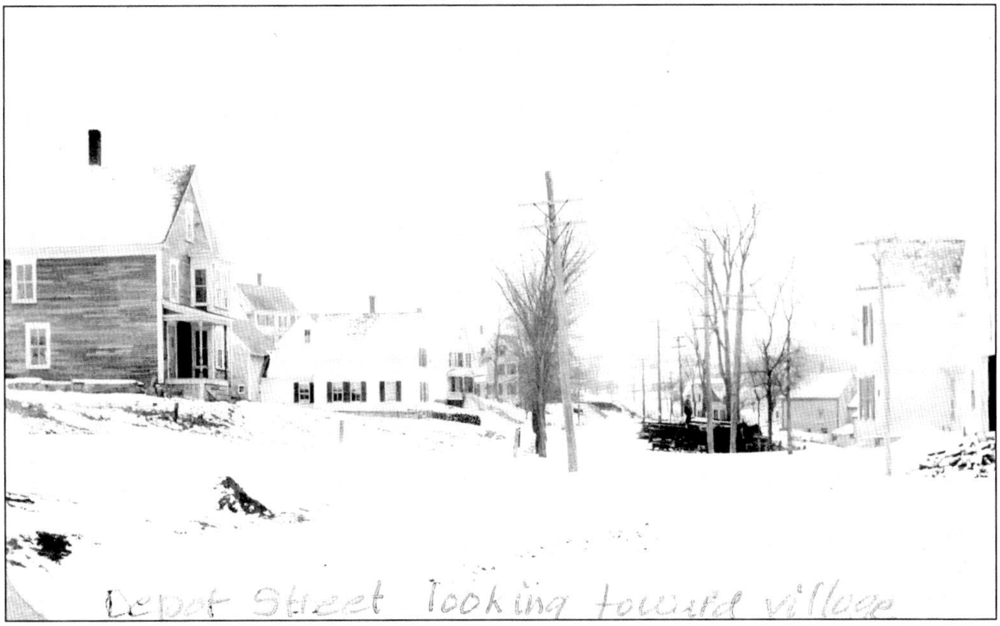

During the 1890s, Gale Street, Spring Street, and School Street were constructed. Several houses were built at this time, and some were moved to these locations. It was common to see homes being moved up and down the streets during this time. Many of the homes moved to these streets are still standing today. The postcard above shows Depot Street, constructed in the 1870s, looking toward the village. The postcard below was taken from the Belmont Mill and shows the footbridge leading to Depot Street. The remains of John Dearborn's gristmill and the end of the rail line can also be seen in the image.

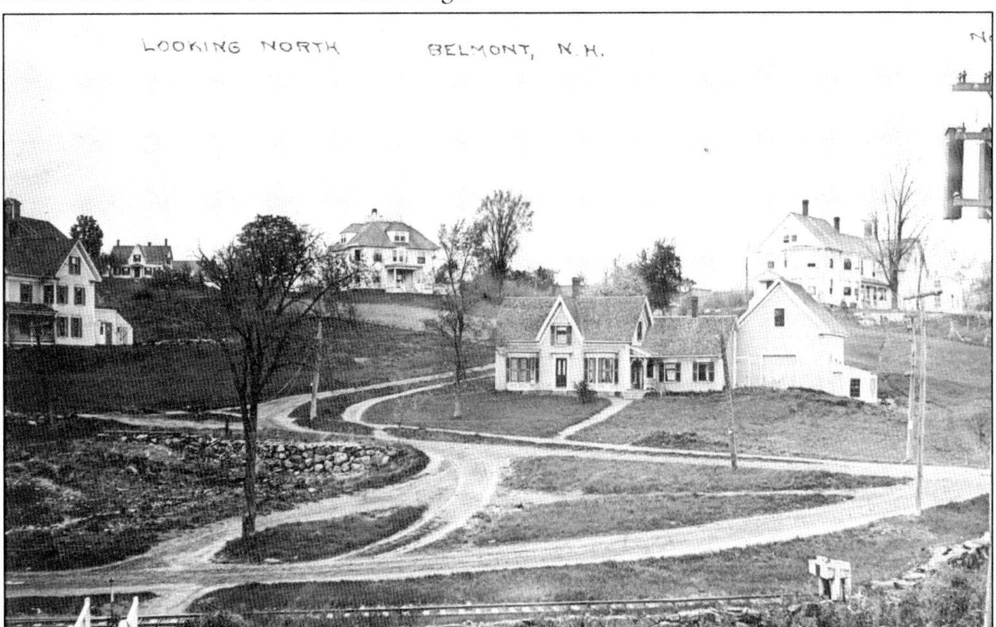

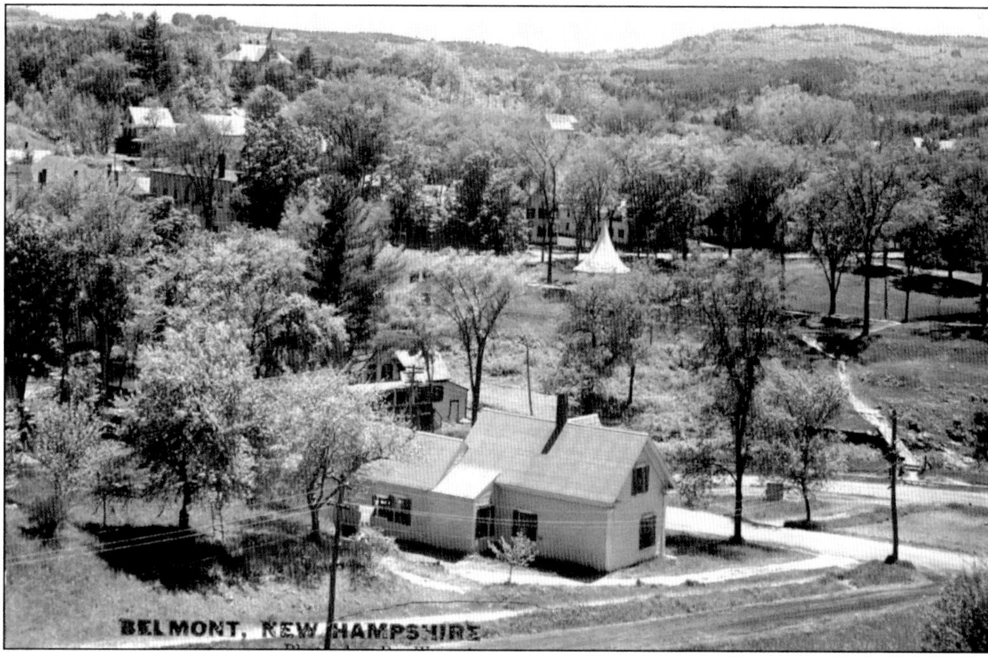

Seen here is a view of Belmont from Johnson Street in 1926. In the bottom left, the railroad yard can be seen and in the middle of the image the bandstand. Looking off to the far top left of the postcard, the Gale School can also be seen. Johnson Street was also constructed in the 1890s.

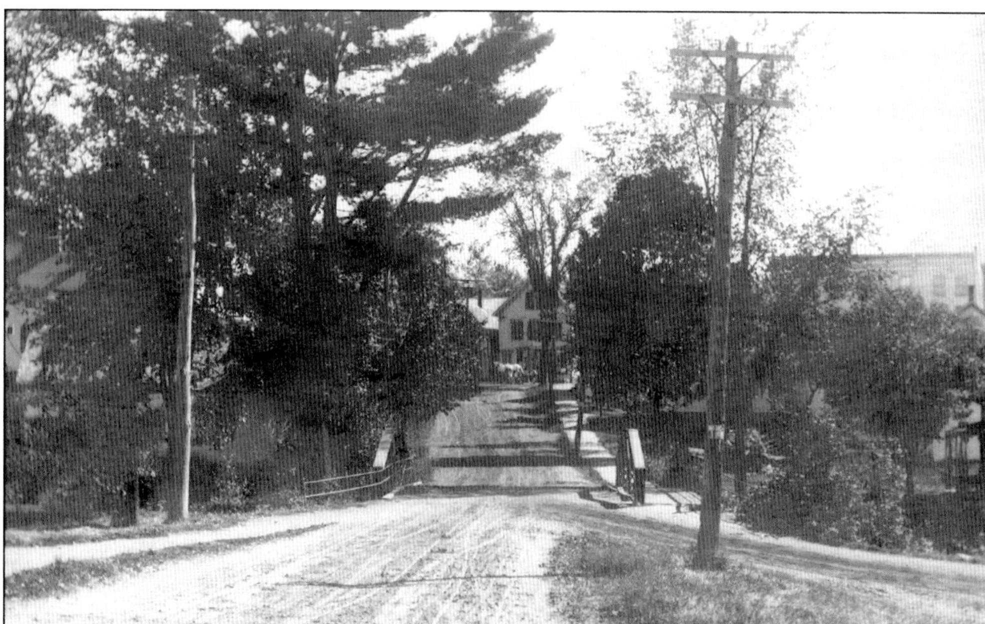

This early postcard shows Depot Street looking toward Main Street. The Depot Street Bridge and the road leading to the Belmont Railroad station can be seen here. The large building in the back to the right of the postcard is Johnson's Block. Notice the unpaved streets.

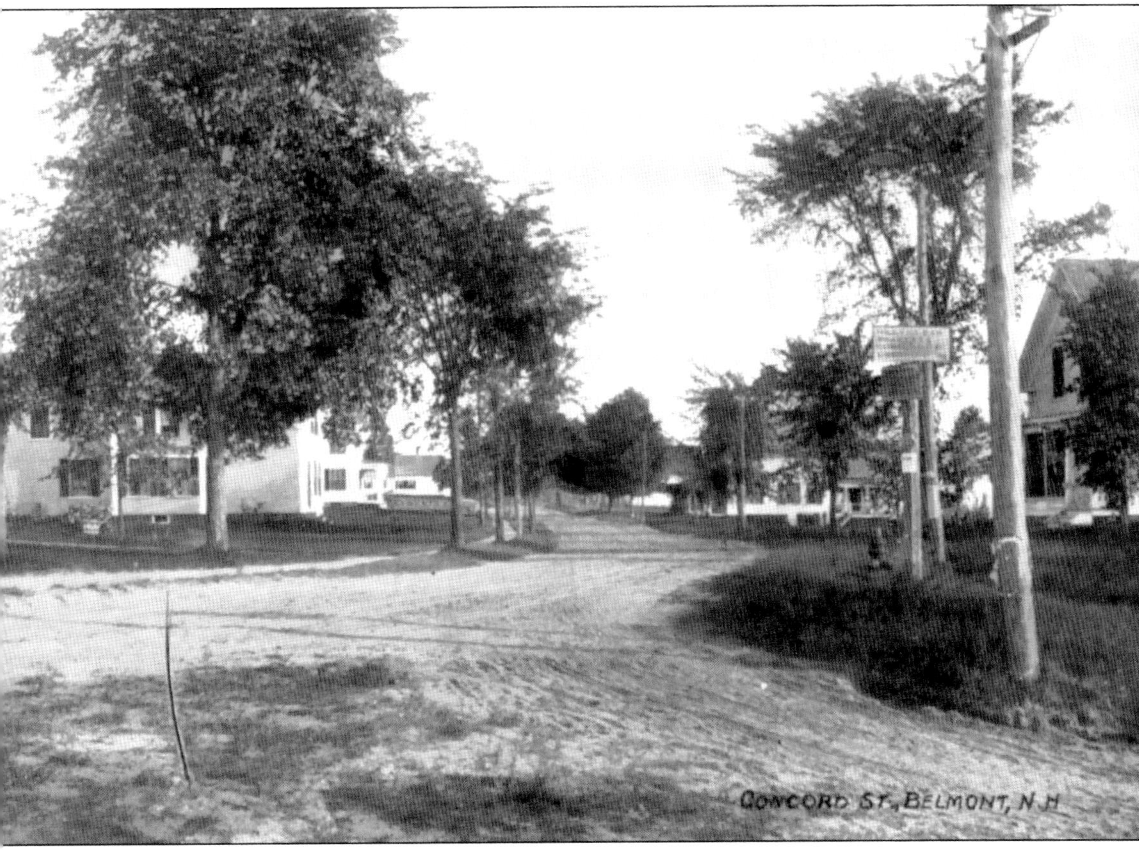

This 1910 postcard shows the corner of Concord Street and Shaker Road. Notice the unpaved streets and wooden street sign. The present-day Moynihan residence can be seen to the right of the image, and Clean Air Technologies is now located on the left across the street.

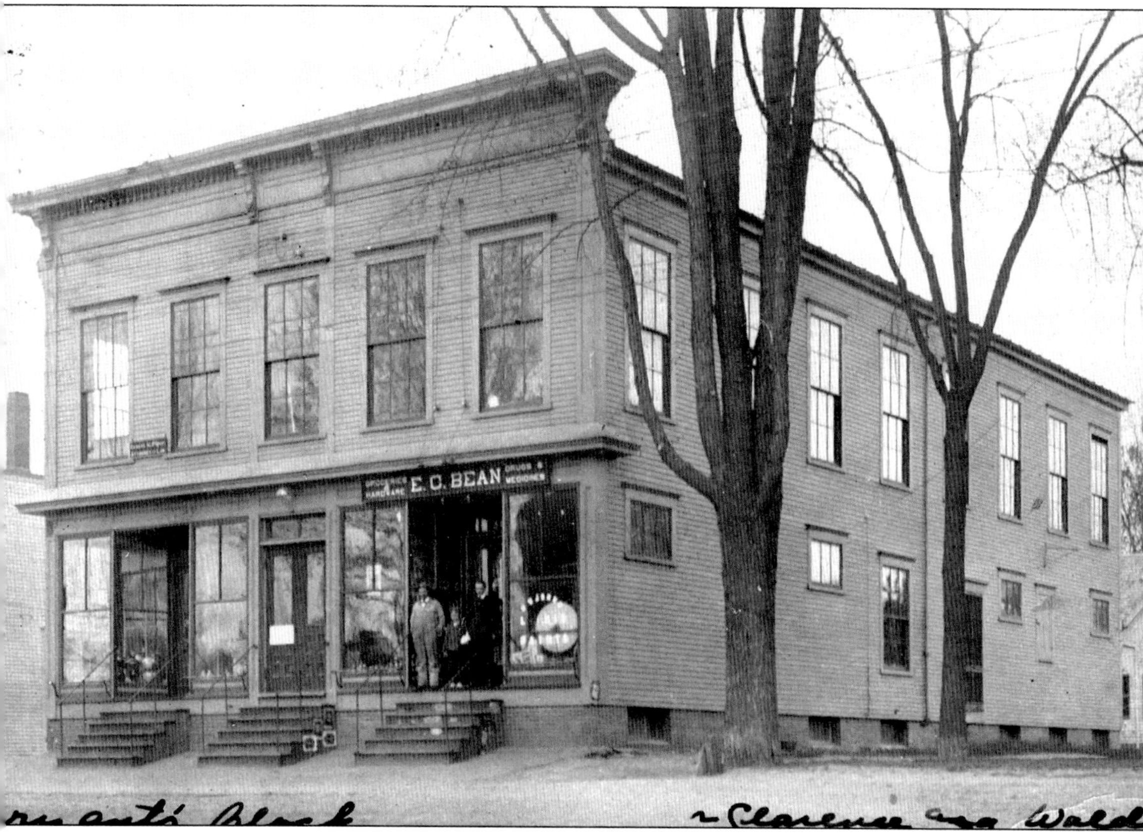

This building was constructed in 1894 by Edwin H. Bryant. This building has had many uses over the years, including stores, a community hall with community dances, basketball games, and concerts, the police station, and the municipal court, as well as today's municipal offices.

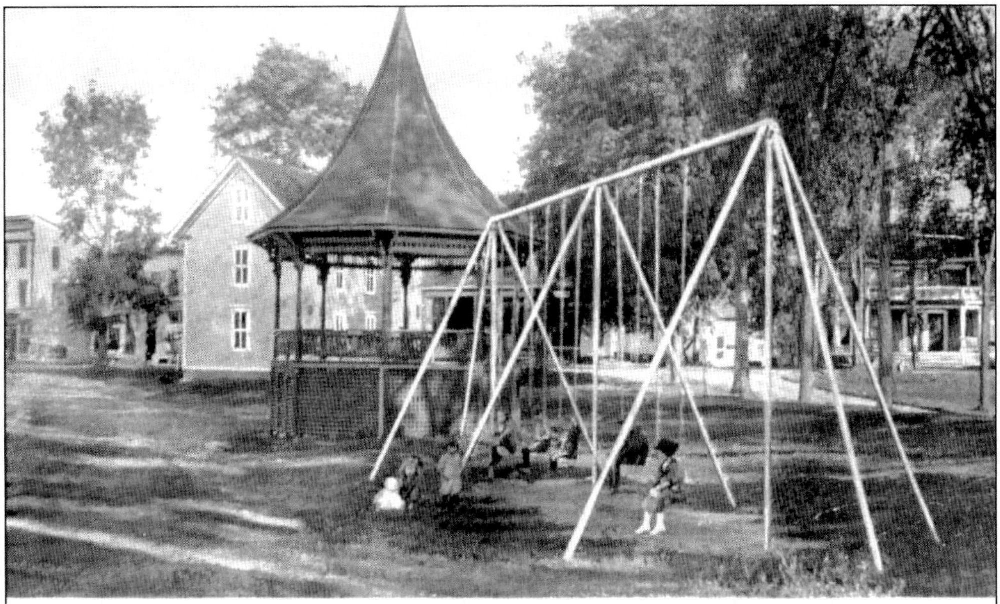

CHILDREN'S PLAY GROUNDS. BELMONT, N. H.

The postcard above shows the bandstand, constructed in 1908, and the "Old Hose House," which at this time was the Belmont Public Library. Main Street is seen in the rear of the postcard. Below, this *c.* 1919 postcard shows homes in the background that were located on Depot and Johnson Streets. In the foreground, Lawrence Street, which is known today as Mill Street, can be seen. This area was used as the first town park, and many events have been held here over the years.

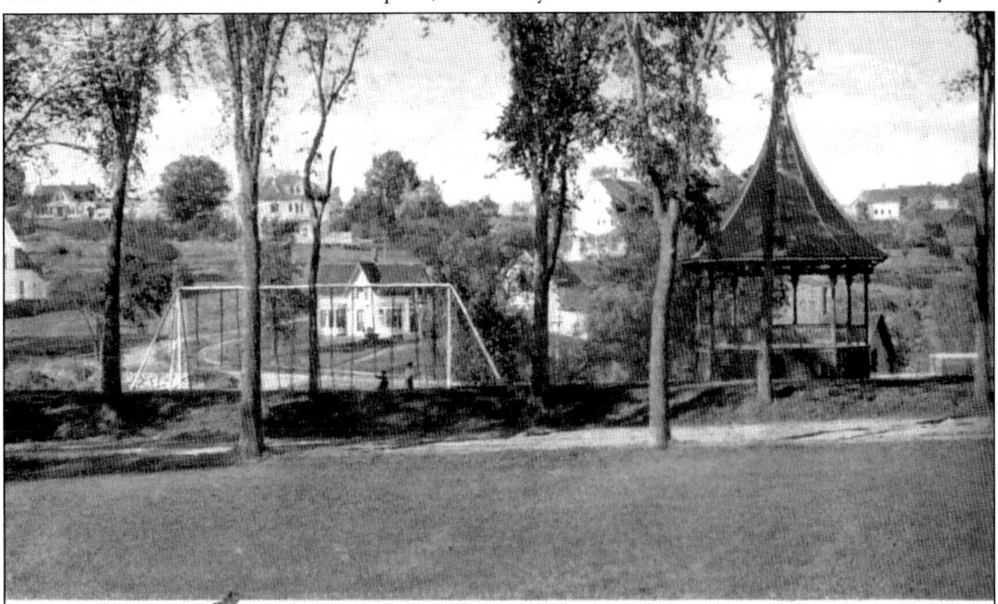

VIEW IN BELMONT, N. H.

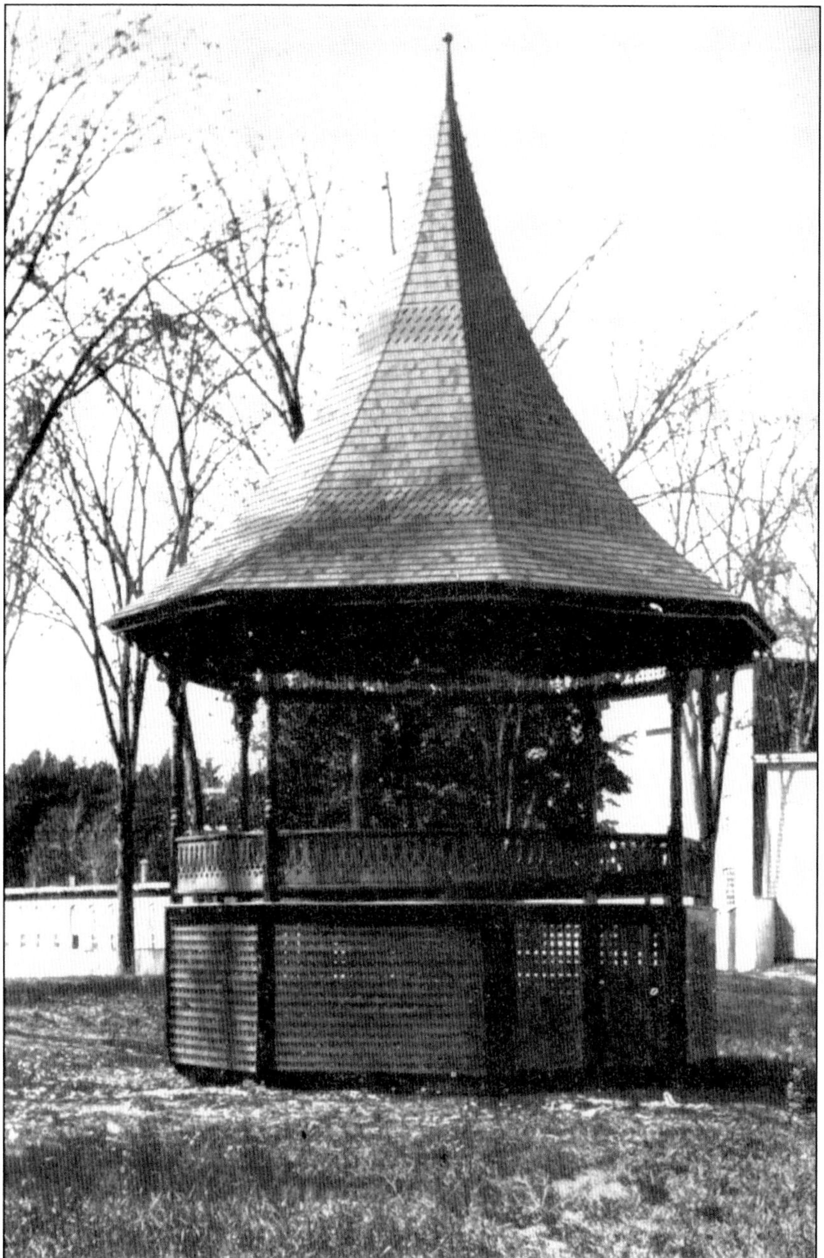

Published by E. W. Johnson. I. B. B. Bandstand, Belmont, N. H.

Belmont Old Home Day celebrations each year are centered around this still-existing bandstand, which stands behind the Belmont Public Library today. Prior to this, the library was in the upstairs of the Hose House building near this location. The Hose House was moved to Fuller Street when the library was constructed. The upstairs of Hose House was used as the selectmen's office, and downstairs was used as the fire station at the Fuller Street location. When these uses stopped, the Charles Kilborn Post No. 58 American Legion used the building, and for a time, the Belmont Fire Department used the downstairs as cold storage. The building was torn down in the spring of 2002, and it is now a municipal parking lot.

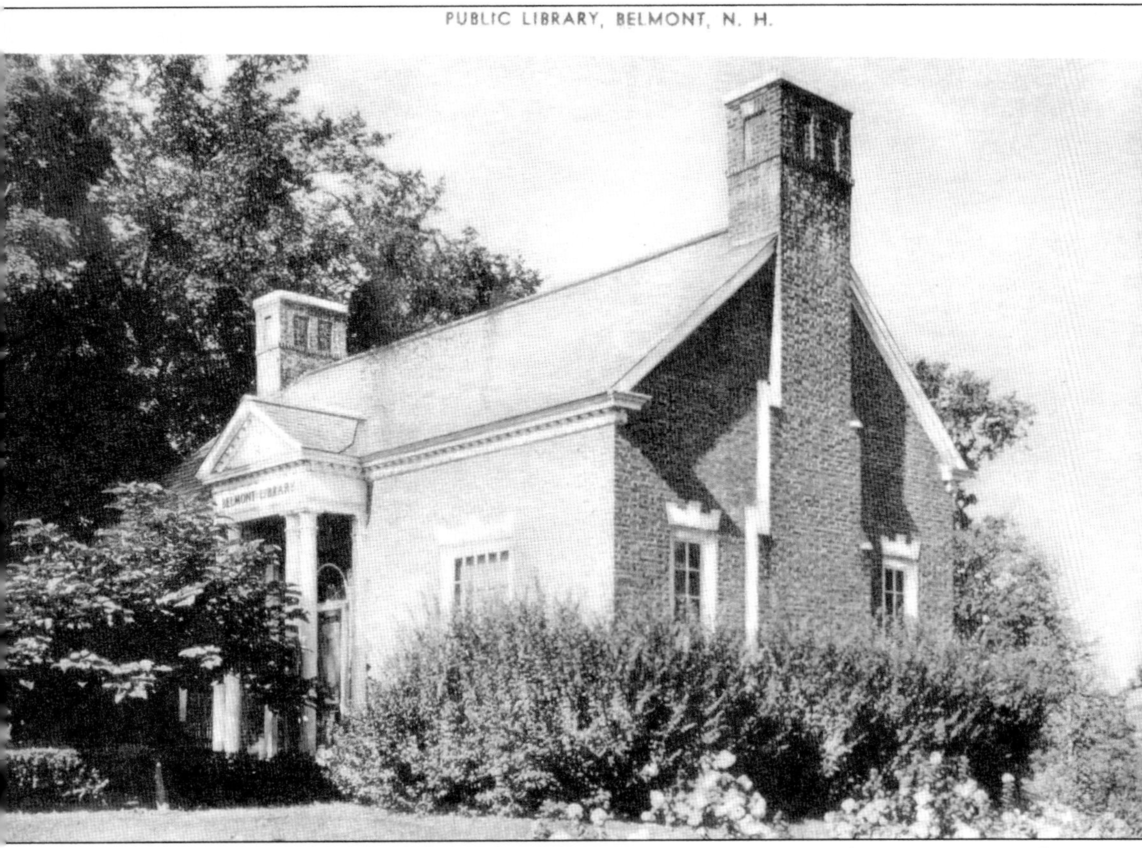

This building housing the Belmont Public Library was dedicated on February 4, 1928. The building was given to the people of Belmont by George and Walter Duffy, along with a trust fund to help in its support. Etta Belle Dearborn was the librarian for 20 years. Other librarians include Antoinette (Nettie) Haggett, Pearl Sanborn (serving this position for 17 years), Evelyn C. Morse, Joanne Stevens, Norma Roulx, Elizabeth Hoey, Joanne Ricard, Mary Bognaski, and Jackie Gardner, the current librarian.

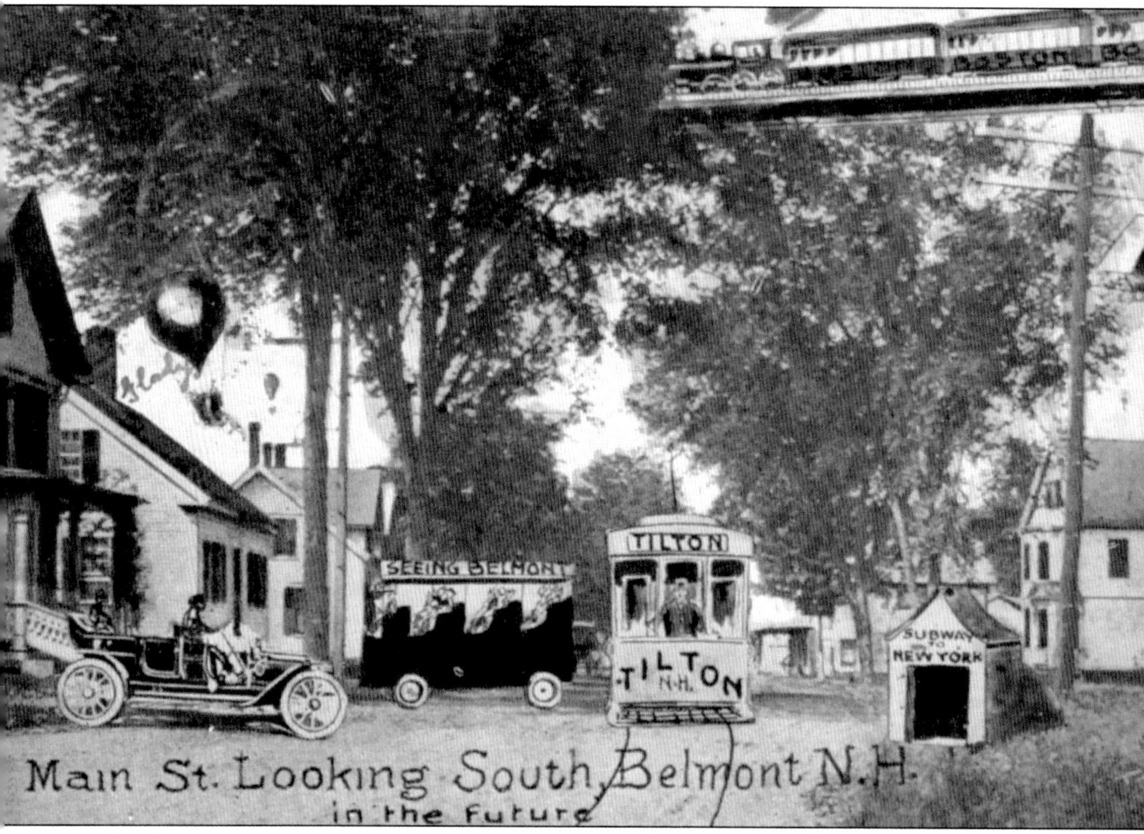

This futuristic 1908 postcard is interesting for those who could imagine what Belmont would be like in the future. Note the flying train in the upper right corner hovering over the blimp and hot air balloons. Below that is a doghouse structure marked "Subway to New York," as the trolley from Tilton makes a stop on Main Street. The "Seeing Belmont" bus is full of people, while a native of Belmont cautiously picks up his aunt, who at any minute will depart for her trip on the trolley.

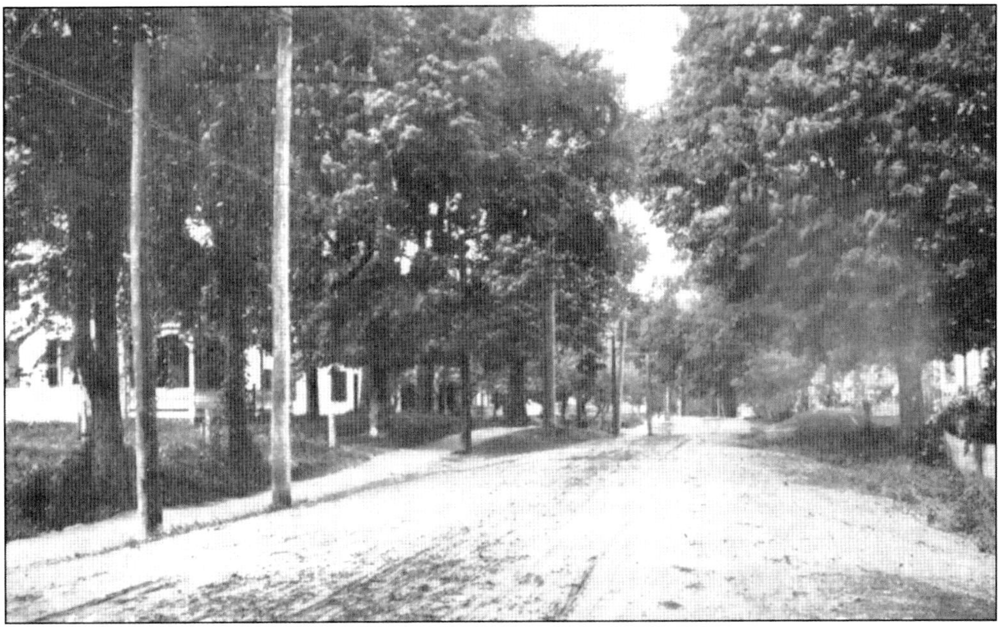

According to a newspaper clipping, one of Belmont's first automobile accidents occurred when Fred LaFlamme and Horace Hancock bumped into each other in front of Hall's store. Both cars were damaged, but no one was hurt. The speed limits first posted in the town of Belmont appeared on July 1, 1904. Automobiles were restricted to 6 miles per hour on any town or public roadways and 10 miles an hour on any said highway running through the town.

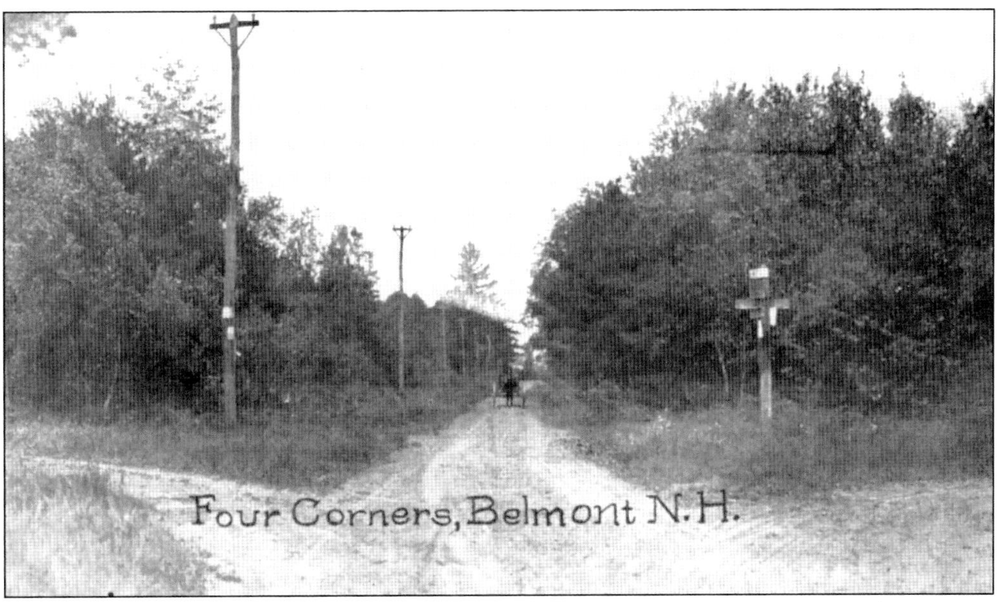

This is the site of the first-known "Four Corners" in Belmont, situated at the corners of Jamestown Road and South Road. In the rear of the image, a horse and buggy can be seen approaching on what is now known as Depot Street (State Route 140 West). Following an easterly direction, the next street at this time would have been Dearborn Street, which led down Church Street onto Main Street.

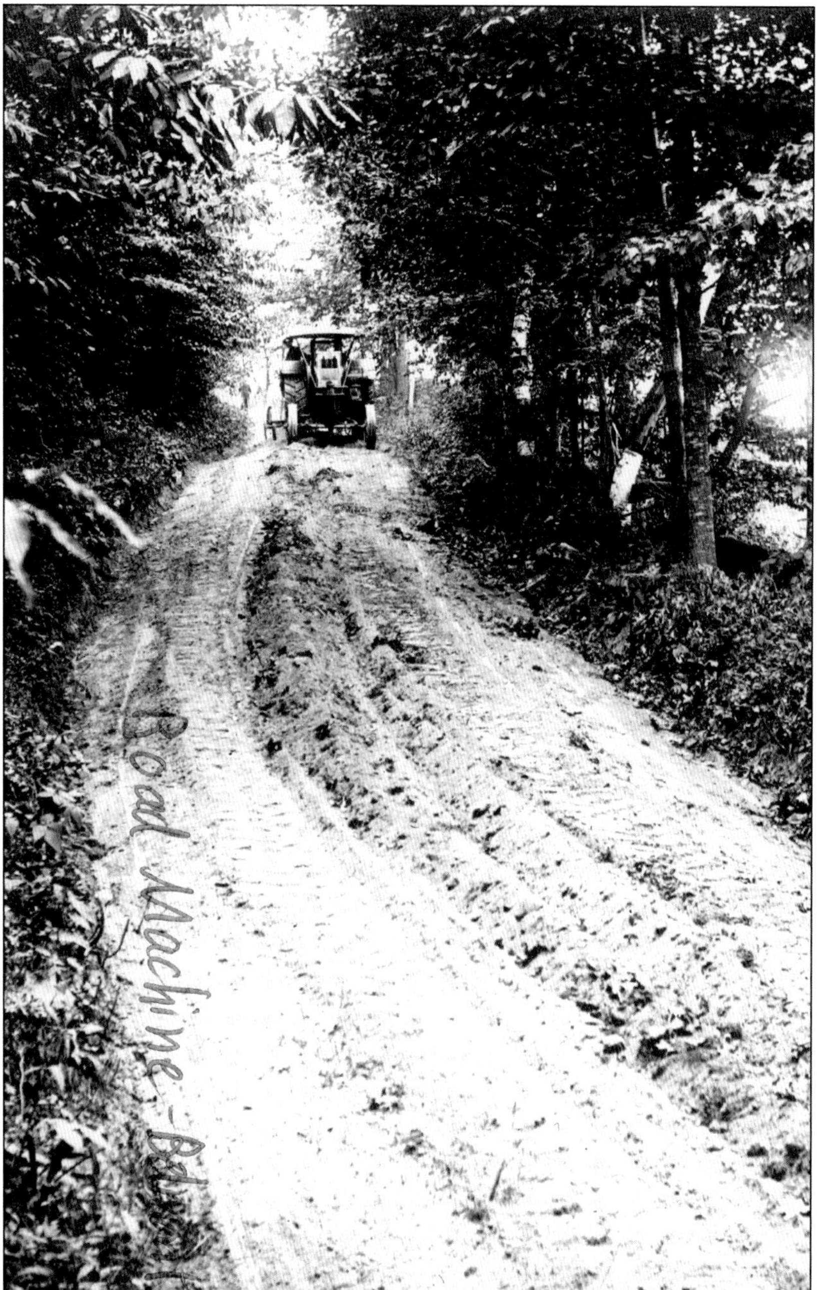

This gas-powered road machine was used for many years to maintain the town's many miles of roadways. This machine was first mentioned in the town's annual town reports in 1887, indicating the growth and development of early town roads. S. F. Hill, Prescott Hall, and John Lyford were operators of this machine. Some of the early village roadways constructed with this machine were Gale Street, High Street, Johnson Street, Sargent Street, School Street, and Spring Street, constructed in the 1890s. In these early days, landowners were either paid for their land to construct roads upon or paid yearly for the use of their lands. Districts were set up throughout town consisting of groups of men who would clear and maintain the roadways.

Five

Schools

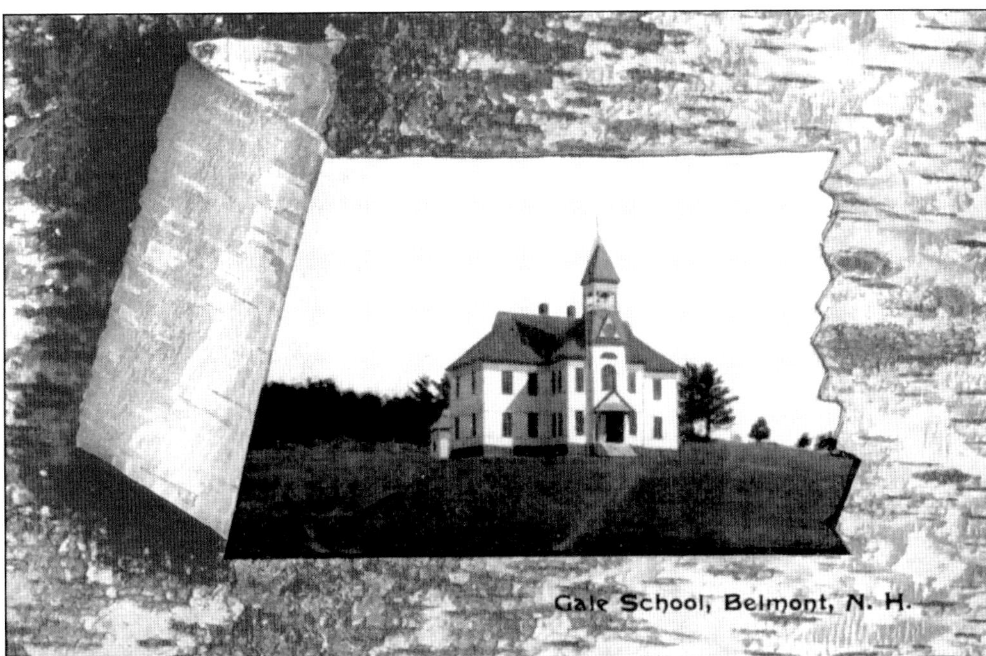

In 1894, the first primary school was constructed by the Town of Belmont. It was later named Gale School after Napoleon B. Gale, who left $10,000 to the town. Gale was born in 1815 at his father's farm on Mile Hill Road and was for years prominent in banking circles in Laconia. The remainder of Gale's estate was left to the City of Laconia and used to construct and fund the Gale Memorial Library.

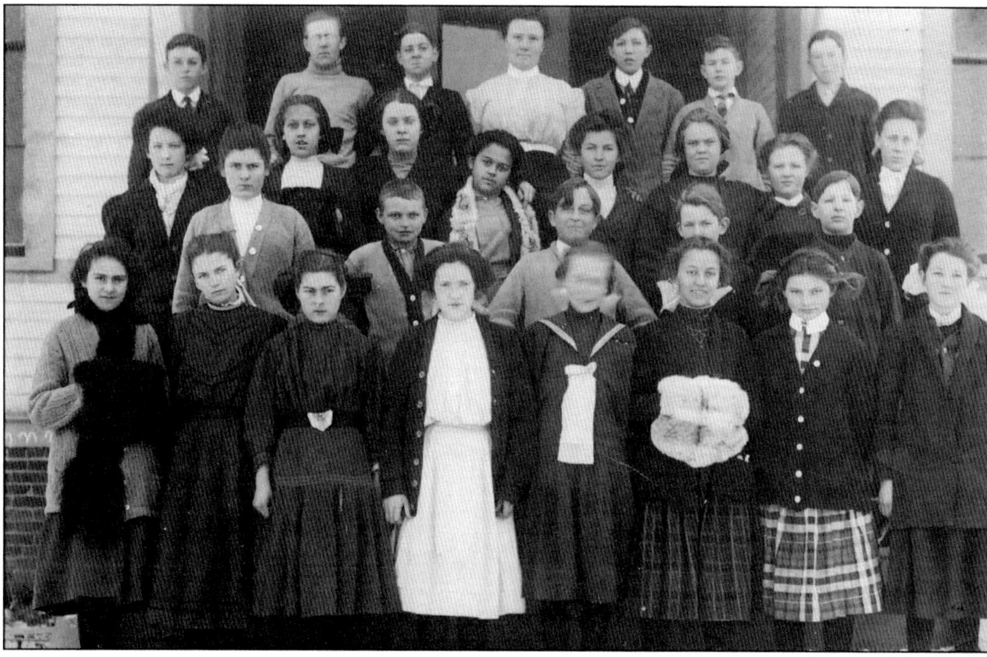

In 1845, there were 33 school districts in the town of Gilmanton. In 1859, when Belmont divided from Gilmanton, there were 12 school districts. At this time, there were no grades in schools, and each student was instructed at the level and subject they could handle. Tax collectors collected school tax from each district, and the operational budgets in each school district varied considerably, resulting in some school districts being able to afford good instructors and longer school sessions. Until 1887, the town's schools were overseen by individuals called the Superintending School Committee, which consisted of one person. This was filled by Lowell French for many years and later by John Sargent. In 1890, 20 weeks of school were conducted, and by 1898, a third, or winter, term was added to most districts.

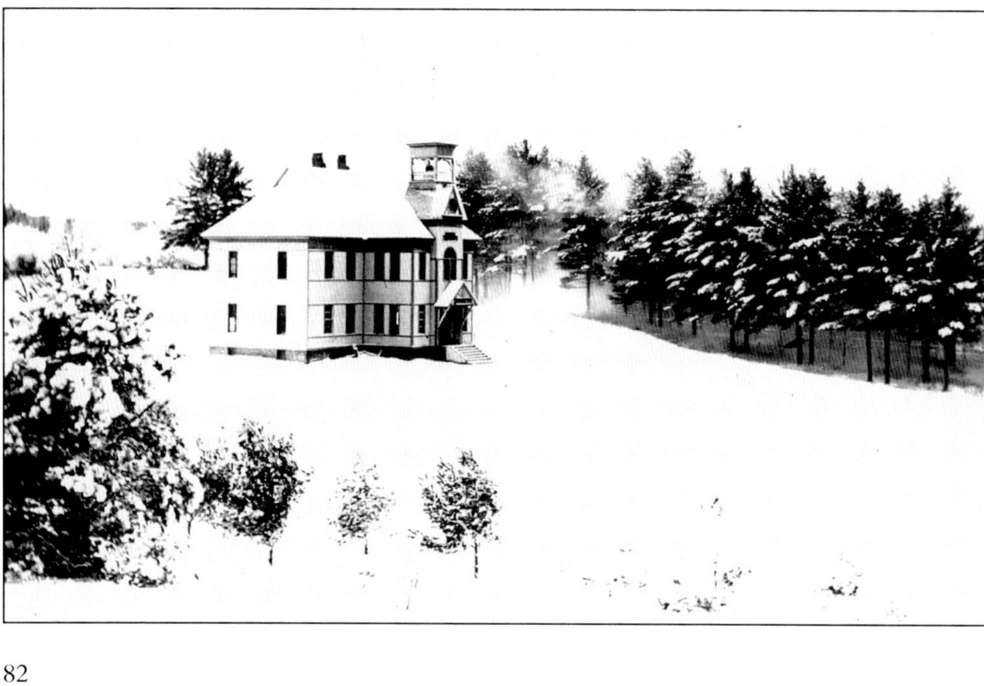

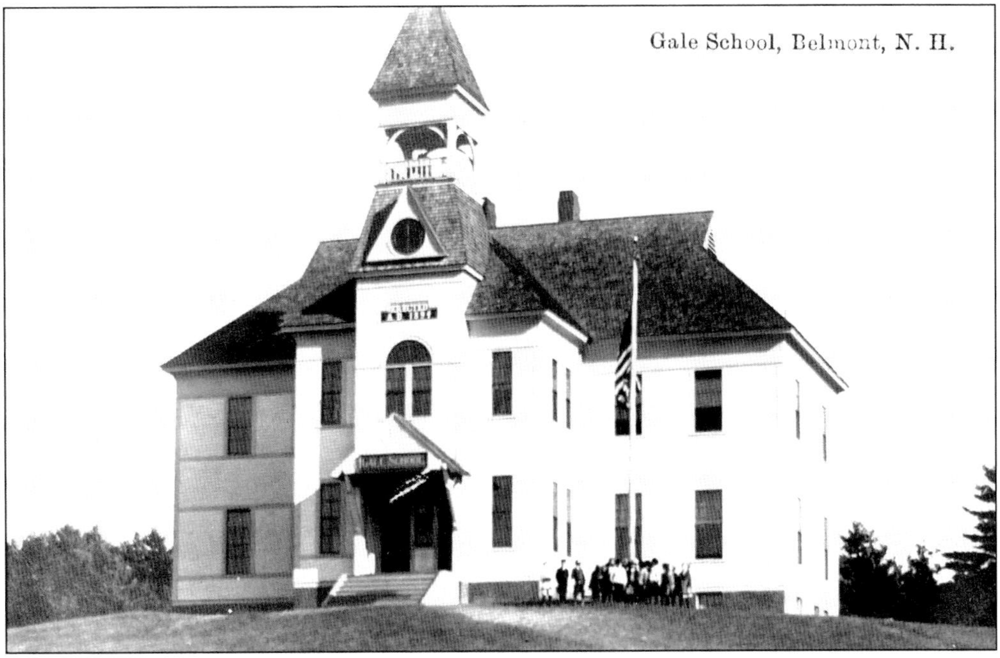

These postcards show the Gale School and its class of 1912. In 1898, a new schoolhouse was constructed to replace the Bennett and Clay Schools. This school was named Plumer School after Joseph Plumer, who had served on the school board since its origination. Shortly after, the neighborhood schools continued to disappear from existence. Belmont's one-room schoolhouses closed one by one as their need diminished. The Jamestown School House closed in 1912, Union in 1923, Upper Province Road in 1928, Ladd Hill in 1932, Plumer in 1939, and the last, Lower Province Road, in 1942. Agnes Moulton has the distinction of being the last teacher at both the Plumer and Lower Province Road Schools and, consequently, the last person to teach in a one-room schoolhouse in Belmont. By 1913, school districts were operating for 36 weeks, and the budgets had substantially increased.

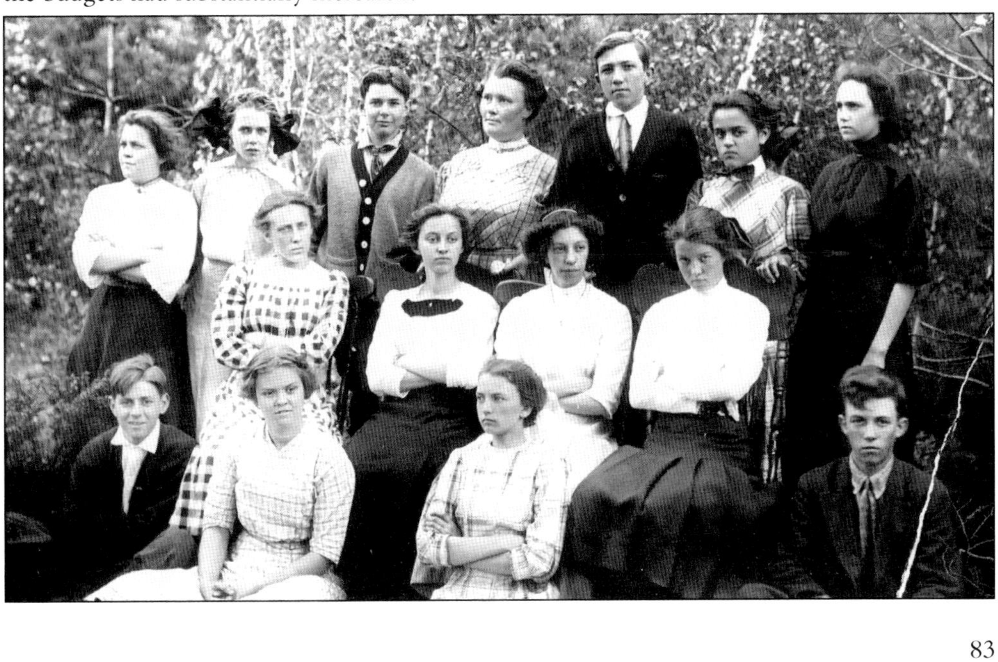

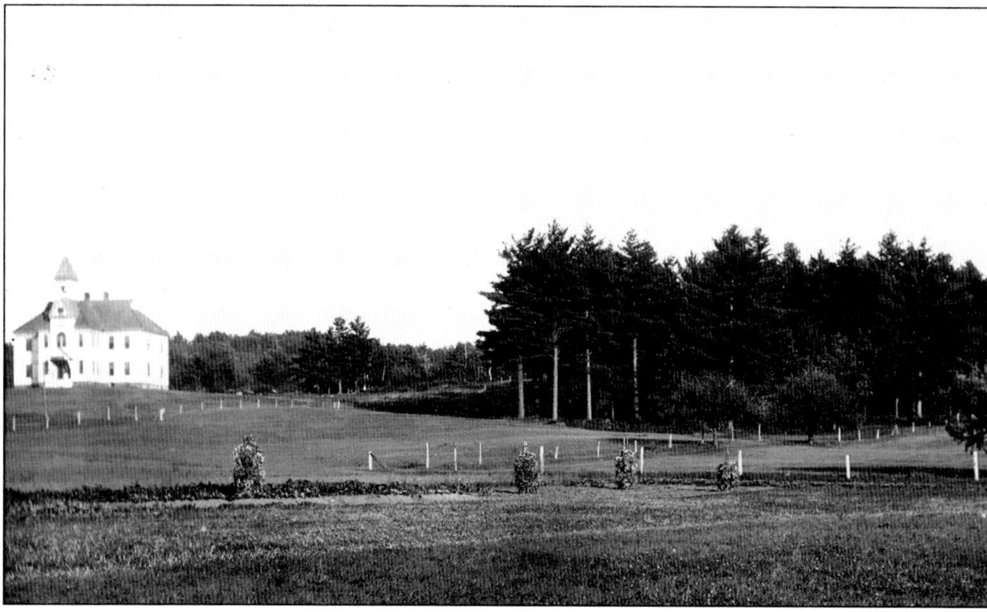

Few students in the 19th century went to school past the grammar school level, and most felt they were lucky enough to have covered the three R's. It was rare to be a high school or academy graduate, more rare than it is to be a college graduate today. This was primarily due to the expense of attending advanced schools, and often when a child was old enough to provide for the family, he or she would be expected to do so. Those who did attend usually ended up becoming teachers, lawyers, or clergymen. Belmont residents traditionally attended Gilmanton Academy, Tilton Seminary, Gilford Academy, or Laconia High School. The town was responsible for the tuition of students choosing to attend higher education. The family was responsible for transportation, books, and room and board.

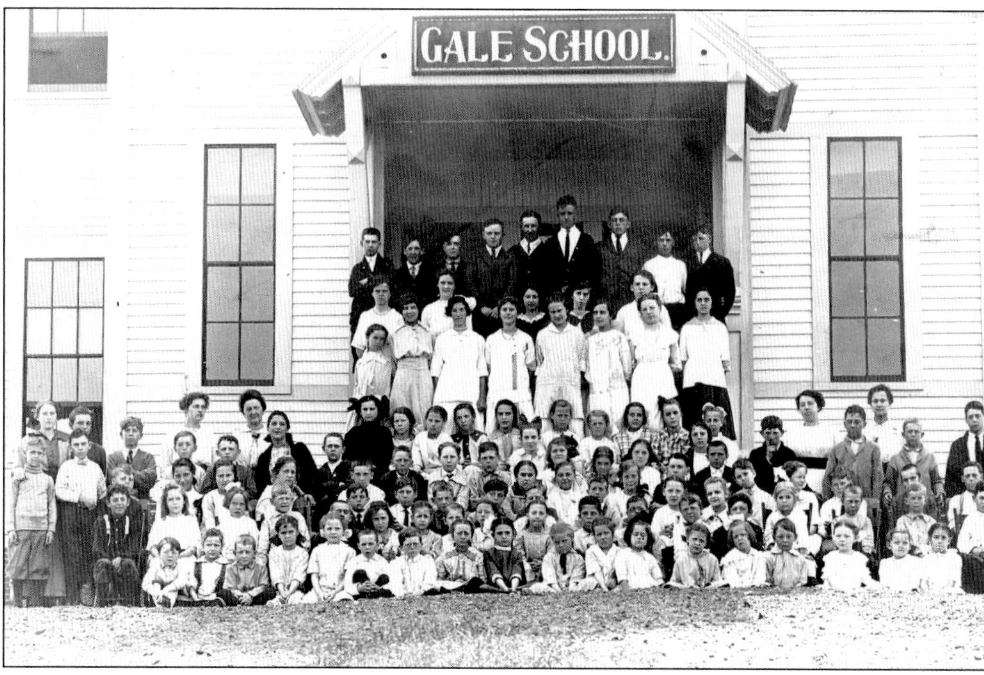

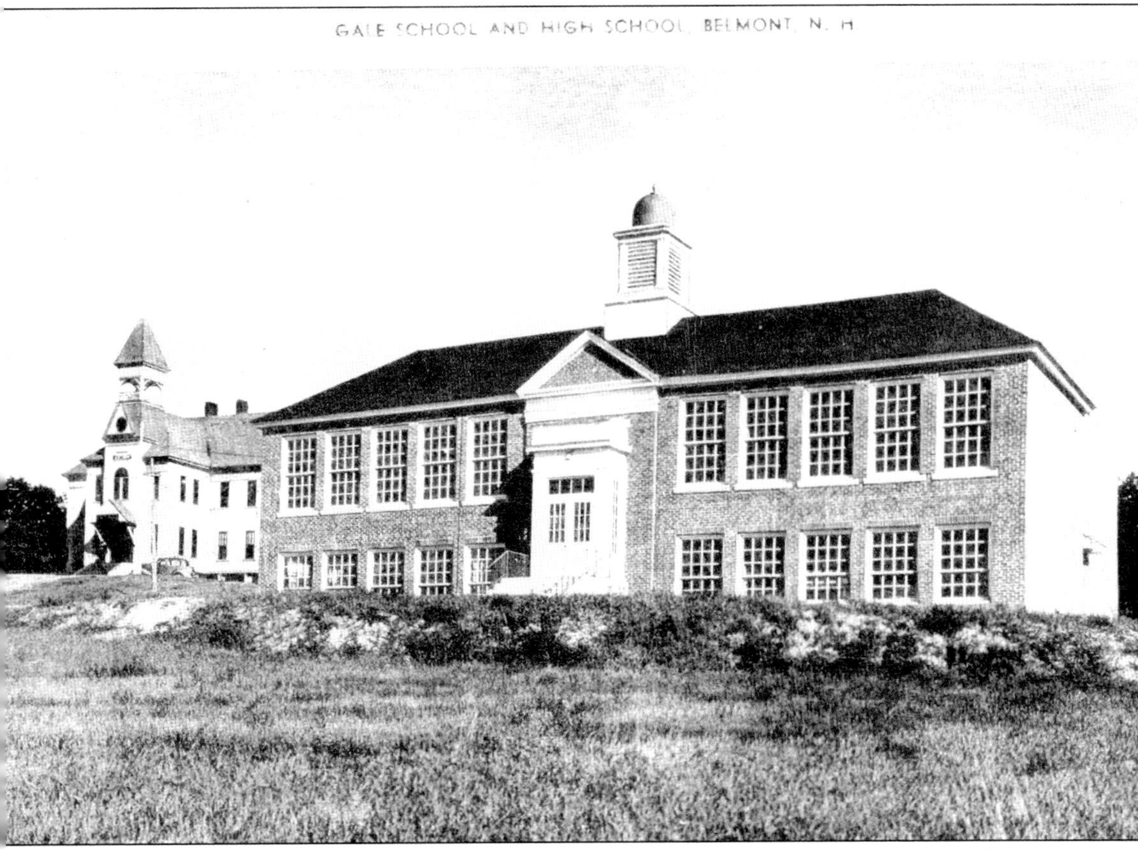

Many students rushed to the train depot early in the mornings to catch the train to Tilton. In 1924, it was voted to add a ninth grade to the second floor of the Gale School. In 1927, the seventh- and eighth-grade classrooms were partitioned to allow for more room for the high school. The first Belmont High School graduate was Kenneth F. Muzzey on June 7, 1928, and he was the only student to graduate this particular year. The high school was finally constructed in 1937, as many wanted their children to get a higher education. In 1955, the Memorial School was constructed for grades one through three. The Gale School at this time was being used for the administrative offices, grades five through eight, the school nurse, and secondary art on the upper level. By 1960, another space problem was encountered at the high school, and classrooms, an auditorium, and a gymnasium were added.

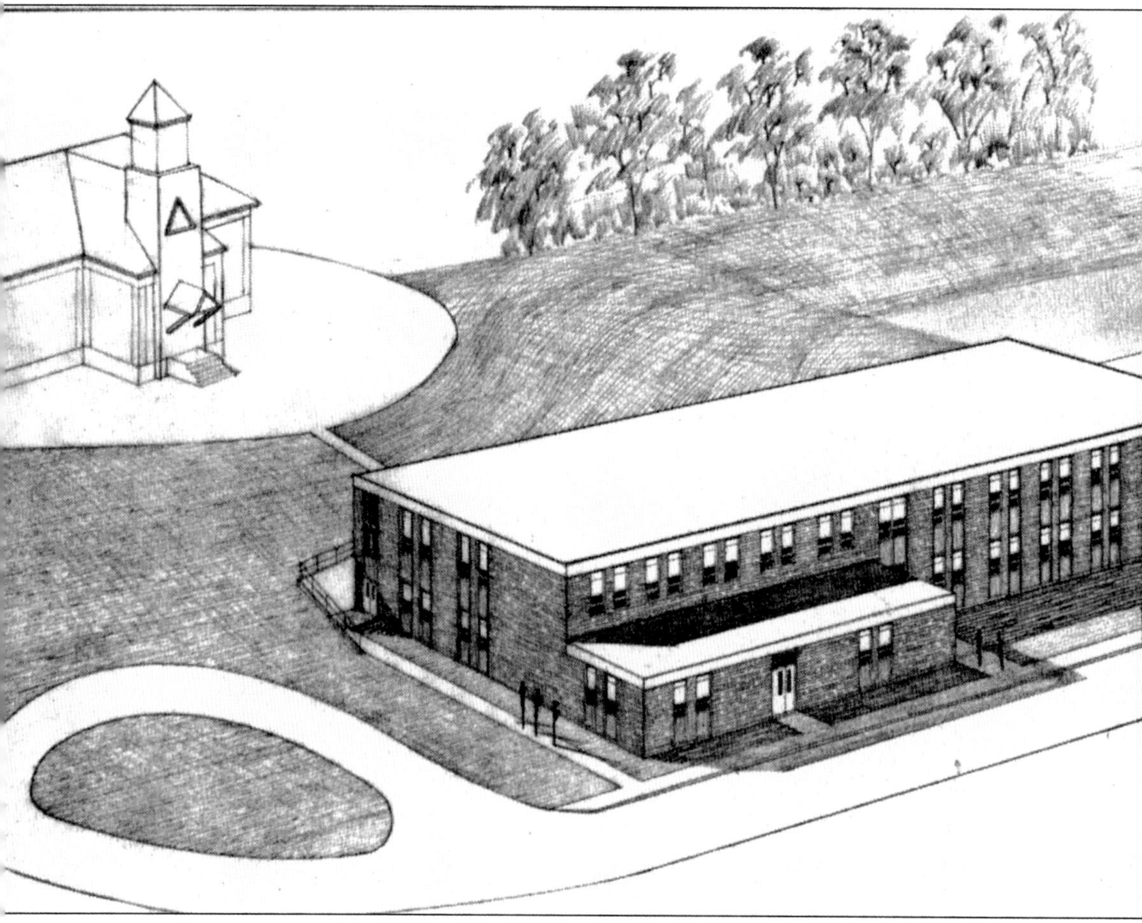

During the 1970–1971 school year, Canterbury students grades 9 through 12 started attending Belmont High School and by 1972 became a part of the school district permanently. Growth throughout Belmont schools continued at a steady pace, and in 1971, a cafeteria and additional classrooms were added to the high school (shown above). In 1985, the Belmont Elementary School was constructed on Gilmanton Road (State Route 140 East), and the use of the Gale

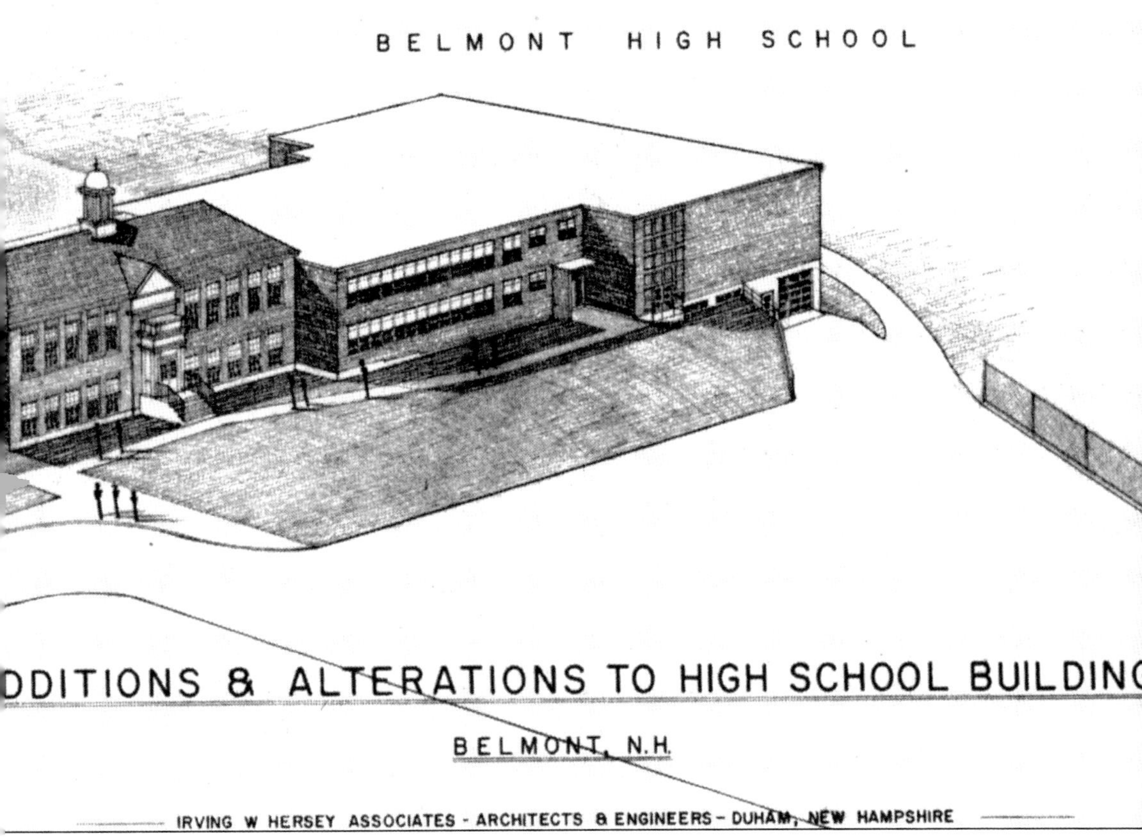

School ceased operation, being used for cold storage. The new high school on Seavey Road was constructed in 1997; therefore, the old high school became the new Belmont Middle School. Today the Memorial School is used for administrative offices, and after 100 years of educating Belmont's youth, the Gale School stands abandoned, overlooking the progress of the Belmont school systems.

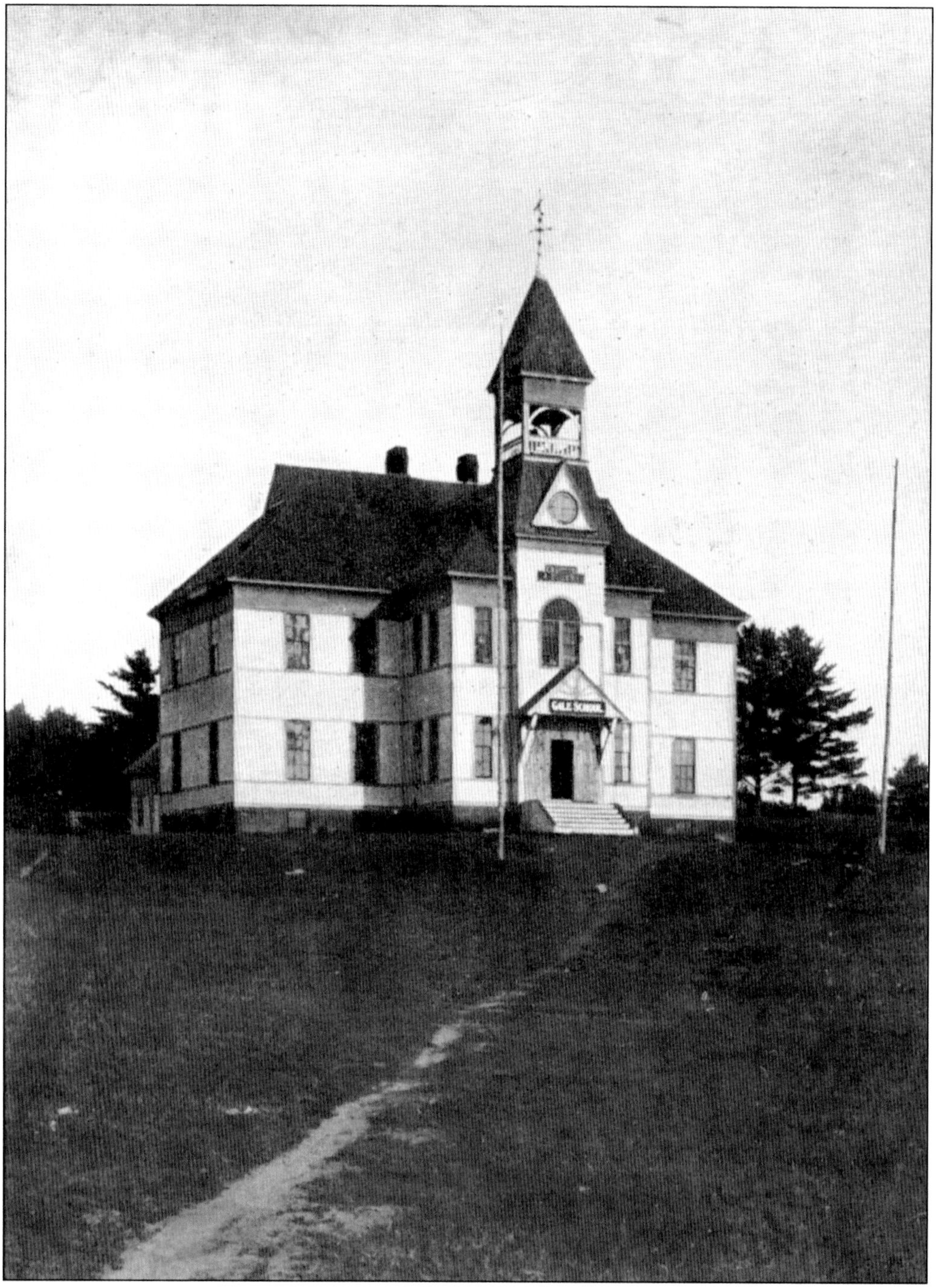

Many postcards have been printed over the years showing the Gale School building. It appears to be a monument in which many past and present citizens seem to remember the most about Belmont. For each person, the Gale School has its own special meaning, whether it is a past teacher, good times with friends, a walk to school, or simply an appreciation of fine architecture and craftsmanship. This monumental building stands tall upon the hill, watching over the town and its people for 112 years, and now this great structure needs the townspeople to watch over it.

Six

Churches

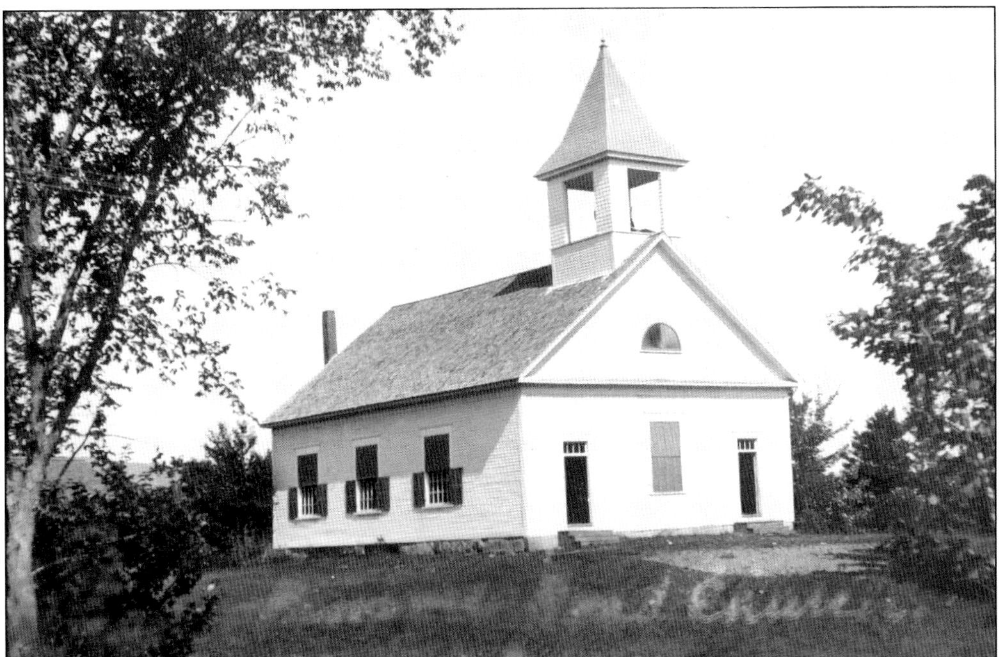

The Province Road Meetinghouse is the oldest church in Belmont, predating most church structures in this part of the state. This church was built in 1792 by no particular denomination and was used by several denominations intermittently. As was the style of churches then, it was fitted with box pews and contained a gallery on three sides and a high pulpit. The members adopted the tenets of the Freewill Baptist denomination in 1816, and in 1835, an organization known as the Third Free Will Baptist Meeting House Society of Upper Gilmanton (Belmont) was organized. In 1844, one acre of land was given to the church for the construction of a parsonage across the street from the church building (236 Province Road). In 1854, the pulpit was rebuilt, and in 1857, the church was turned to face the road. In 1910, the bell and belfry were donated by members of the Lamprey family. Today it is owned by the Belmont Historical Society.

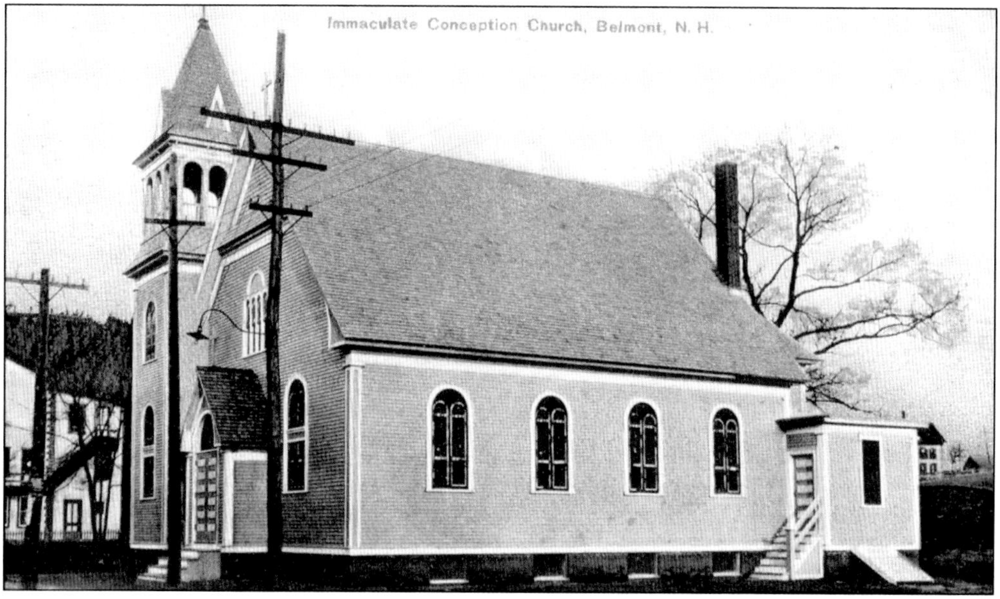

In 1914, St. Joseph's Church was organized as a mission assumption parish in Tilton. By 1949, the rectory was purchased on Gale Street. The church was established as a parish with Rev. Arthur L. Massacotte as the first pastor. In 1989, the 1907 structure was demolished because it was too small and needed substantial repairs. In addition, the stream under the building was deteriorating the structure. A new building was constructed in 1990, the building was moved farther back on the lot in order to accommodate needs at that time.

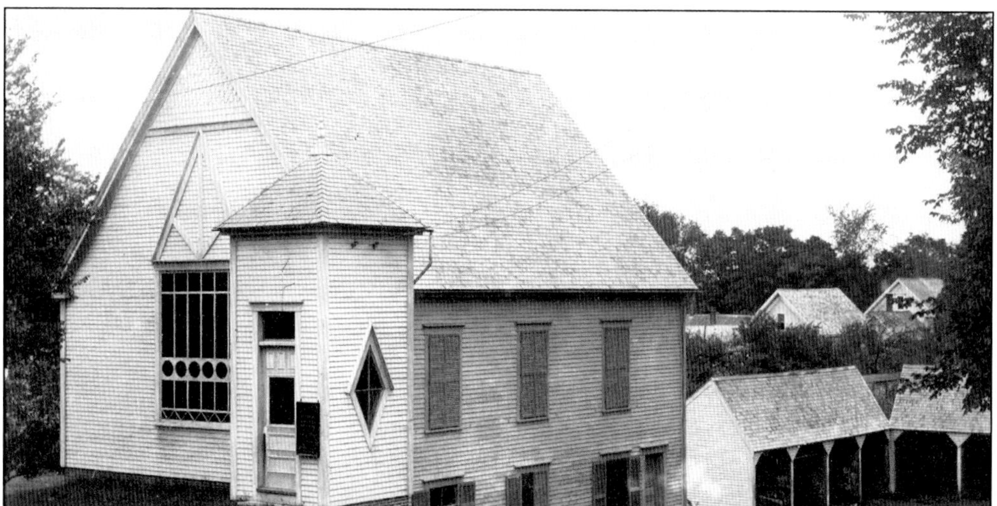

This building was organized in 1899 as the Advent Christian Church. The church was constructed in 1900 and dedicated the same year. Prior to the construction, members met in Hall's store for a short period of time. In 1904, Rev. David Jack was called to the church, and on May 20, 1951, the name of the church was changed to Belmont Full Gospel Assembly. Today this building is owned by the Town of Belmont and is called the Corner Meeting House. Currently it is used for town purposes and community organizations as a meeting spot. Notice the horse stables on the right of the postcard, formally the site of the Belmont Fire Department and today the site of the Belmont Police Department.

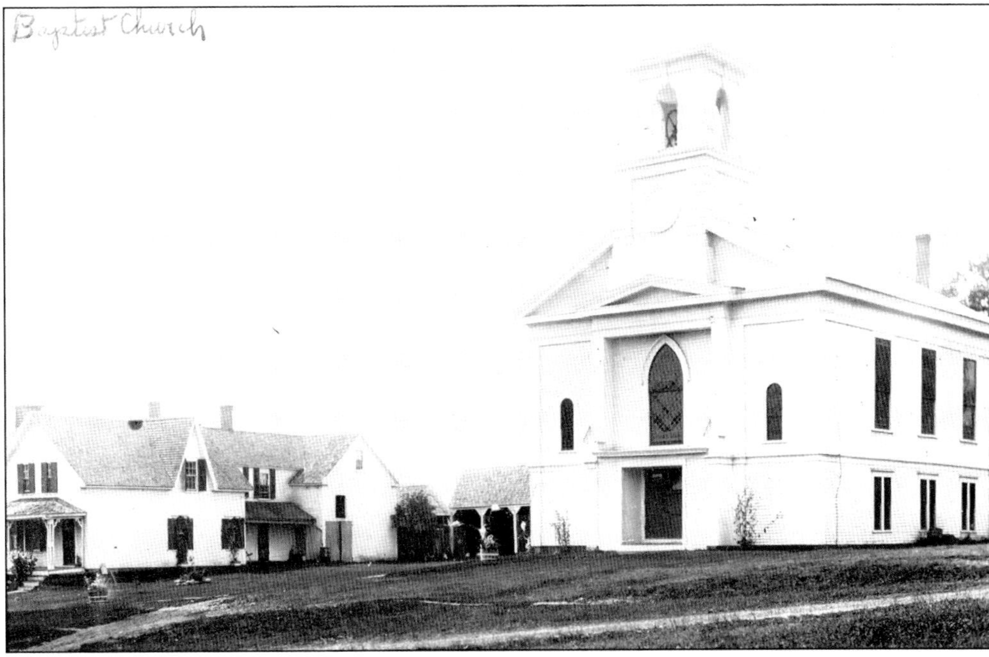

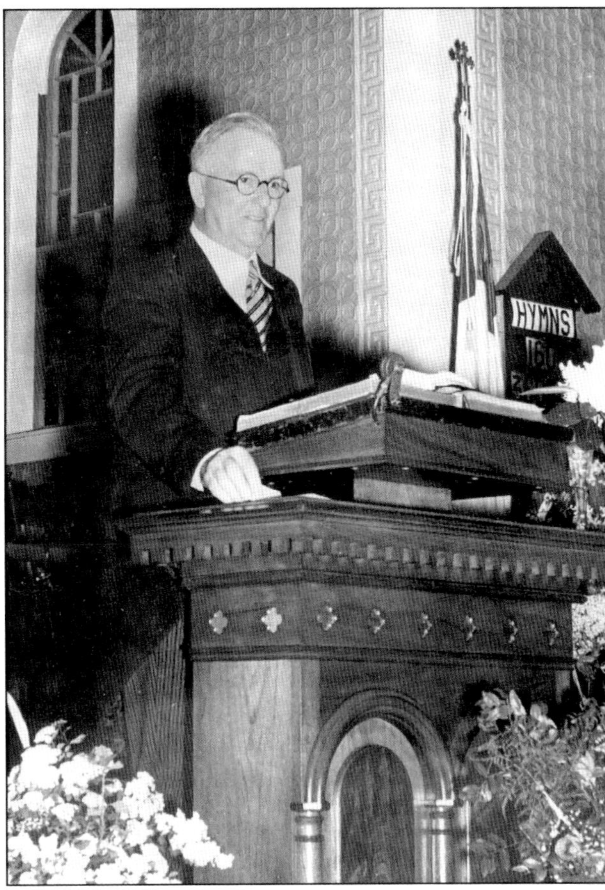

The Third Monthly Meeting House, as it was first known, was organized in 1810. A meetinghouse was erected in 1811, possibly of brick, but was removed in 1852 when the structure above was built. In 1860, the parsonage was constructed, and by 1889, the church had been raised to accommodate a vestry and the installation of new memorial windows. The postcard above shows the Baptist church stables to the left of the building. By 1907, the Baptist church added the organ loft, and in 1917, a pipe organ was installed as a gift from Moses Sargent Jr. John M. Sargent, the son of the organ donor, donated the chimes in 1946. The first minister was Elder Peter Clark, from 1810 to 1841. Since then, the church has had approximately 25 pastors, the longest tenure being that of Rev. Frederick W. Fitzpatric (right), who served for 42 years. This building burned on December 19, 1975, and was rebuilt in 1976.

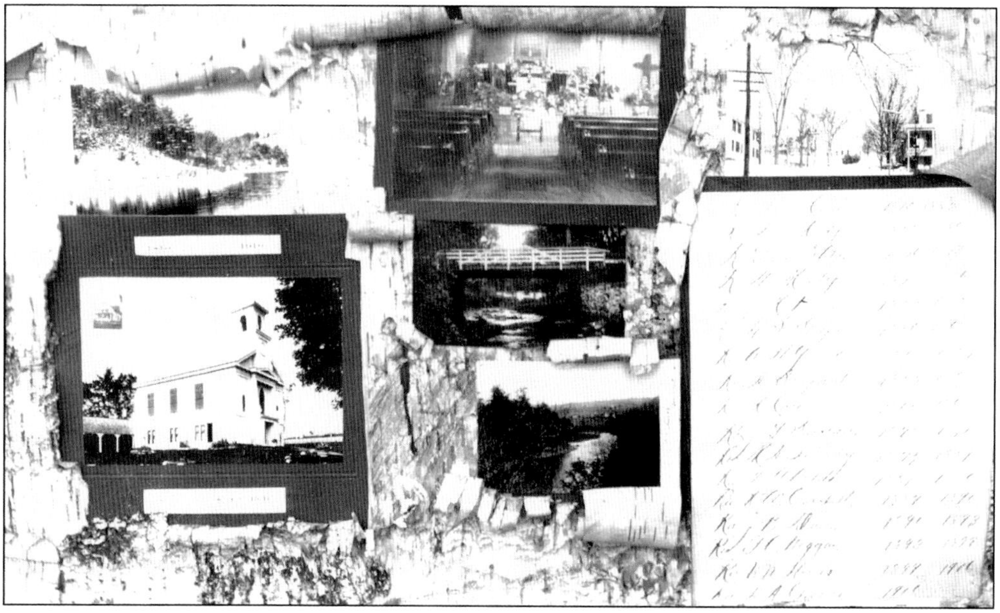

This postmarked 1910 postcard is the centennial postcard produced to celebrate the Belmont Baptist Church. It shows a series of images on the front from 1910, including the Baptist church with the horse stables located on the left of the building, the inside of the Baptist church, the Church Street Bridge, and a view from the top of Church Street looking toward North Main Street. A list of pastors is seen in the image to the left.

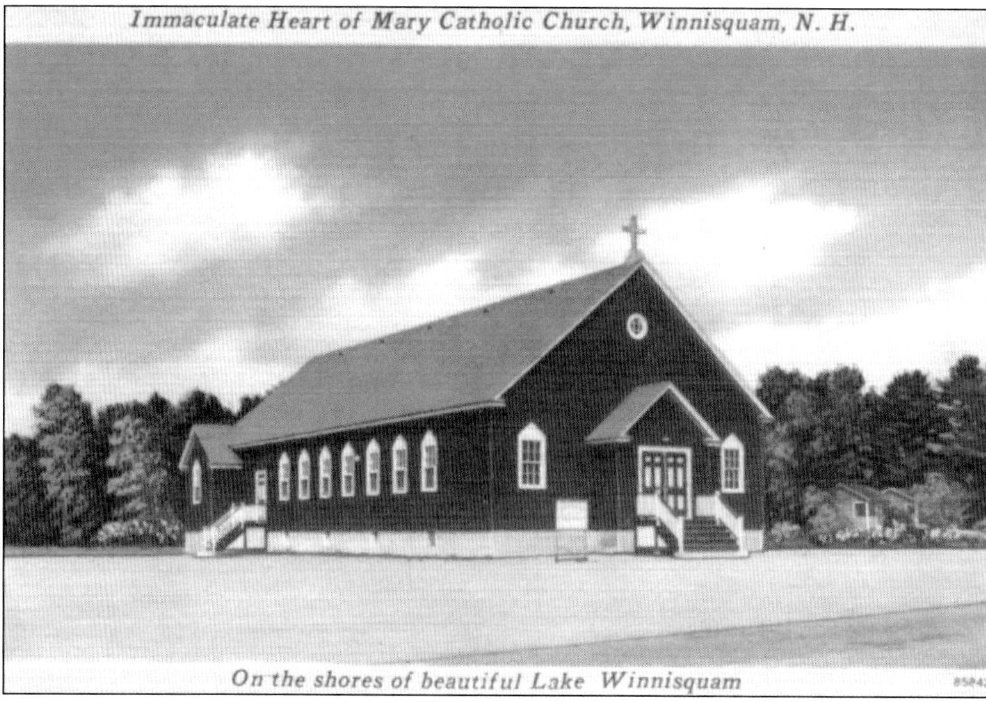

The Immaculate Heart of Mary was built in 1951 to serve the residents in the Winnisquam area. Today this building is the home of Piche's Ski Shop, located on the Daniel Webster Highway (State Route 3) at the end of Union Road.

Seven

Homesteads and Eateries

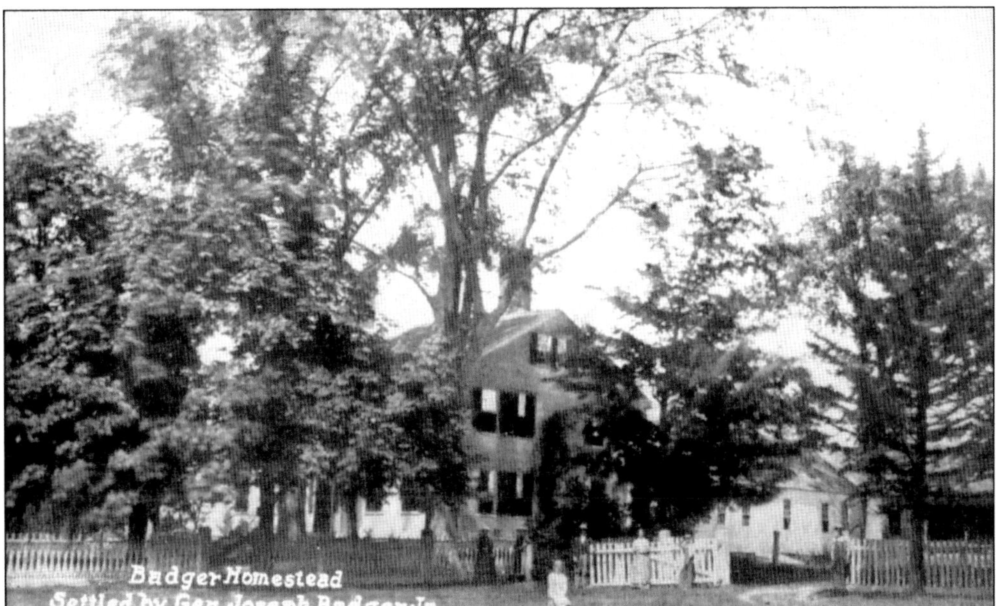

Located on Hackett Road off Gilmanton Road (State Route 140 East) between Belmont Village and Gilmanton Corners is the Badger homestead. This impressive two-story home was the residence of William Badger, Belmont's most noted citizen of the 19th century. The house is situated on the crest of the hill, offers impressive views, and exhibits such details that only a person of considerable wealth could have acquired. The title to 70 acres was given (a portion of the eventual 600 acres) to Joseph Badger Jr. by the proprietors of the town in 1772 as compensation for collecting taxes assessed to construct Province Road (State Route 107).

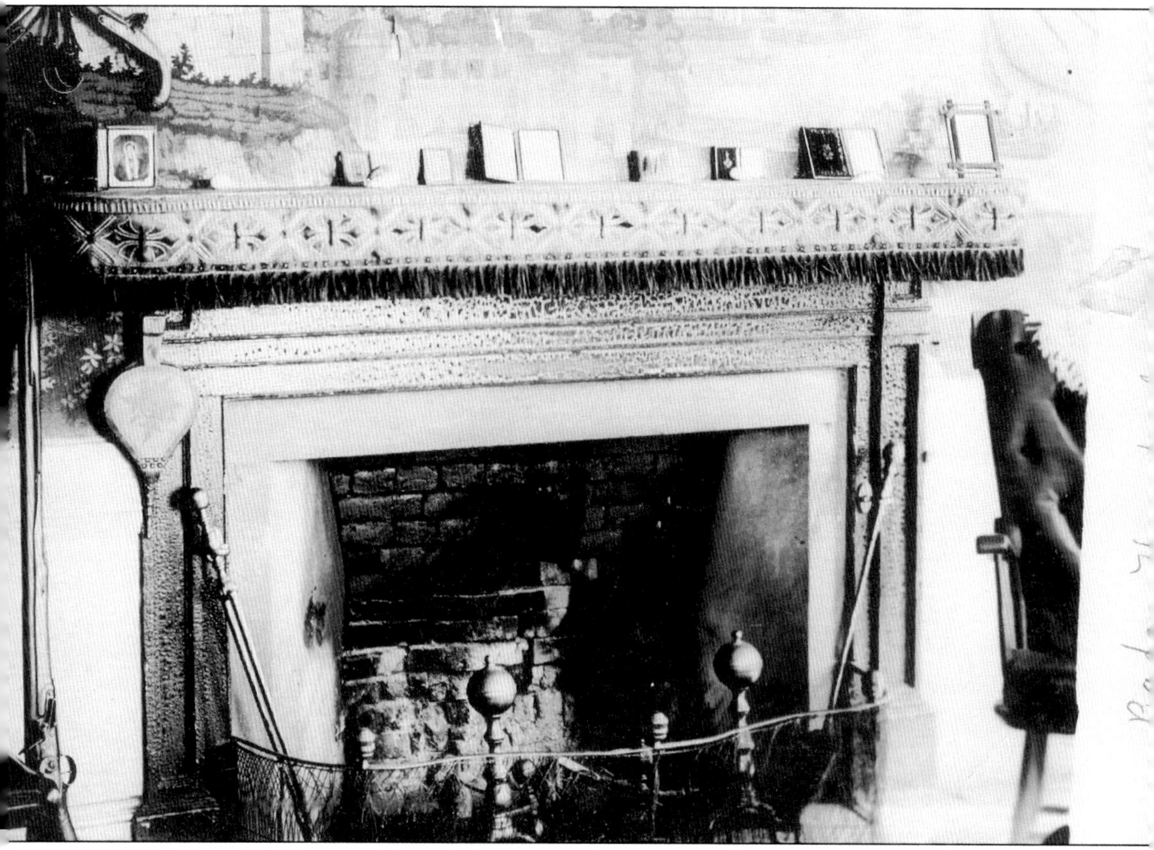

Joseph Badger Jr. had first settled in the town of Gilmanton in 1766. The exact date that he moved to the Badger homestead property is not documented. The ell portion of the present house may well be the first building constructed on the property. A cape-style dwelling was built on the site around 1784 and replaced by this structure around 1816. Joseph Badger Jr. held offices in the New Hampshire militia for a period of 30 years, passing from the rank of captain to brigadier general. This postcard shows the fireplace in the Badger homestead.

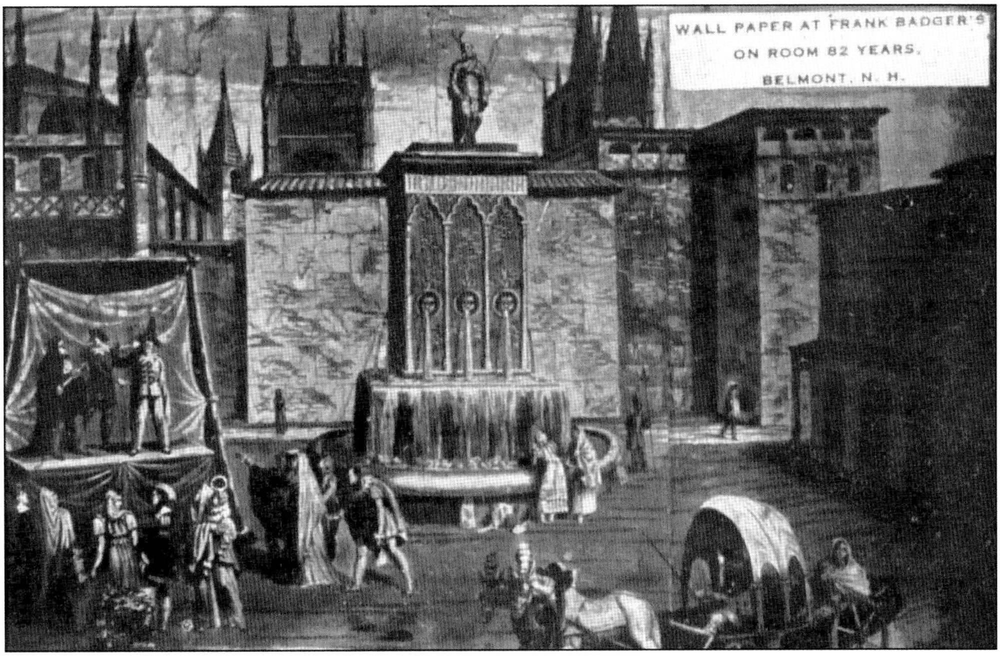

This is the wallpaper that lines the walls of the Badger homestead. It had been on the wall of this room for 82 years when the postcard was printed around 1900 and is still present in the home today. William Badger in politics was a Jeffersonian Democrat and attained several high offices, including the office of governor in 1834 and 1835.

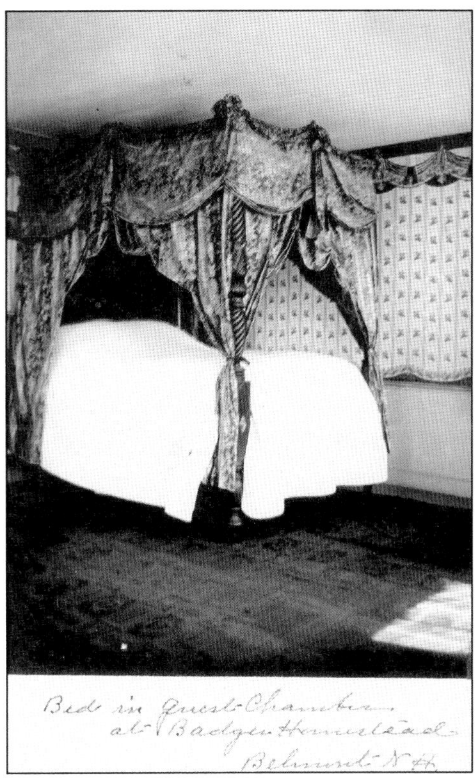

Shown here are the guest chambers at Badger homestead. Joseph Badger Jr. died in 1809 and his son William inherited the property from his father. The two-story house was probably built around 1818, after the 1784 house was moved to make room for the new house. The 1784 cape was moved to Belmont Village at the corner of School and Main Streets. William Badger was undoubtedly the most prominent man to come from Belmont during the 19th century.

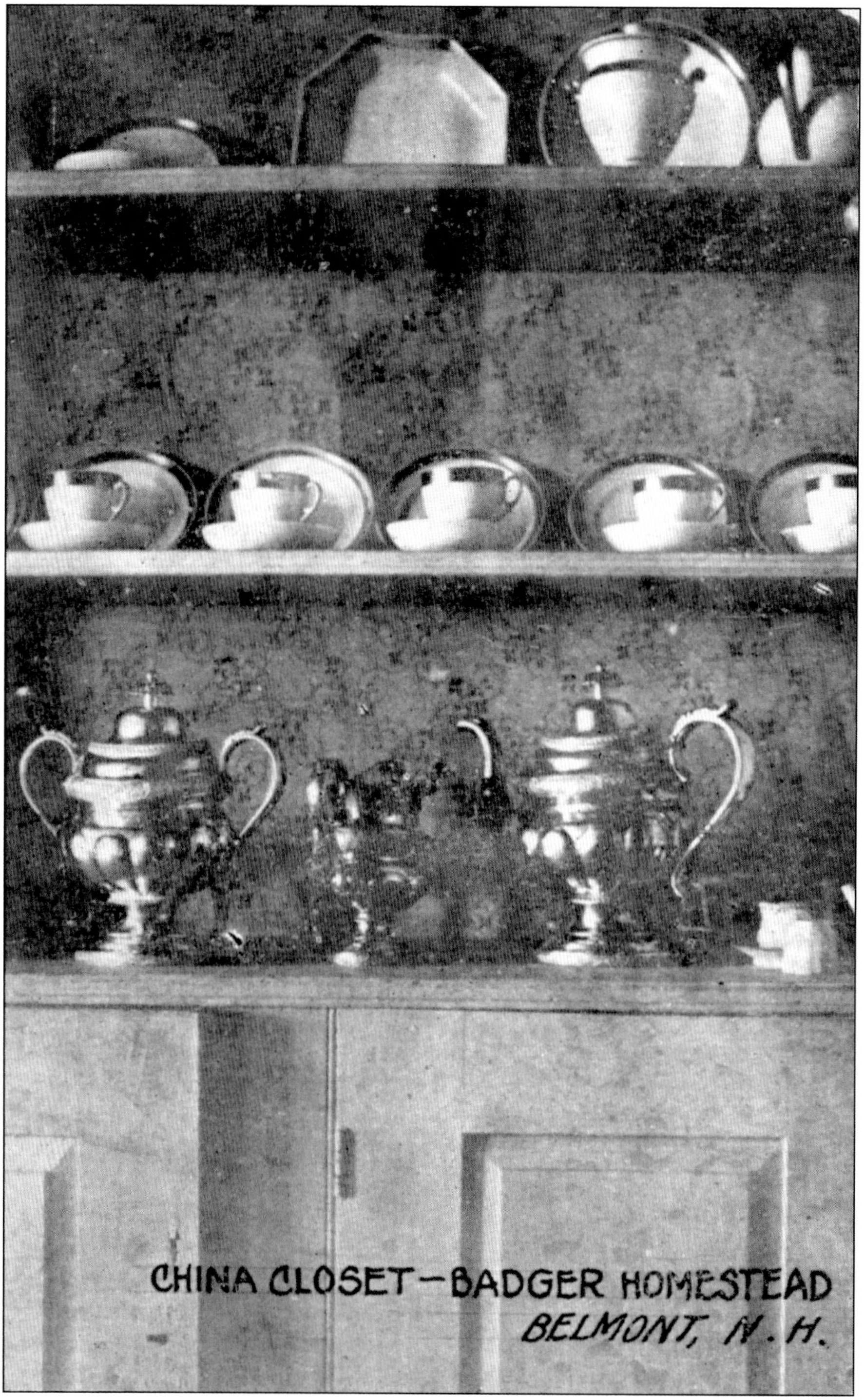

The front parlor is decorated with imported English wallpaper for which Joseph Badger Jr. is said to have paid $100 and carried from Portsmouth in saddlebags. William Badger, who later acquired the property, is said to have hosted many prominent people of the time here, including Benjamin Pierce and his son Gen. Franklin Pierce, who became the 14th president of the United States.

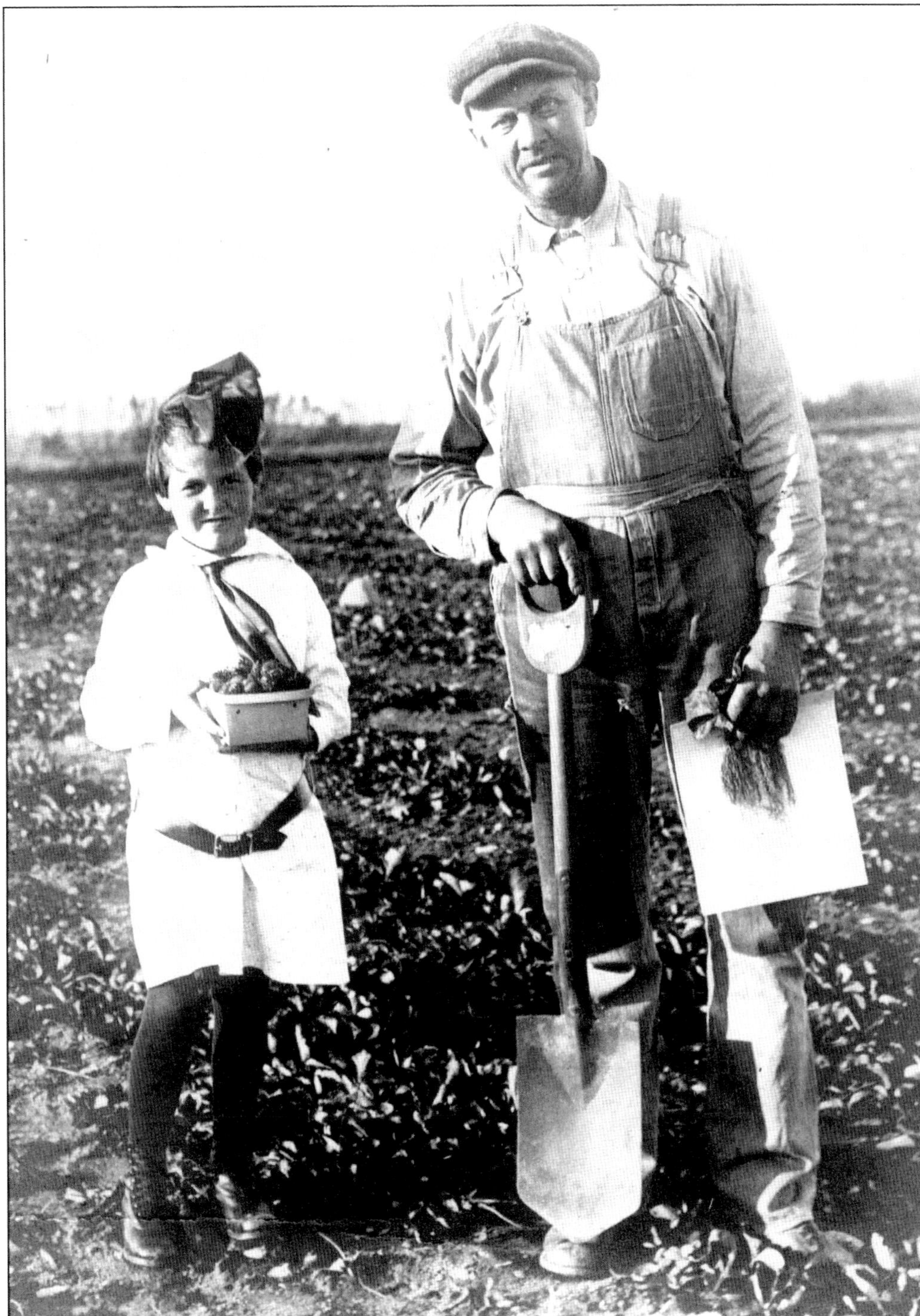

The Badger property remained in the family until 1928 when, after the death of Francis Badger, the buildings and contents gathered over several generations were sold at auction. Today the property is owned by Suzanne Roberts. Francis Badger and his daughter are seen in this postcard working in the strawberry field.

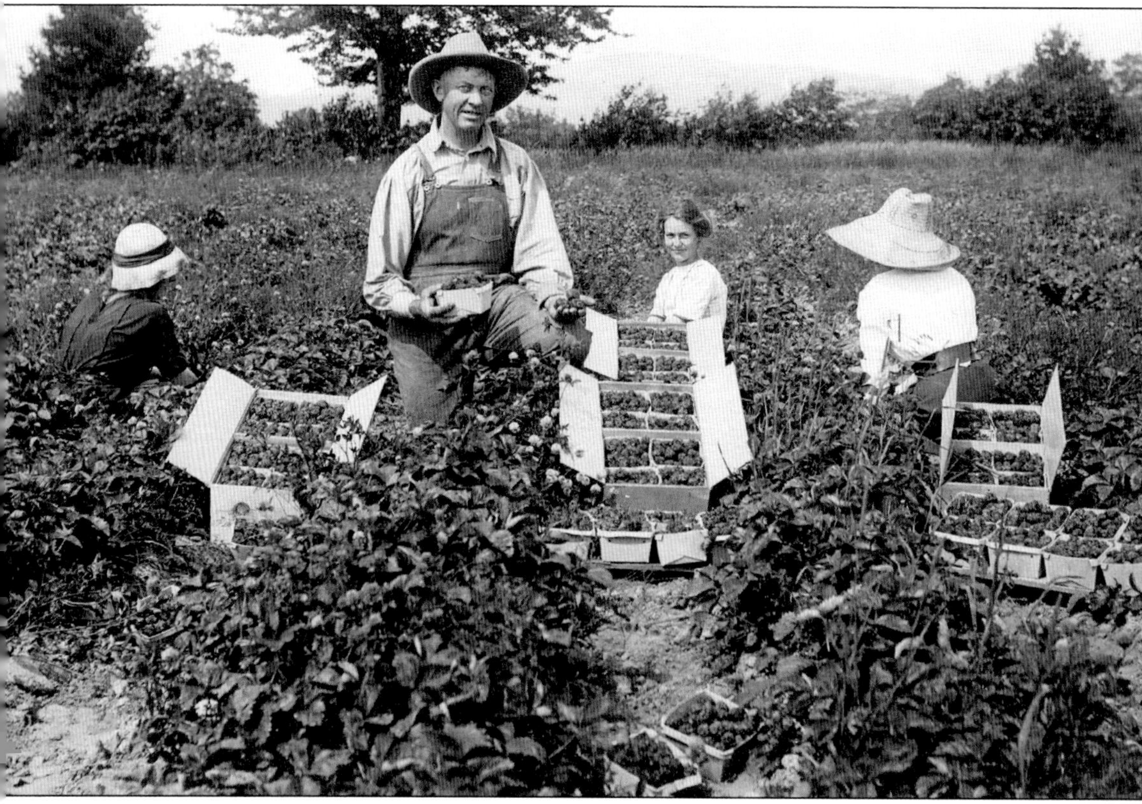

Francis Badger was the grandson of Gov. William Badger. His father's brother Capt. William Badger was the author of the 1875 *History of Gilmanton*. Francis Badger was born in 1868 and died in 1927. He operated the farm and, as seen in the picture, one of his crops was strawberries. The homestead was auctioned in 1928 to settle his estate. Contents that had been accumulated for generations were also auctioned at that time.

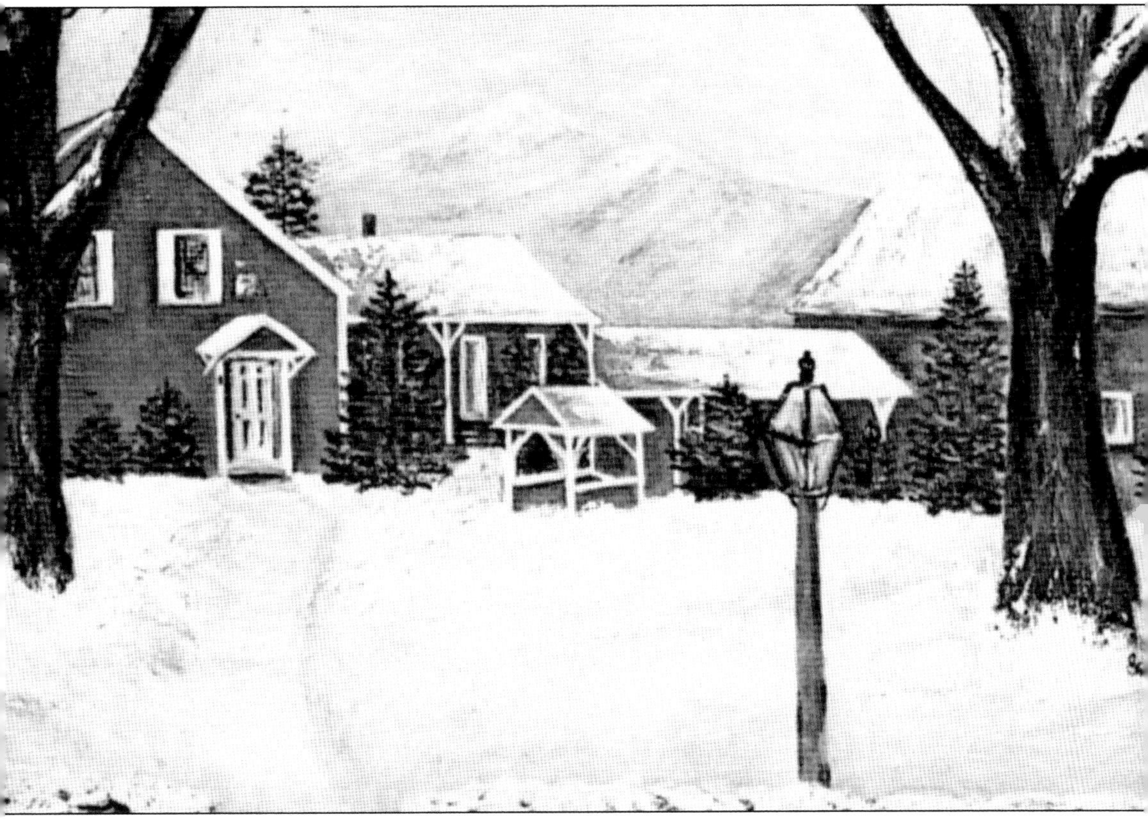

Hickory Stick Farm Restaurant, located on Bean Hill Road, occupied what was previously known as the Grant Farm. Frank P. Grant purchased the farm around 1890 and lived there with his wife and children for the remainder of his life. The farm had previously been known as the Lamprey Farm. Bean Hill Road was named for the Bean family that built and occupied several dwellings farther up the hill.

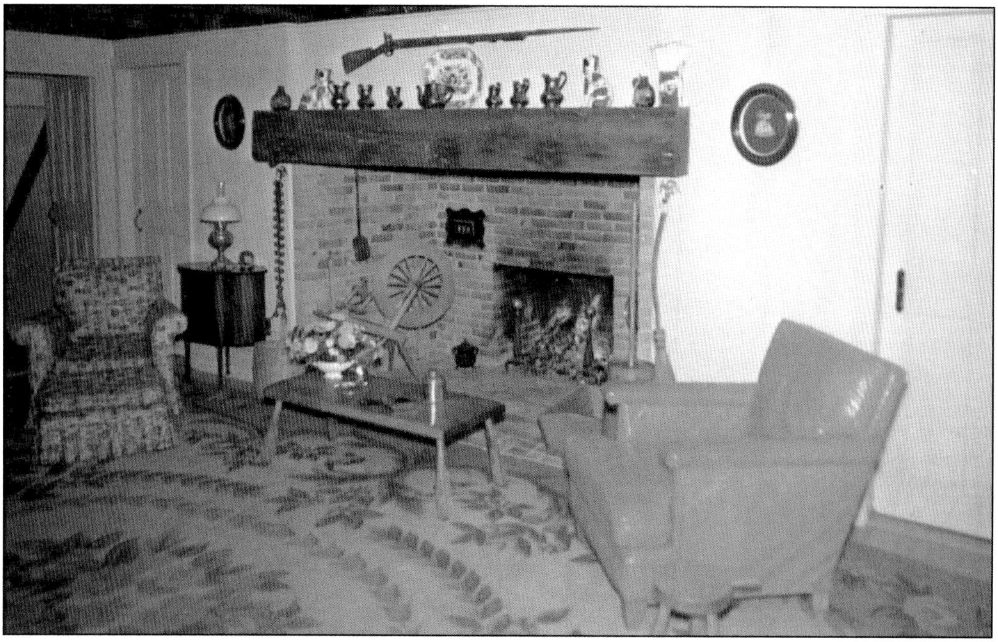

This impressive fireplace evokes the feel of colonial America. In reality it was built in the early 1940s after the farm had left the Grant family and was remodeled by the Donovan family to be occupied as a summer home. The 1940s remodeling was tastefully done so that the best of the old house was preserved and often enhanced, such as with this fireplace.

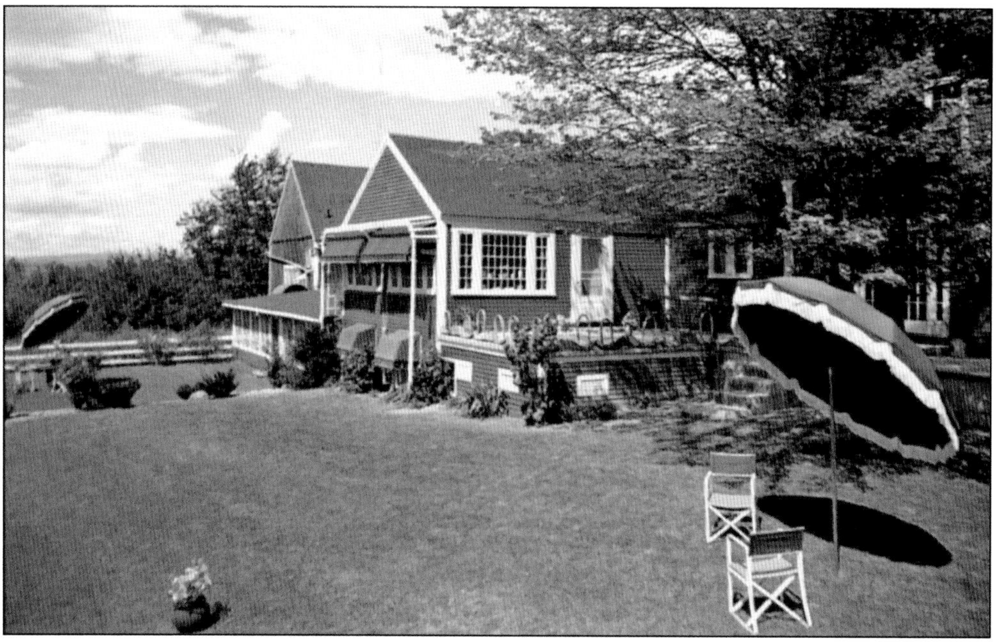

The last Grant to occupy the property had constructed a series of greenhouses behind the house, which were removed at the time of the remodeling in the 1940s. In 1948, Charles Roeder and his wife purchased the property and named it Hickory Stick Farm, possibly in honor of "Old Hickory," as Andrew Jackson was often called. This view is of the outside of the Hickory Stick Farm Restaurant to the rear of the building.

Hickory Stick Farm

In 1635 Capt. John Mason obtained a grant of the Province of New Hampshire from Charles I, the reigning King of England.

When Capt. Mason died, he gave almost all of the grant or province to his grandson, John Tufton Mason, who for many years owned and controlled what is now virtually the entire state of New Hampshire. Late in life, Mr. Mason sold his claim for 15,000 pounds to a group of Portsmouth people, among whom was a Joshua Wentworth Bean. Early in the 18th century Joshua and his family migrated from Portsmouth and settled on the plot of land from which Bean Hill Road takes its name.

In 1751 a son of the family married and the buildings erected for their home were called the "Bean Farm". In 1846, fire destroyed the farm, then occupied by the third generation. Shortly thereafter, friends and neighbors gathered to raise the present set of buildings which were then called the "Grant Farm". These buildings and the surrounding land were used continuously for the next 94 years, for farming. This reconstruction took place when Andrew Jackson, known as "Old Hickory", was successfully campaigning for the Presidency, and the present name of the farm reflects the durable tradition of the hospitality of those days.

In 1940 the name was changed to "Rolling Acres" and with this change complete restoration and modernization took place. Eight years later the property was purchased by the present owners, Mr. & Mrs. Charles Roeder, who again changed the name, this time to "Hickory Stick Farm". With the addition of the breezeway, used for our restaurant, and landscaping, completed in 1950, "Hickory Stick Farm" stands as you find it today.

LUNCHEONS 12:00 TO 2:30 **DINNERS 5:30 TO 9:00**

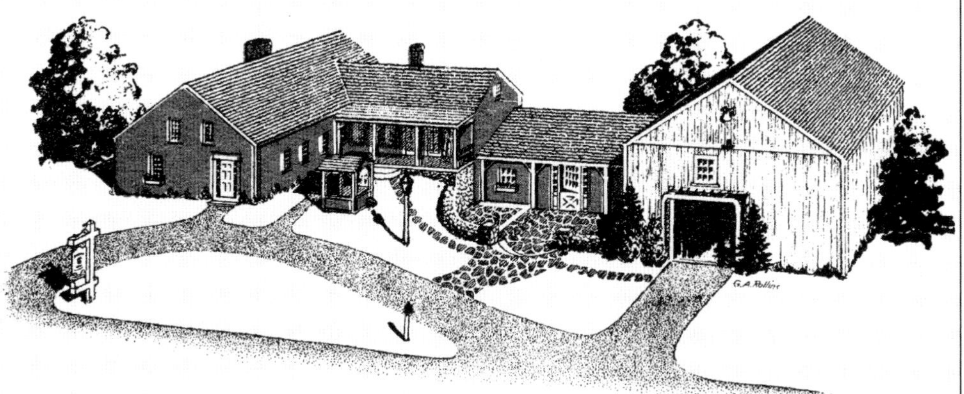

Hickory Stick Farm

TEL. 294
LACONIA, NEW HAMPSHIRE

After the Roeders added the breezeway, additional landscaping, and commercial kitchen facilities, the property was ready to begin its new life as a restaurant. For over 50 years, the restaurant was known for its casual country dining and was famous for its roast duck in orange sauce as well as several other unique offerings. Because of the inability of the Roeder family to continue the operation, the restaurant was closed in 2004, when contents were disposed of.

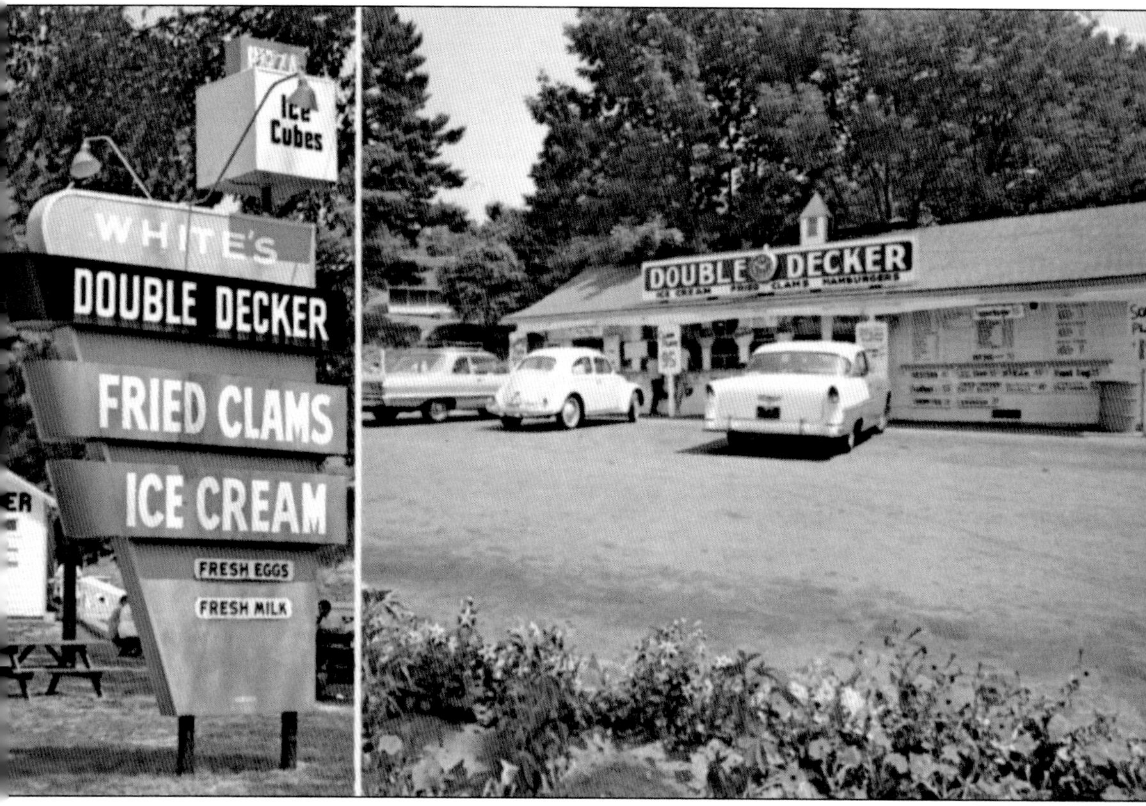

In 1957, George and Faith White constructed a restaurant known as White's Double Decker located on the Daniel Webster Highway (State Route 3) in Belmont. Later it was sold to Laurence Tanner, who continued operating the business until 1974, when it was purchased by Double Decker Inc. Today it is the location of a car dealership and is on the left at the end of Union Road.

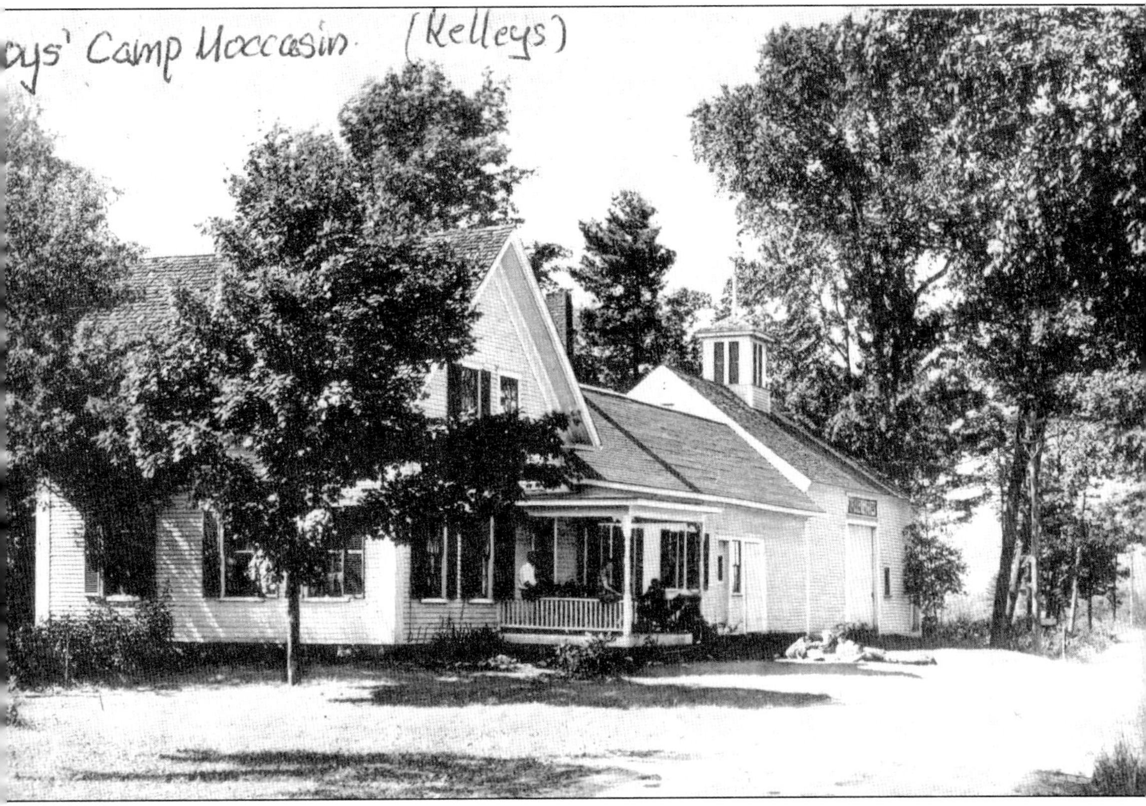

Located on Jamestown Road on the shore of Silver Lake, a summer camp for boys, Camp Moccasin, operated here in the 1930s and 1940s. The house at one time belonged to Dexter Webster and included a barn and shed, which no longer exist. The camp was operated by Carl Buckheister, who came from Massachusetts. The barn was used for a dining hall, and the shed served as the kitchen. The boys slept in tents that were pitched near the lake. Verne and Nancy Bryant purchased the property in 1969. Verne was an outstanding citizen who served on the Belmont School District since its beginning. Active in early Belmont youth athletic programs, the Belmont ball field was named Bryant Field after his death in 1975.

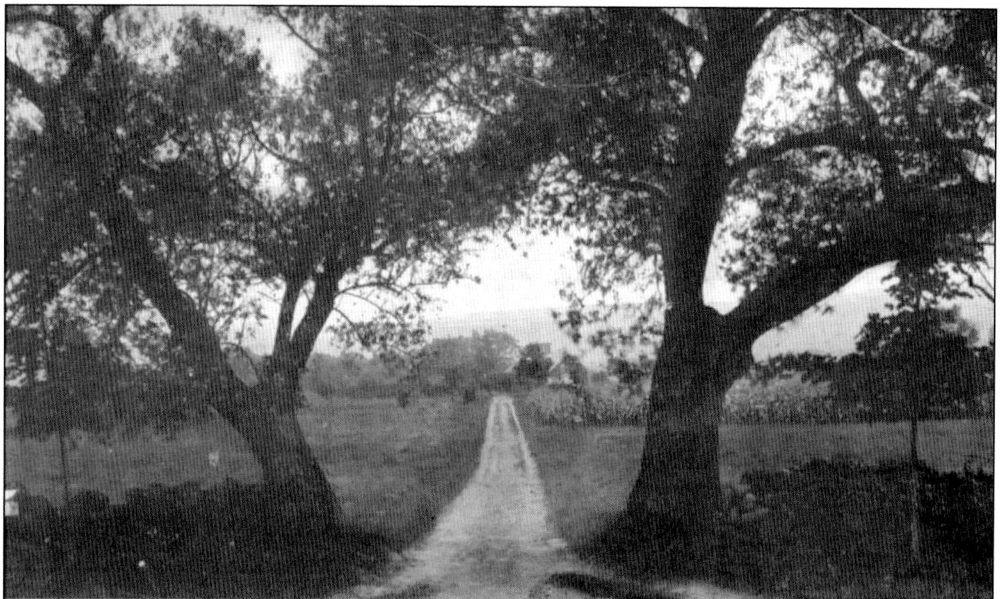

Entrance to Maple Grove Farm, Belmont, N. H.

Located on Jamestown Road, the Maple Grove Farm was both a working farm and a summer boardinghouse. The first house located on the property was constructed by John James in the late 1700s. The property then was sold to John Barker, whose daughter married Ebenezar Currier. The property remained in the hands of Currier descendants for many years. The pictured farm buildings were destroyed by fire in 1927.

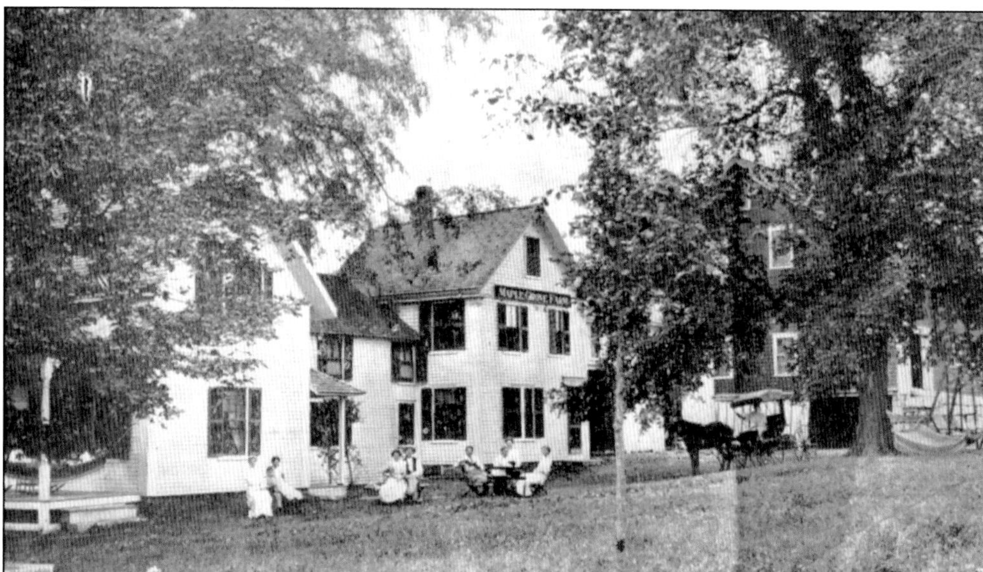

Maple Grove Farm, Belmont N. H.

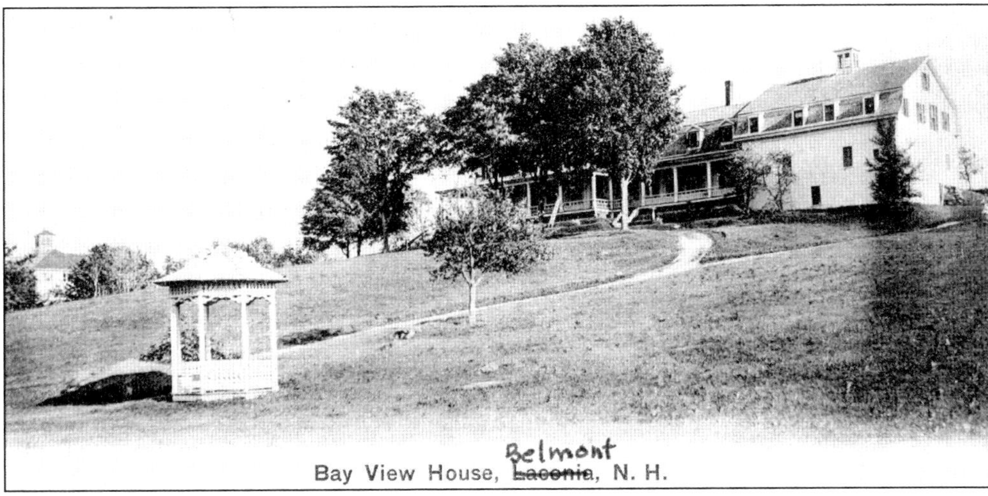

Located on the Daniel Webster Highway (State Route 3) adjacent to the Laconia town line, the Bay View Hotel was established by Stephen Taylor and constructed in 1869. His son Edward was a major benefactor of the Laconia Home for the Aged, now known as the Taylor Community. In 1940, the Bay View Hotel was renamed Terrace Hotel, operating until 1960 when it was closed. In 1963, contents were auctioned, and the building was destroyed by a controlled burn shortly after.

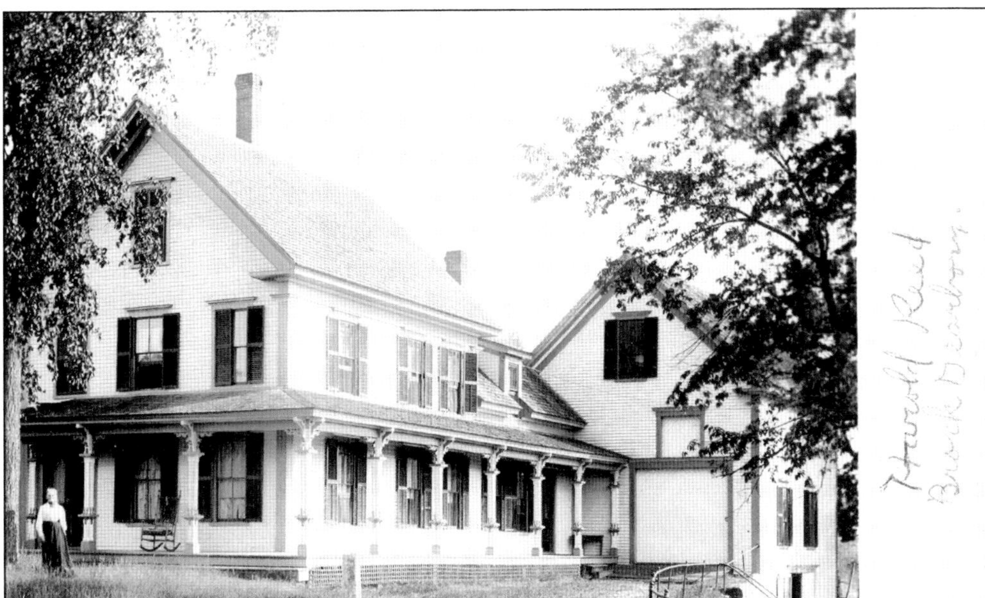

This home dates from the 1800s. It was owned in 1835 by the first-known doctor in Upper Gilmanton (now Belmont). Dr. Joseph and Sally Gould moved here in 1830 and left the area by 1850. The property was later owned by Brock and Etta Belle Dearborn. Etta became librarian and held the position for 20 years. In 1951, Harold and Isabella Reed purchased the property. Harold was the road agent for 26 years, from 1957 to 1983. This building still stands today.

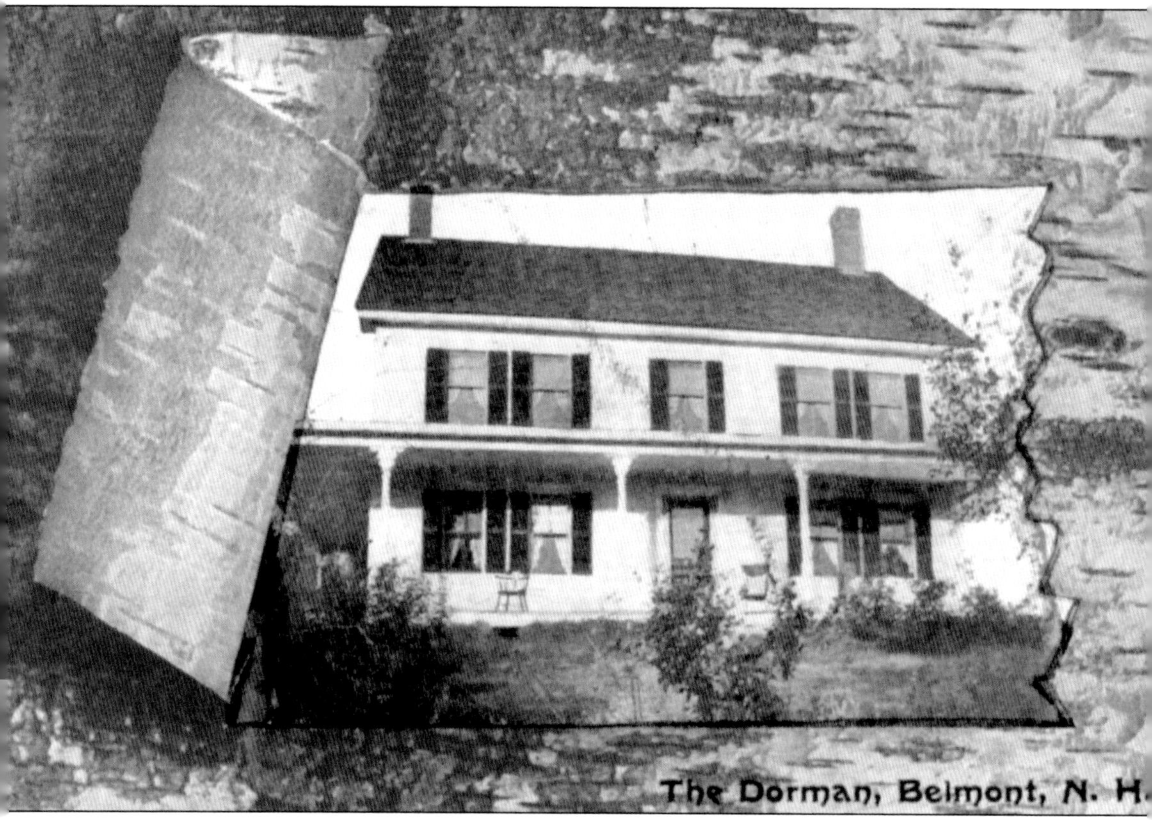

This property was purchased from Hazen P. Weeks in 1905 by George and Alice Dorman. This structure burned prior to 1920, and a new home was built. In 1947, it was purchased by the Moulton family and is still owned by them today.

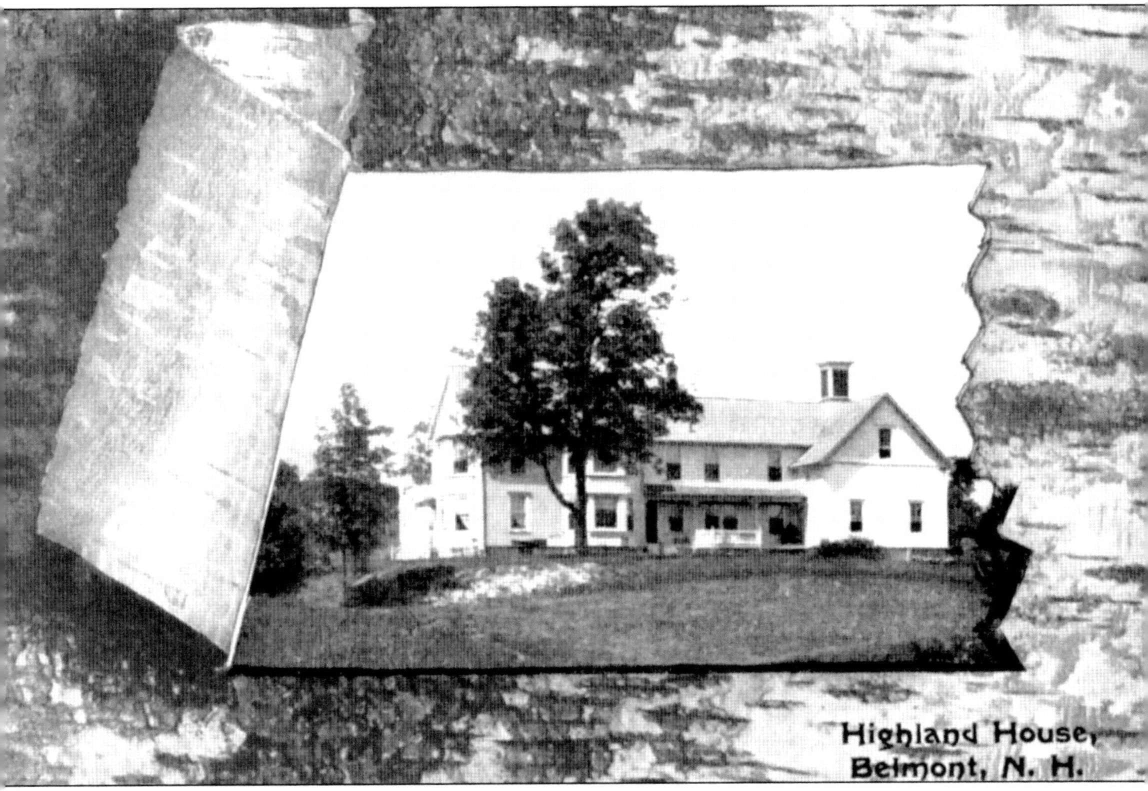

Highland House is seen here in 1910 and was constructed in 1900. This is the original homestead of Charles and Lillian Knowles. Since its construction, it has had several owners, the most recent being George and Murilla Rohach, who purchased it in 1985. It is assumed that the name Highland House was derived from the house's location on the highland at the top of Johnson Street. Today it is known as the Rohach home.

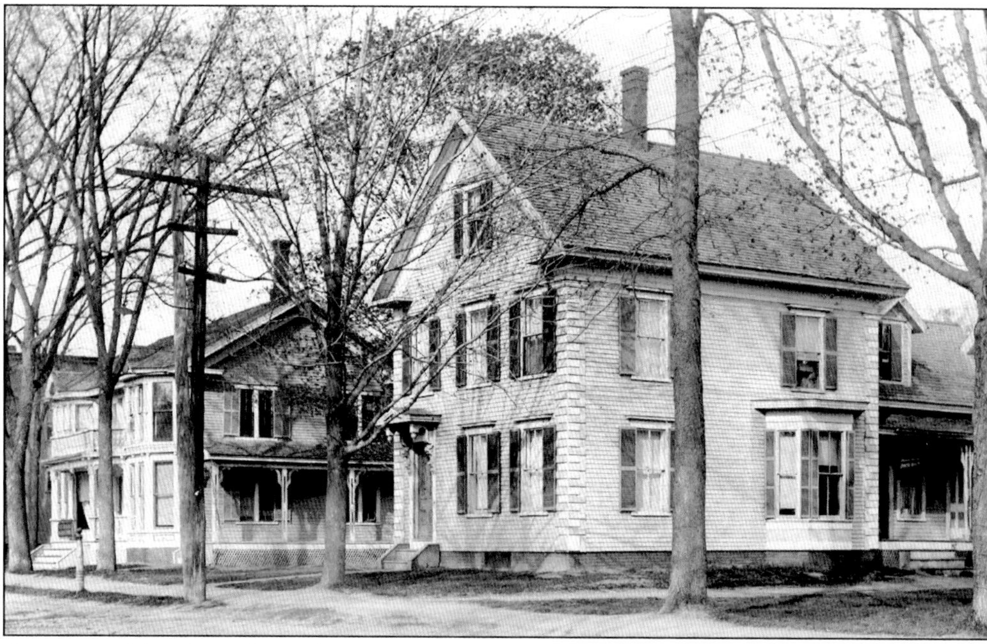

Constructed in 1900, this is the original homestead of Clarence Johnson. He married Mary "Mamme" Belle Muzzey on February 10, 1897. She was from Sunapee. Clarence died on January 25, 1915, and Mary on February 21, 1925. The property was bought by Allen M. Agle in 1925, then Belmont Hosiery Company by 1926, Thomas and Pauline Murphy in 1954, and Andre and Doris (Chapman) Paquette by 1970. Today it is owned by Allan Hart and is a two-family dwelling.

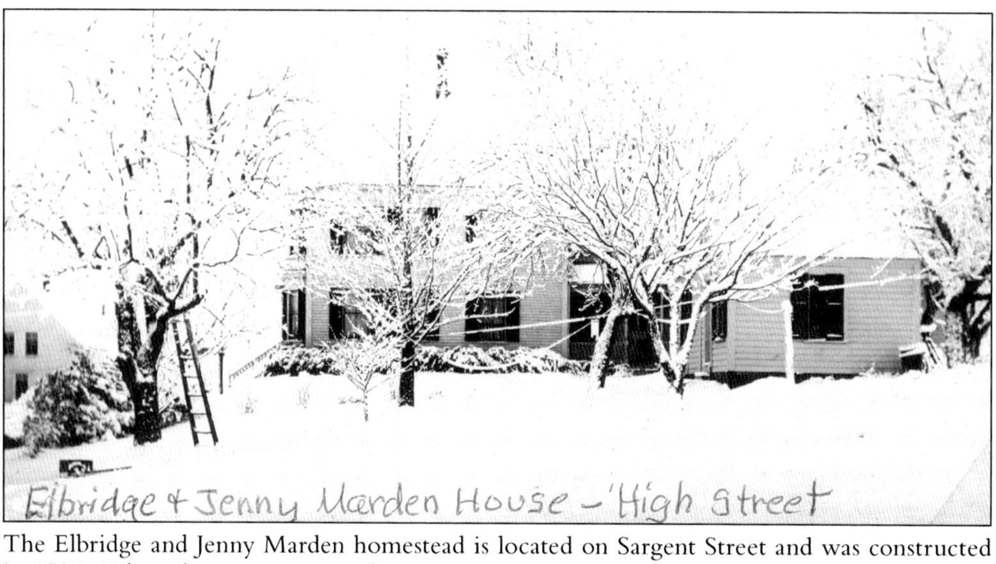

The Elbridge and Jenny Marden homestead is located on Sargent Street and was constructed in 1896. When the property was first purchased in 1894, High Street was present, and the property was considered to be on High Street. After the construction of Sargent Street, the property obtained a Sargent Street address. At one time, Elbridge owned more than 25 acres in the village district, selling most of it between 1919 and 1927. Today the home is owned by Marilyn Pollman.

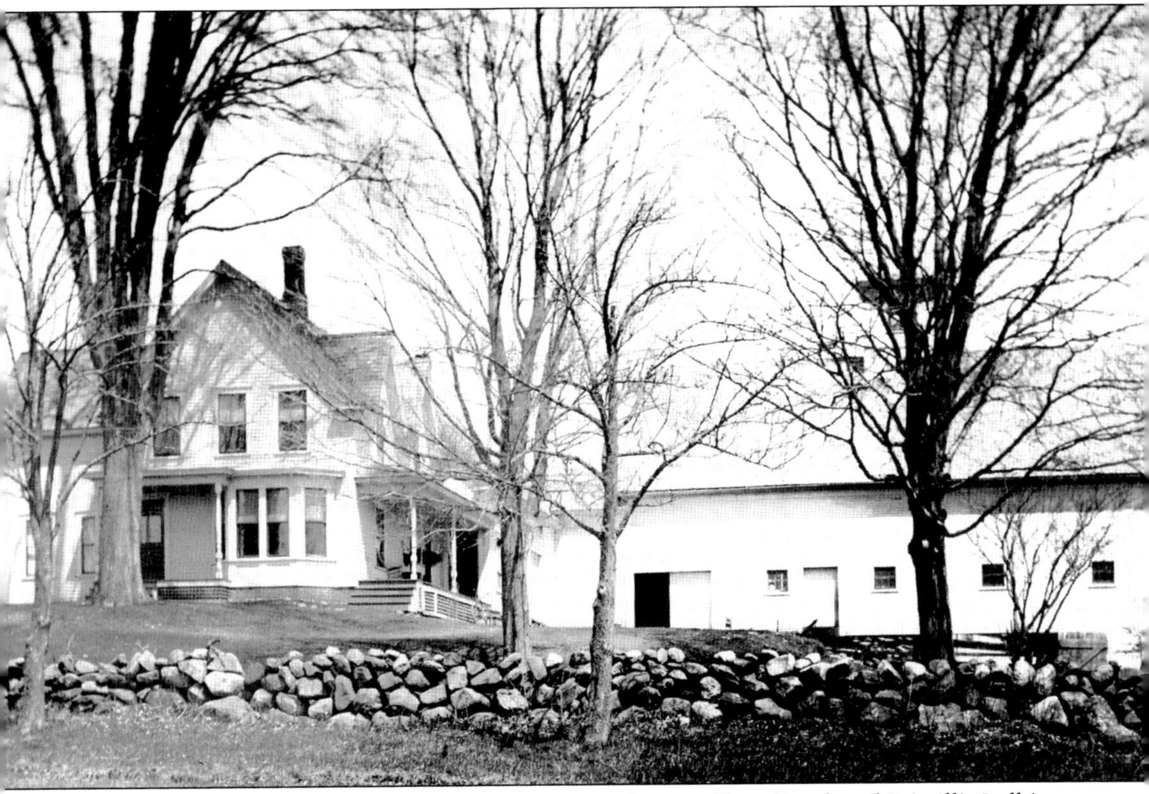

This property was owned by Wilbur and Winnie Mudgett and later Frank and Priscillia Judkins. Part of the original property consisted of the land around Pout Pond, which was transferred to the Town of Belmont for use in the municipal water system. Today the building is owned by Charles Hampe.

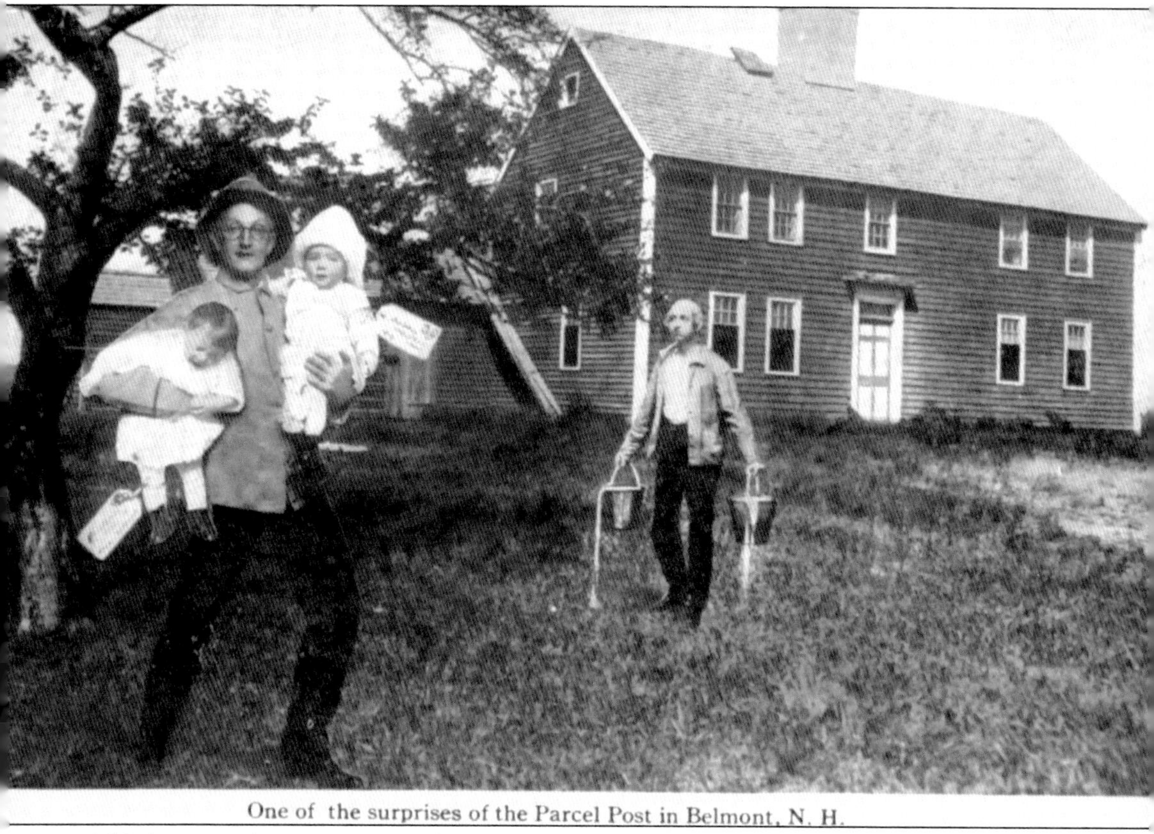

This home no longer exists. Walter and Marguerite Clavett purchased the property in 1961; a few years later, the structure burned to the ground, but the cellar hole still remains on the property. Today the property is owned by Alfred E. Wentworth. This postcard pokes fun at the parcel post in Belmont.

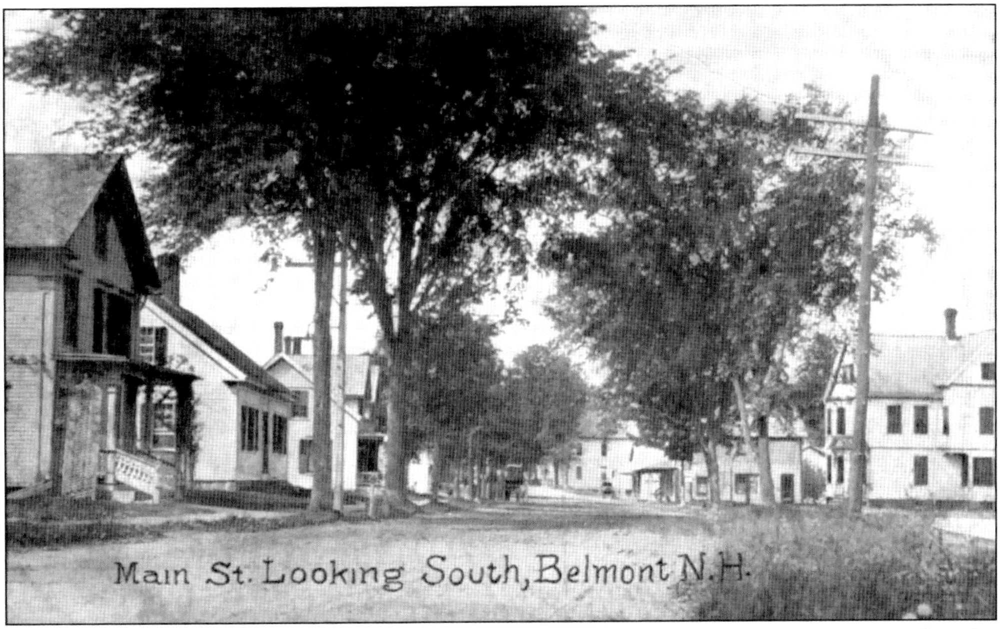

The postcard above shows Main Street looking south around the early 1900s. Note that the street is unpaved. The Moses Smith house appears on the left side of the photograph (third in) where the Belmont Hardware Store is now. The first house on the right is the Abbie Fifield house. Currently this building is the home of the Village Image.

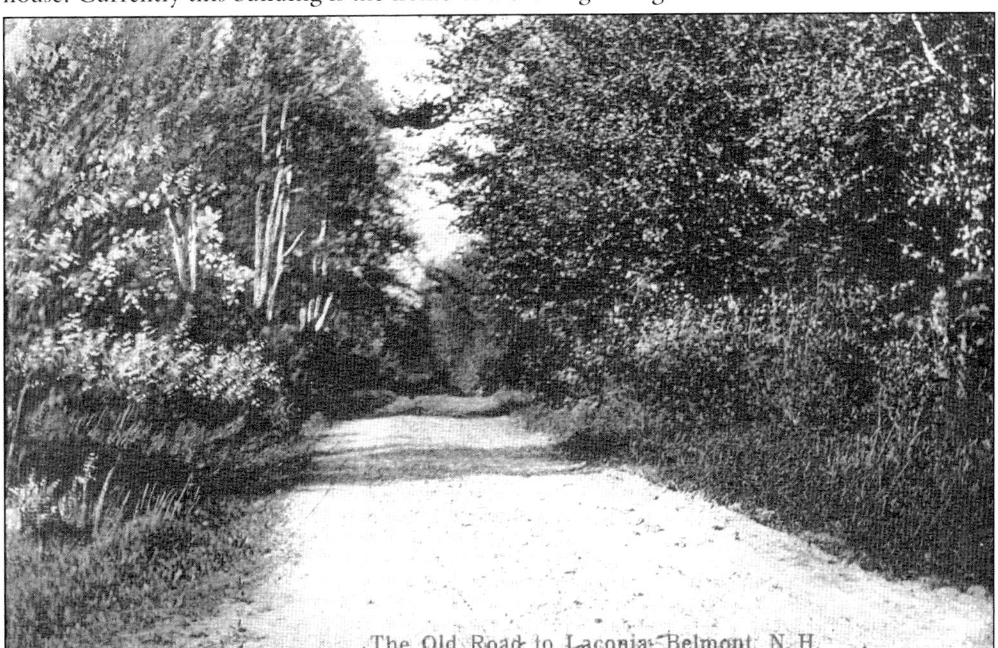

The first telephone lines in Belmont came to town from Laconia and were strung on short poles so that the snow sometimes drifted almost to the wires. These poles were along the Old Laconia Road leading from Church Street. From Belmont, the lines ran to Gilmanton Corner. The first homes to have telephone service in town were the Moses Sargent Sr. house and Hoyt's store. At a later date, the telephone office was located in the post office.

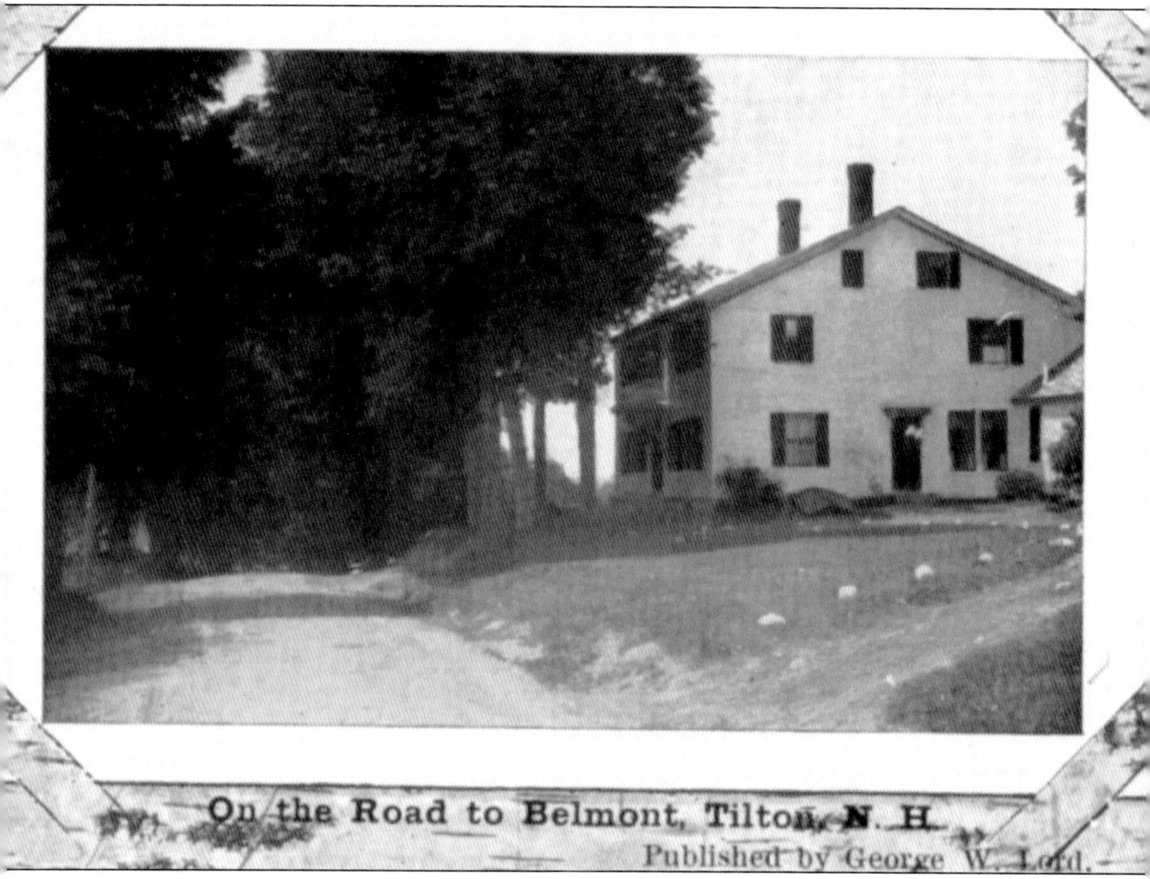

One of the earliest automobile accidents is said to have occurred when Dr. H. S. Bickford and Sumner Gardner were thrown out of Gardner's vehicle on Tilton Road when they came into collision with another vehicle. Dr. Bickford was reported saying that he now understood the truth in the saying "It is nothing to fall out of a balloon, but the stopping so quick is what hurts."

Eight

Town Views

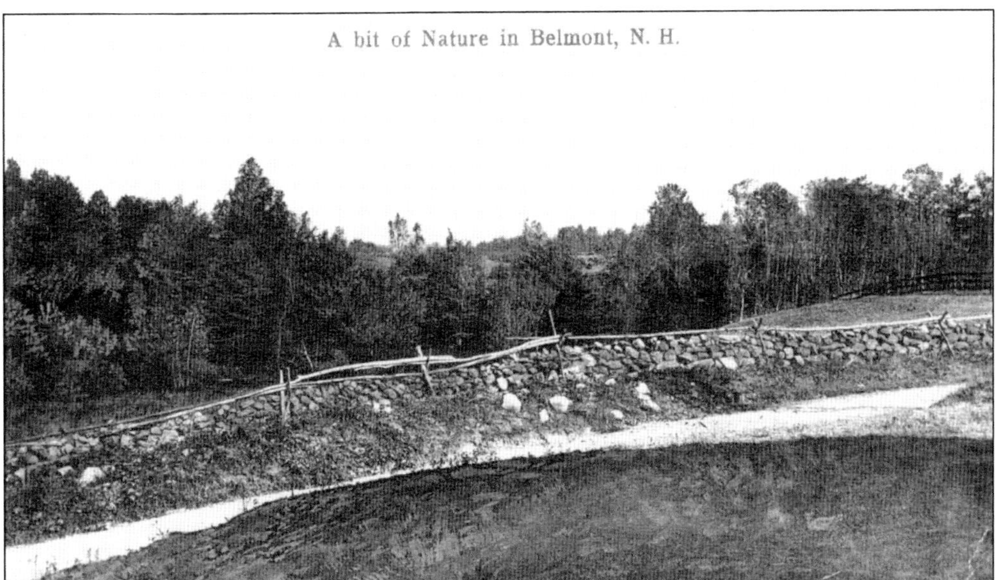

This countryside postcard of Belmont shows the hillside and farmland of an unknown location. Notice the unpaved road, the long stone wall, and the wooden fence posts. To the right, just beyond the pasture, another fence can be seen, probably constructed to contain cattle.

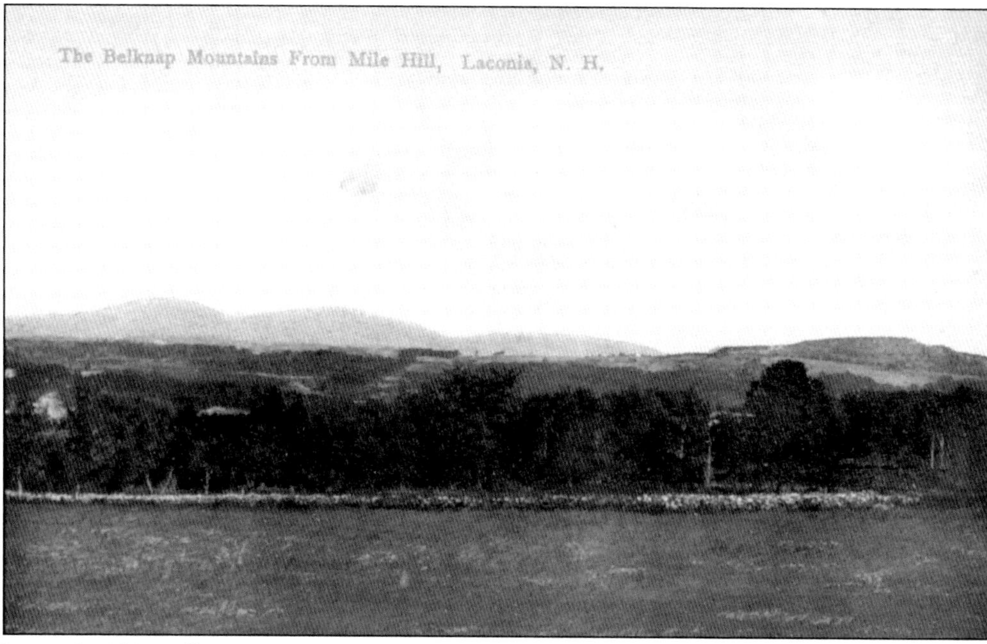

Located within Belknap Mountain State Forest is the New Hampshire Lookout Tower. Constructed in 1915, the 34-foot steel tower is standard but is constructed with a unique wooden cabin. In 1979, an additional 10 feet was added to the tower. It can be reached by trail directly from the Gunstock Recreation Area in Gilford. The tower has had many visitors since 1915 and is still actively reporting fires within the Lakes Region. The State of New Hampshire's Department of Resources and Economic Development has 16 fire towers within the state.

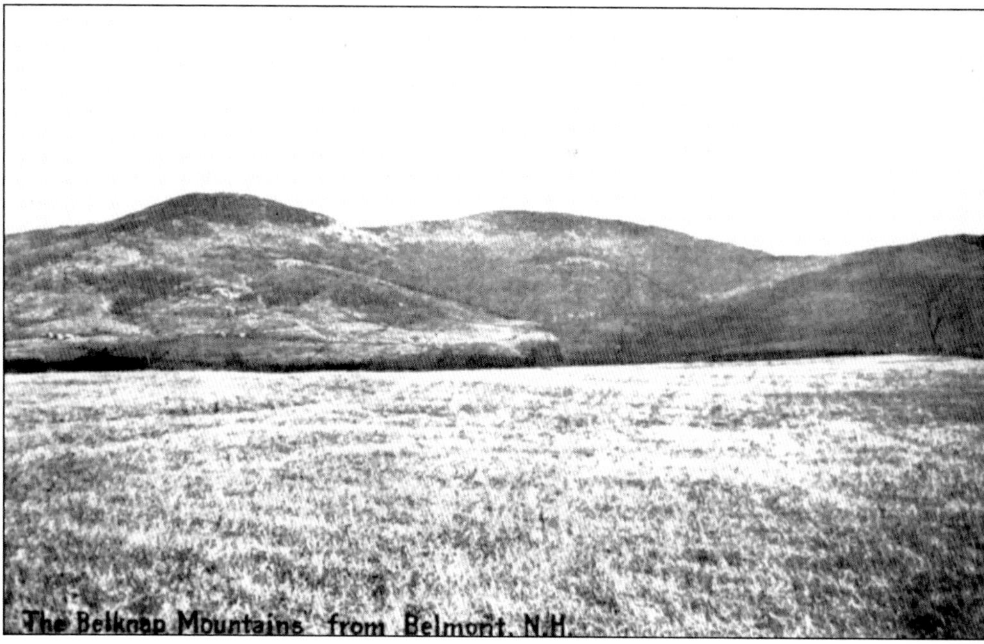

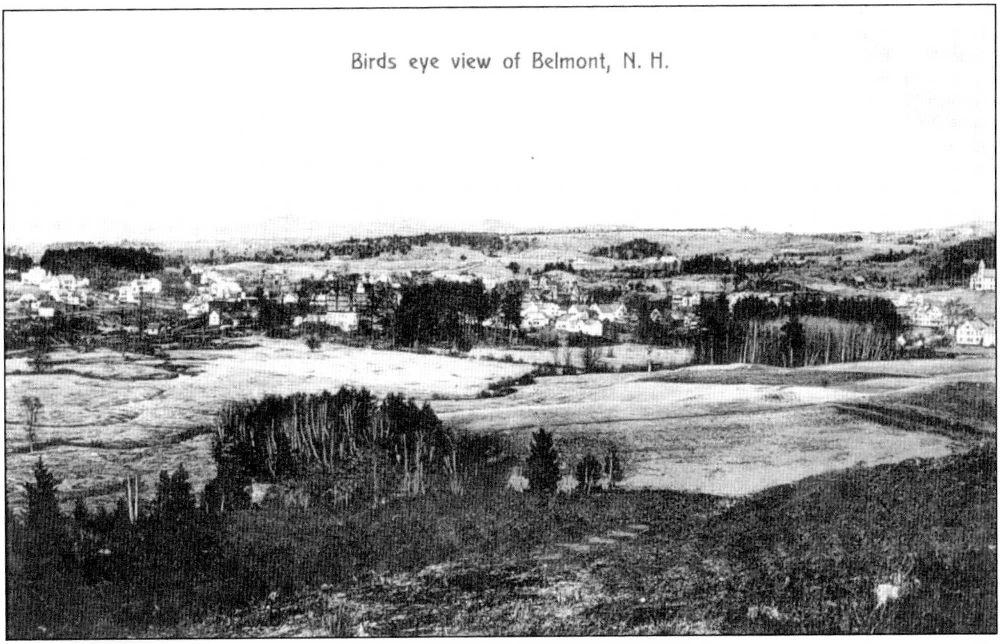

This is the village of Belmont as seen from the hills southwest behind the Belmont Mill. Originally part of Gilmanton, this area changed its name to Upper Gilmanton in 1859 and to Belmont 10 years later. Until 1859, the name Gilmanton applied to the present town of Gilmanton and Belmont; prior to 1812, it also applied to the town of Gilford.

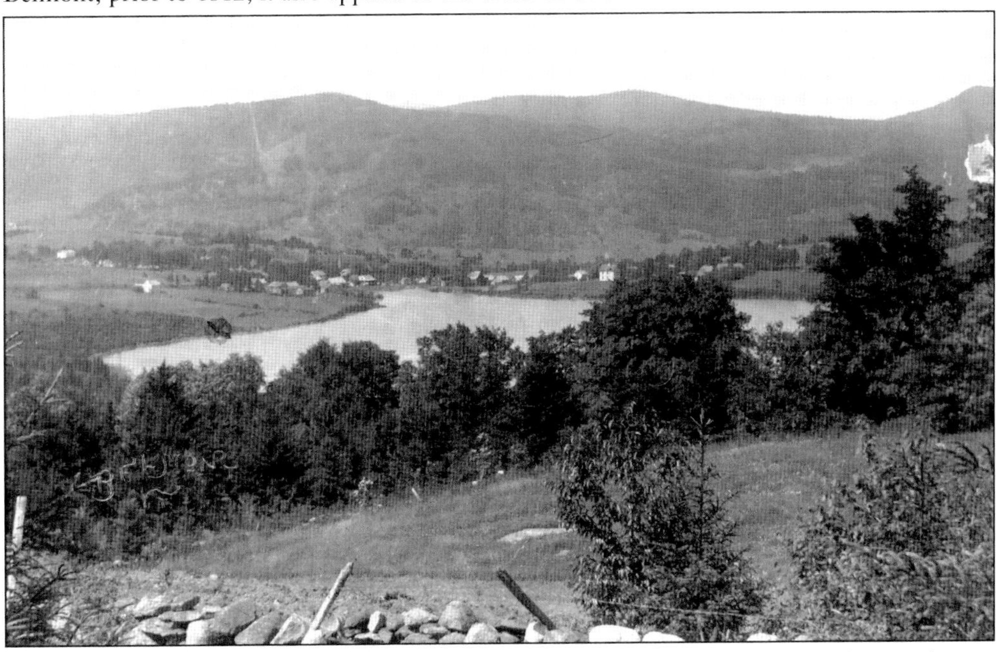

This postcard from October 13, 1958, made its way to Newark, New Jersey, from Belmont. The message on the back reads, "Mom & Dad, Here's the Lake where we've been fishing and enjoying all the fall colors from the big picture window of my mother's cottage- where X is marked on front of card. This is looking south down on the Town of Belmont. See you all soon! Love, Freddy."

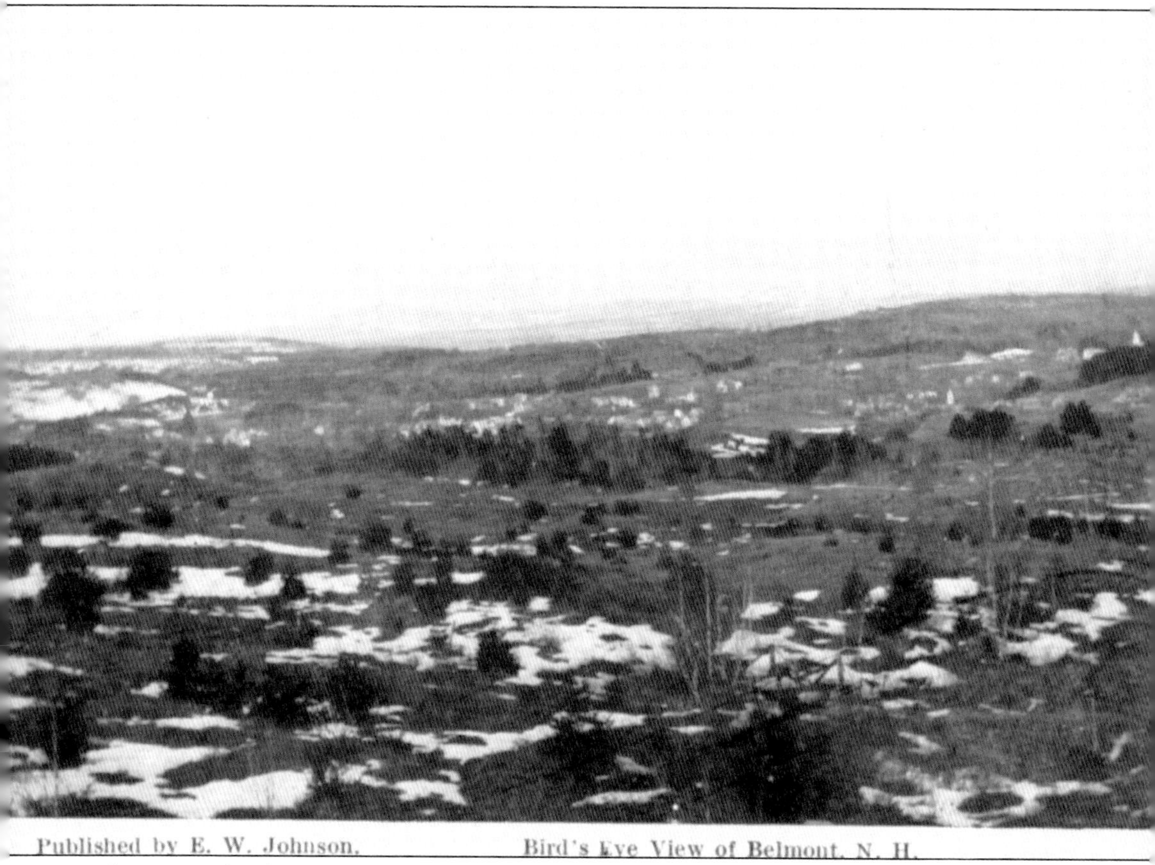

The town of Belmont is located in the southern portion of New Hampshire's Lakes Region in Belknap County. The village area, found at the intersection of State Route 106 and State Route 140, is 4 miles from Interstate 93, exit 20, 7 miles south of Laconia, and 24 miles north of Concord. There are 30 square miles of land area, and over one and one-half square miles of lake area in Belmont. Today the current population is 6,228, although the seasonal influx of temporary residents in both the summer and winter recreational seasons greatly increases this number. Nineteen miles of state highways and 65 miles of town highways provide excellent transportation routes throughout the town. Three town highways have also been designated as scenic roadways. Like much of New Hampshire, Belmont's history centers around the flowage of the Tioga River and the mills that clustered along its banks. The town seal indicates the importance that this industry played in Belmont's past.

Nine

SOUVENIRS

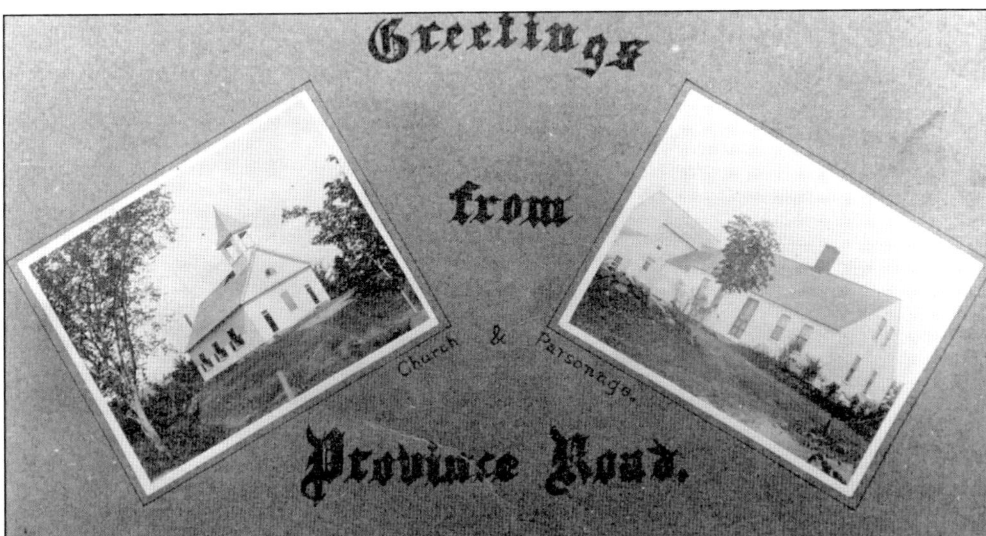

This *c.* 1901–1907 postcard of Province Road shows the Province Road Meetinghouse on the left, which was constructed in 1792. This 213-year-old structure still stands today, presently owned by the Belmont Historical Society. The home on the right was constructed in 1848 by the Third Free Will Baptist Meeting House from land purchased from Asa Lamprey in 1844. Harry Jones and his wife purchased the property in 1951 and sold it to Edward J. Lavallee Jr. in 1955. This building is 158 years old, and Edward L. Lavallee, a descendant of Capt. Leander Lavallee of the MS *Mount Washington*, owns the property today.

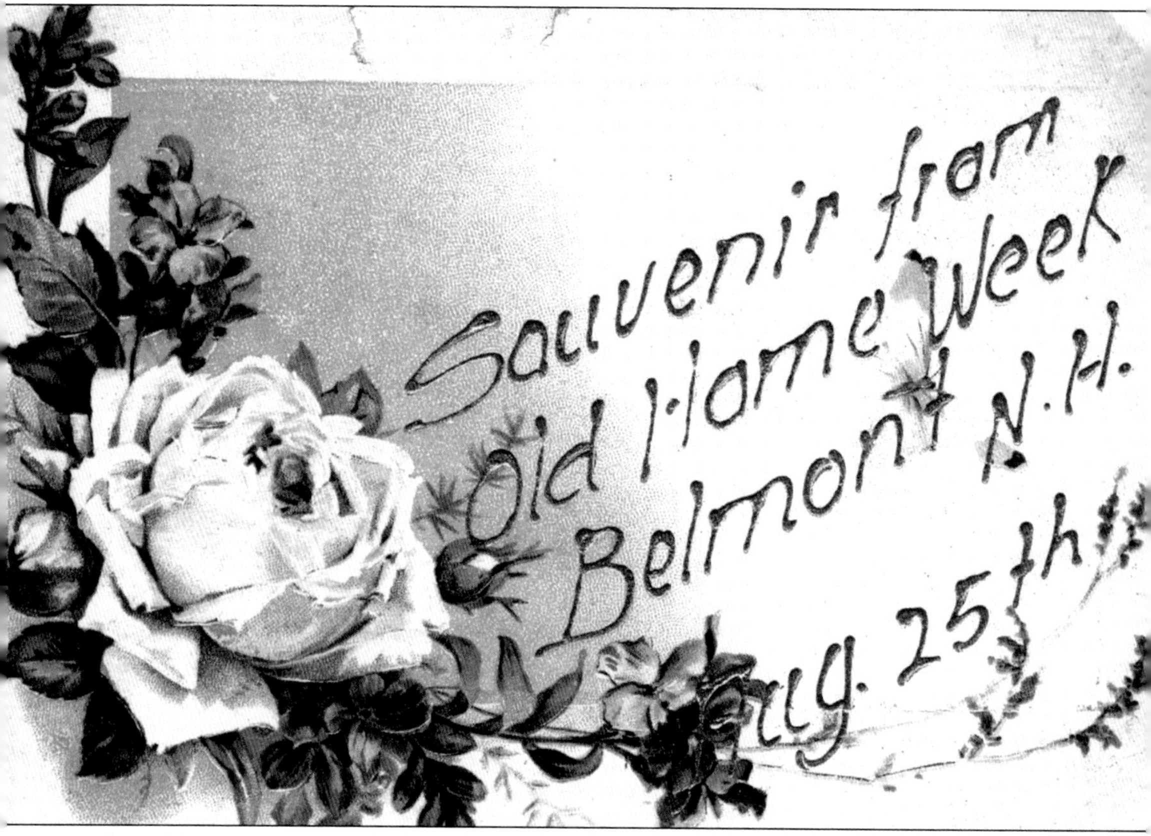

The celebration of Old Home Week originated in New Hampshire when Gov. Frank Rollins proclaimed August 26, 1899, would usher in "Old Home Week." The celebration was unified by bonfires throughout the state. Reasoning for this tradition was that after the Civil War farms were abandoned and people were moving to big cities or out west. The idea was to encourage former residents to come back home to renew friendships, make new acquaintances, and stir up some excitement for the locals. The earliest Old Home Day found in Belmont's history is August 20, 1902, and it apparently was not celebrated every year, as one held on Friday, August 21, 1914, indicated its ninth celebration.

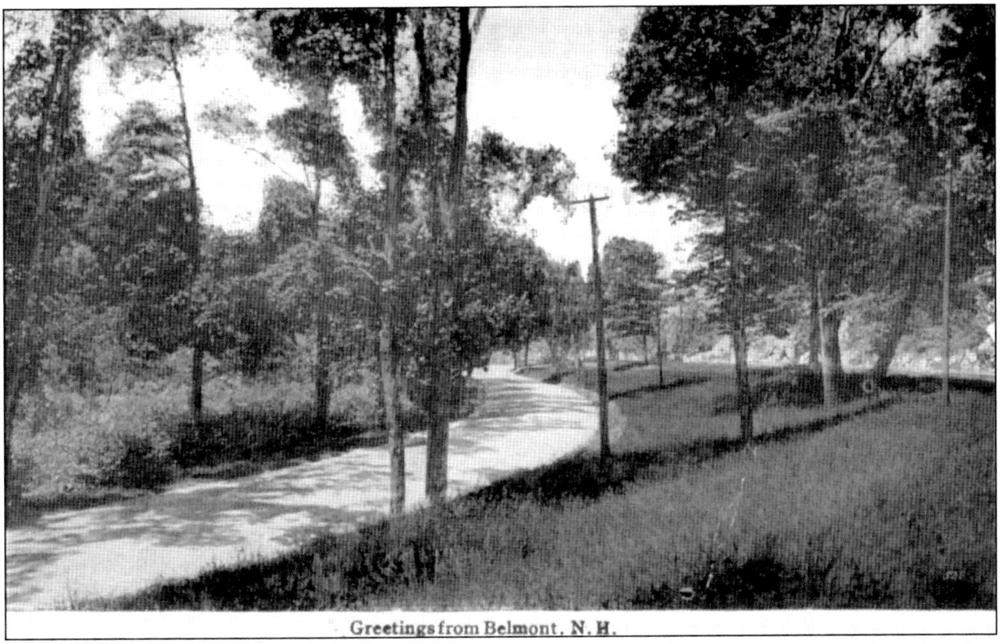

These postcards from the early modern era of postcard history date from 1916 to 1930. During this time period, American technology advanced, allowing quality card production, although often mass-produced in order to saturate the market. Therefore, some cards may say "Greetings from Belmont," but the actual picture may have been taken elsewhere. However, during this period, these postcards remained in demand as a way of telling people where the card came from at a glance, with the writing on the back often offering a sentiment of the day. The back of the postcard below reads, "Dear Walter, Sorry you couldn't get down to see us. Having a fine time—going home Sunday a.m. Hope to see you when you get back. We are having a big party on tonight 16 in all."

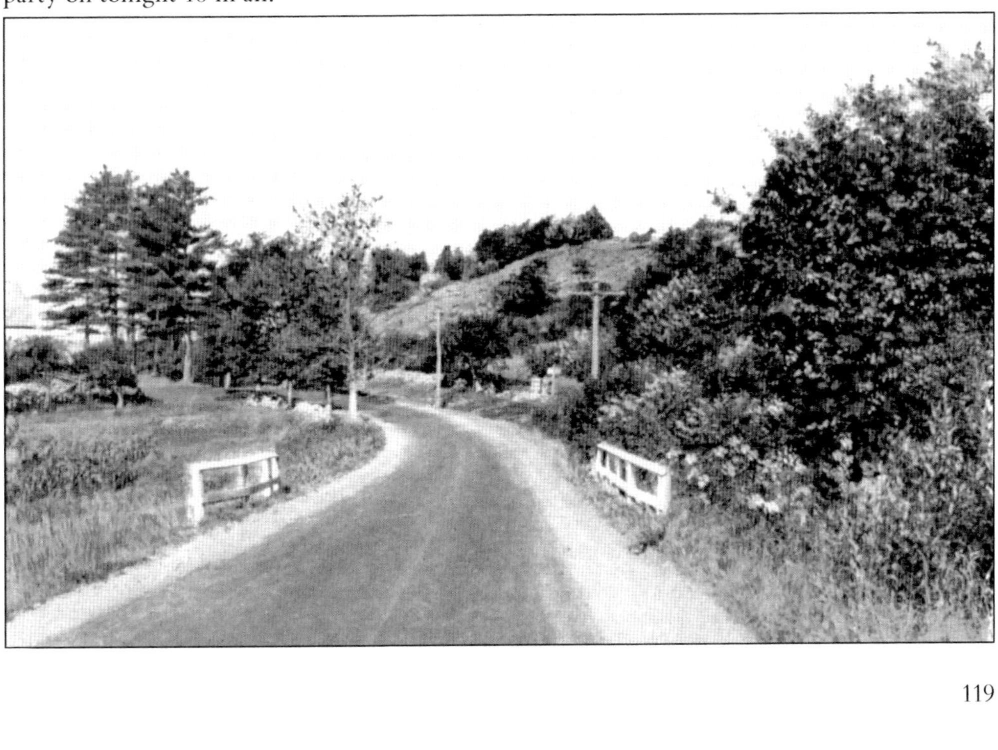

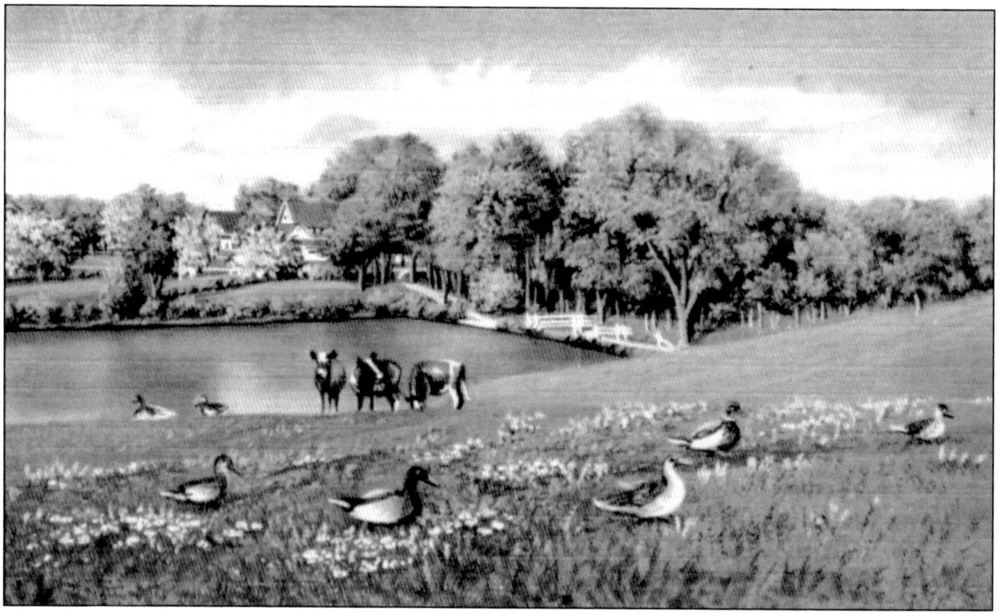

These linen card–era postcards date from 1930 to 1945 and show the change in technology enabling publishers to print cards on linen-type paper stock with very bright and vivid colors. Again, these cards were mass-produced, not necessarily having a picture from Belmont but more of a greeting from Belmont. The back of the card above reads, "Dear Laura, I have been sick, had to have Mildred help me, but wish you might come to see me. I guess things are about the same in Belmont. Love, Mary" The back of the card below reads, "Your letter duly received, many thanks for it. We'll try to get you more films next time we go to the city [possibly the city of Laconia]. You had a nice visit with Harold. Glad the films got there before he left. We're in Belmont for a few days. Expect to go back to Lake when our garden is in shape. Hastily, Eliz."

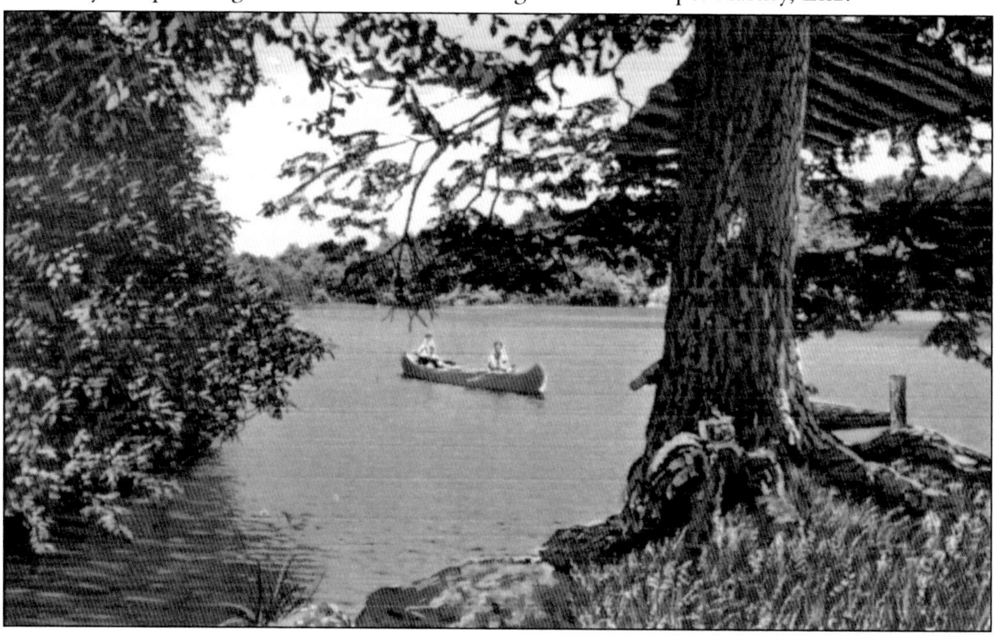

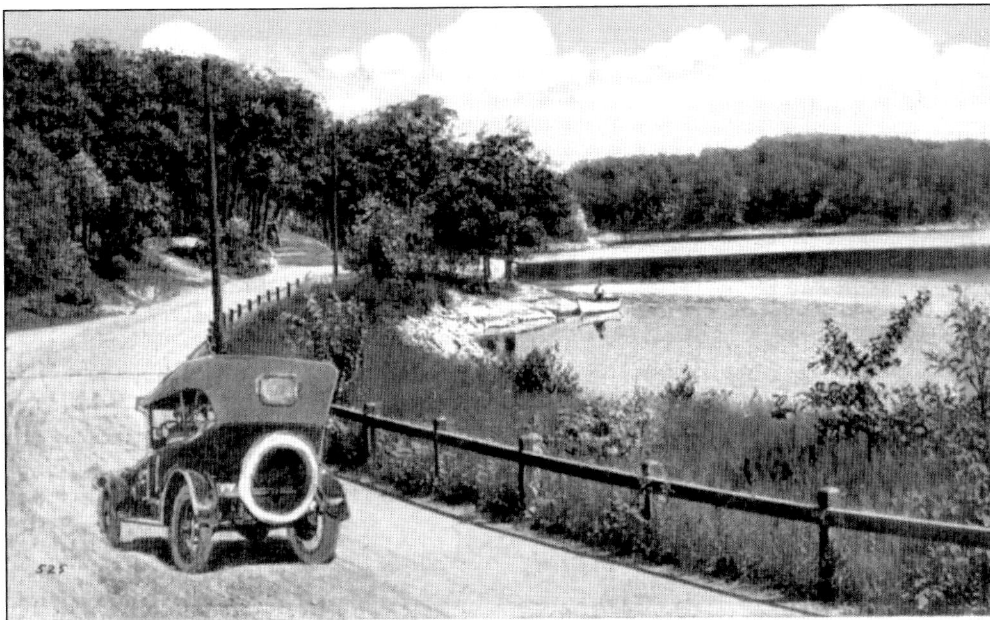

Greetings from Belmont, N. H.

These 1916–1930 postcards show early automobiles portraying a relaxing ride along Belmont's countryside. The back of the postcard above reads, "My Dear Friend, if I may call you my friend. I guess you have forgotten me. I have thought of writing you many times but we are having our hands full. Suppose Marion has told you about mamma, she is a little better, but not out of danger yet. I have to be up nights so much, but we want to do all we can to save her. You know what it is to worry about your mother. I haven't had any nerves I guess they seem to go on me like a rough cracker on the end of a dogs tail like the card I sent you once. Write Carrie." The back of the card below states, "Mr. Cate, The Fifields have moved out Wednesday. Yours truly, Mrs. R.N. Bernier."

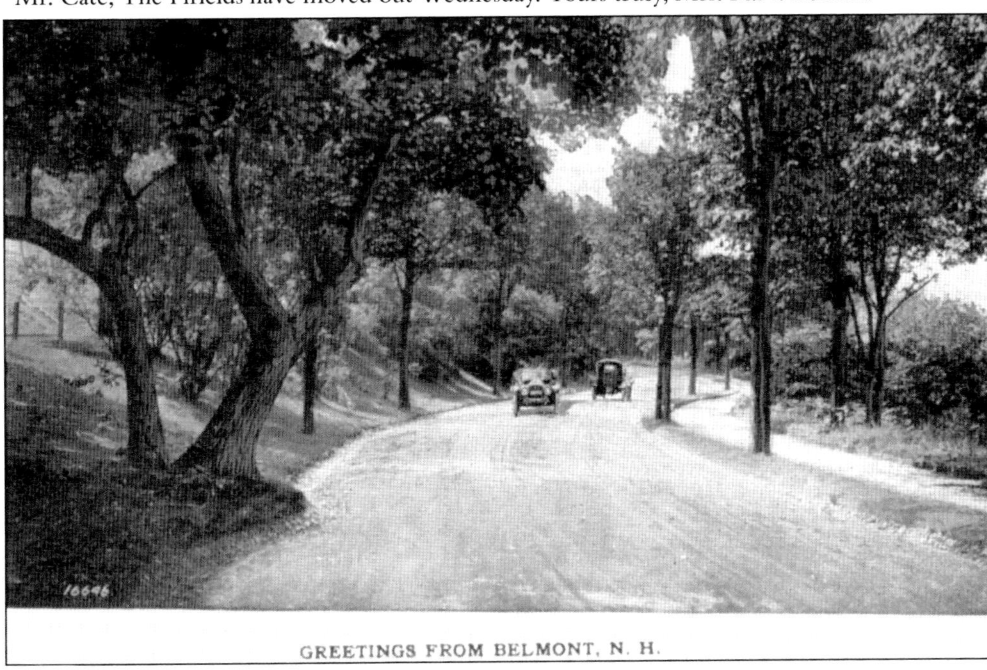

GREETINGS FROM BELMONT, N. H.

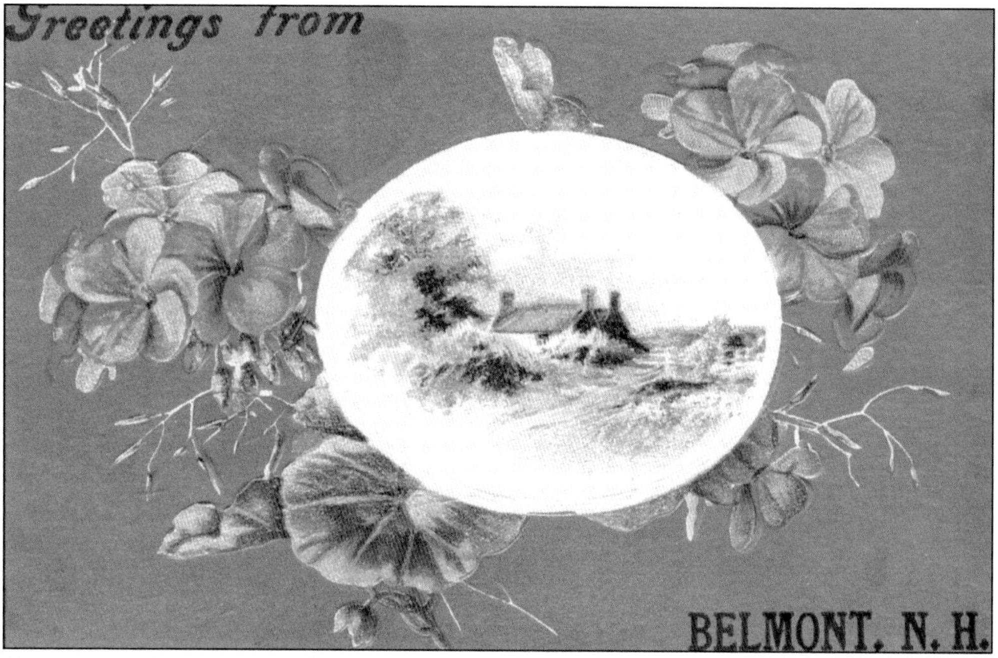

The postcard above was mailed on May 13, 1908, from Belmont at 10:00 a.m. and the back reads, "Received your postal today am all well and glad you are all the same. Love to all Minnie." In 1901, the federal government granted the use of the words "post card" to be printed on the undivided back of privately printed cards and allowed publishers to drop the authorization inscription previously required. As in earlier eras, writing was still limited to the front or in a very small area to the left on the back of the card. The message on the back of the card below reads, "Dear Susie, In this mail I will send you a plant which I think is very pretty. I wonder if you have got one like it if so give it to someone that hasn't got one. With best regards Nellie." This message clearly indicates people were collecting postcards and possibly swapping the cards among one other.

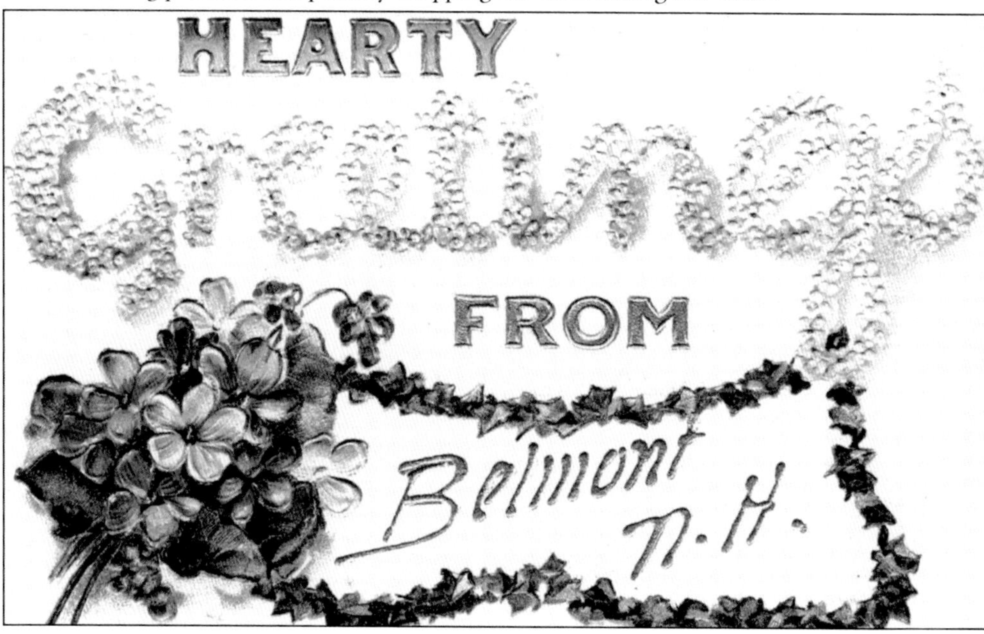

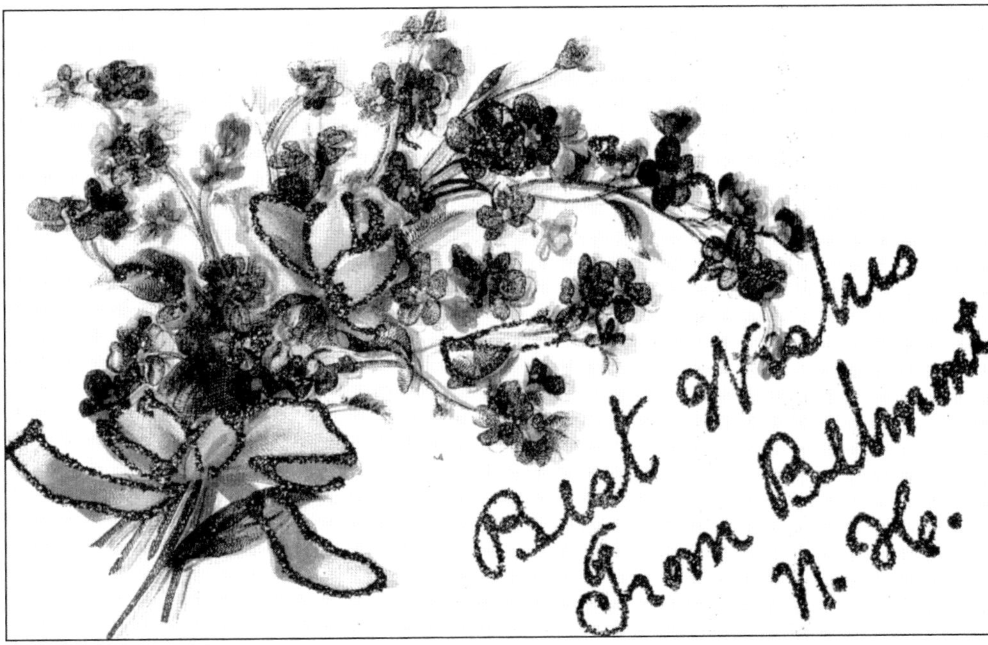

Early greeting cards are some of the most beautiful cards ever printed, as seen above and below. Publishers competing for sales, printed cards using intricate embossing techniques, high-caliber artwork, superior inks, expensive lithographic processes, and even novelty additions such as glitter, ribbons, silk, and feathers. The postcards above and below were universal between 1907 and 1915, except in a few monopolistic governments. During this time, the majority of U.S. postcards were printed in Germany and elsewhere in Europe, whose printing methods were regarded as the best in the world. Although, the trying years during this period, with rising importation of tariffs and the threats of war, caused a swift decline in the cards imported to the United States. These political strains brought about the end of the golden age in postcard history.

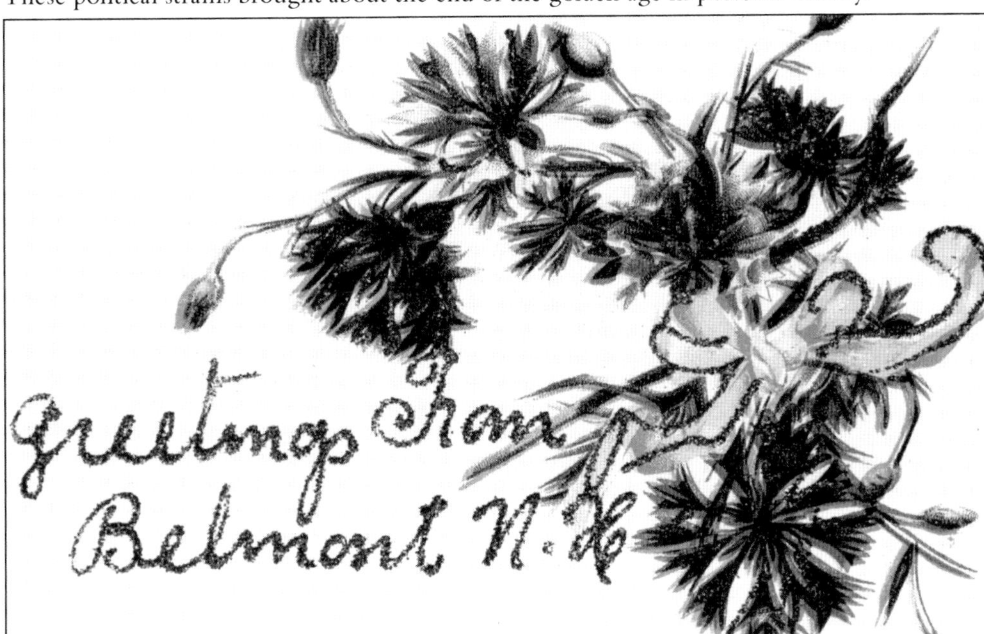

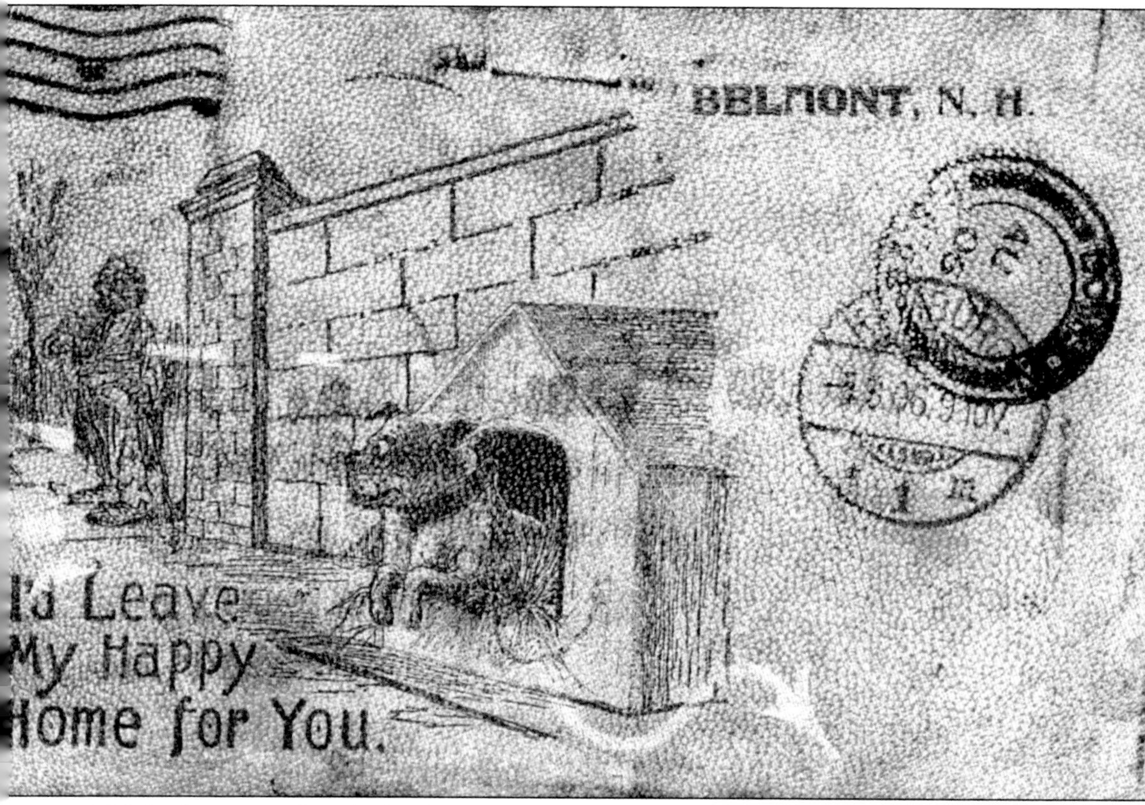

This leather postcard marked Belmont, New Hampshire, is postmarked 1906. Leather postcards are one of the earliest types of postcards. They were produced between 1903 and 1910. The United States Post Office banned their use in 1909 due to the difficulty in processing them and the increasing use of mail-sorting equipment. The leather postcards are all of the undivided back type of card and were usually produced from deerskin. The designs were individually created using a heated iron in a process called pyrography. The same process is used to burn designs into wood.

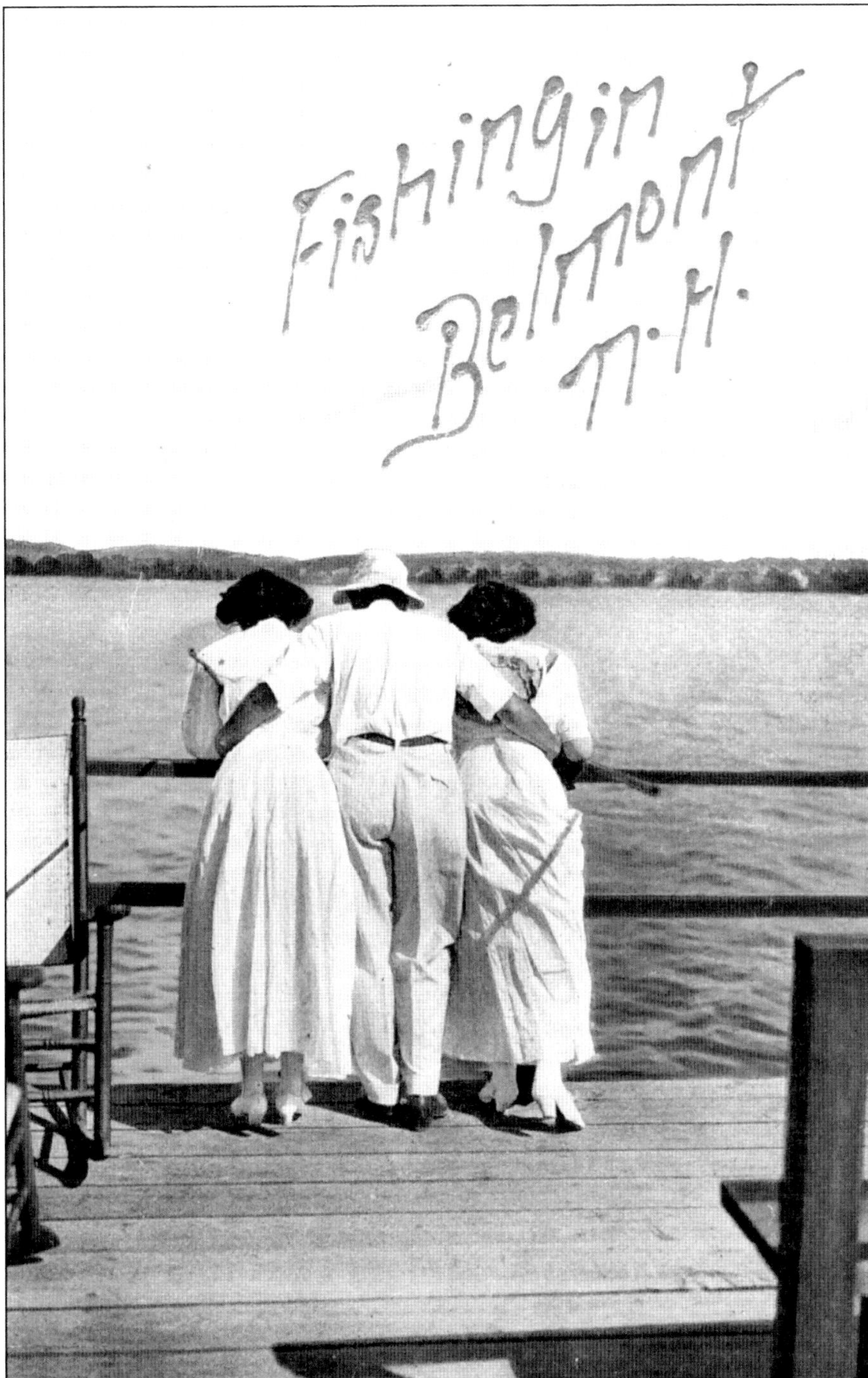

Since Belmont is located at the heart of the Lakes Region, there is an abundance of fishing holes for personal enjoyment. Within miles of the center of town there are Pout Pond, Silver Lake, Lake Winnisquam, the Tioga River, and the Winnipesaukee River. This postcard invites friends and family to come join the fun. Pickerel, trout, shad, perch, and salmon have been caught in the waters surrounding Belmont.

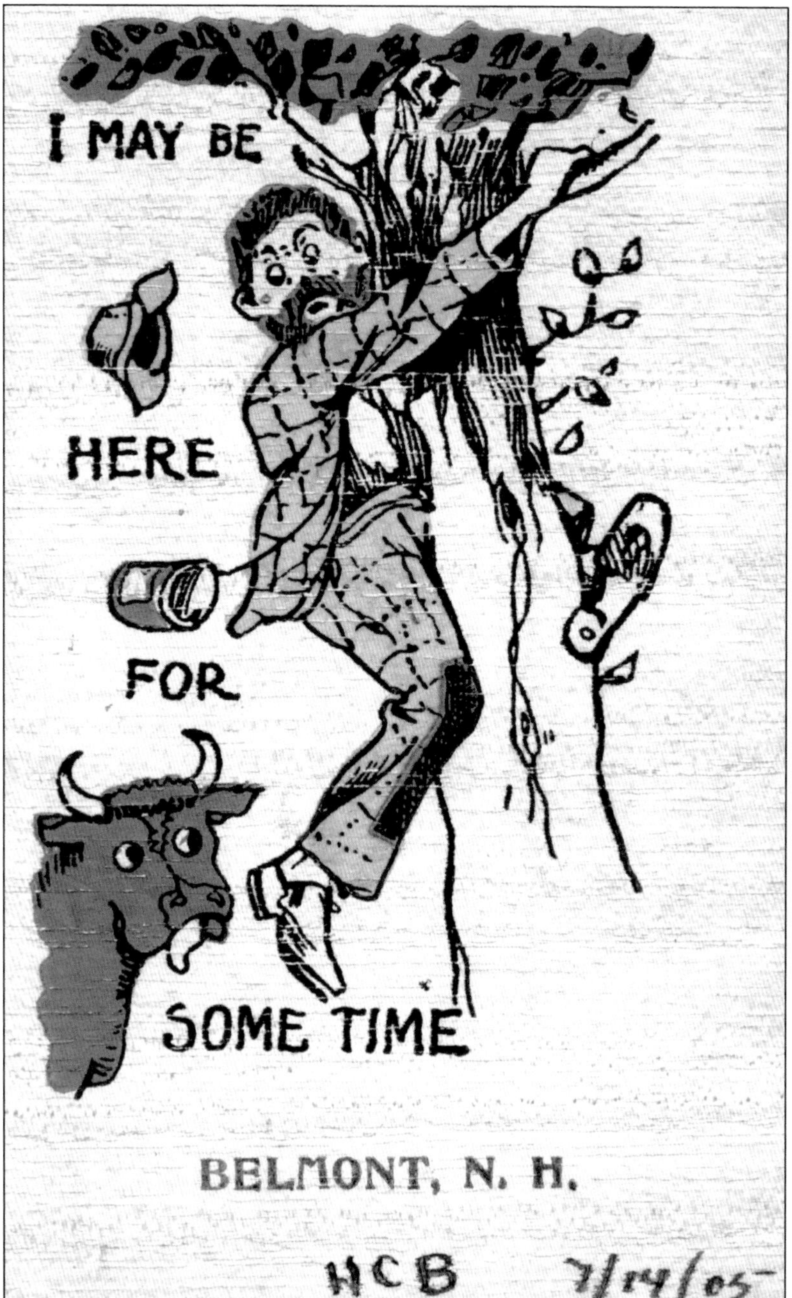

This 1905 postcard shows a gentlemen hanging onto a tree for life, indicating the grand time he is having in Belmont. Postcards began to be widely used in the United States soon after governmental restrictions on the private publishing of postcards were lifted in 1898. In the following years, the demand for postcards grew rapidly. The official figures from the United States Post Office for the fiscal year ending in June 1908 cite almost 680 million postcards mailed. Putting this into perspective, the total population of the United States at this time was only 89 million. Telephones were common, but postcards were a fast, reliable, and inexpensive means of keeping in touch.

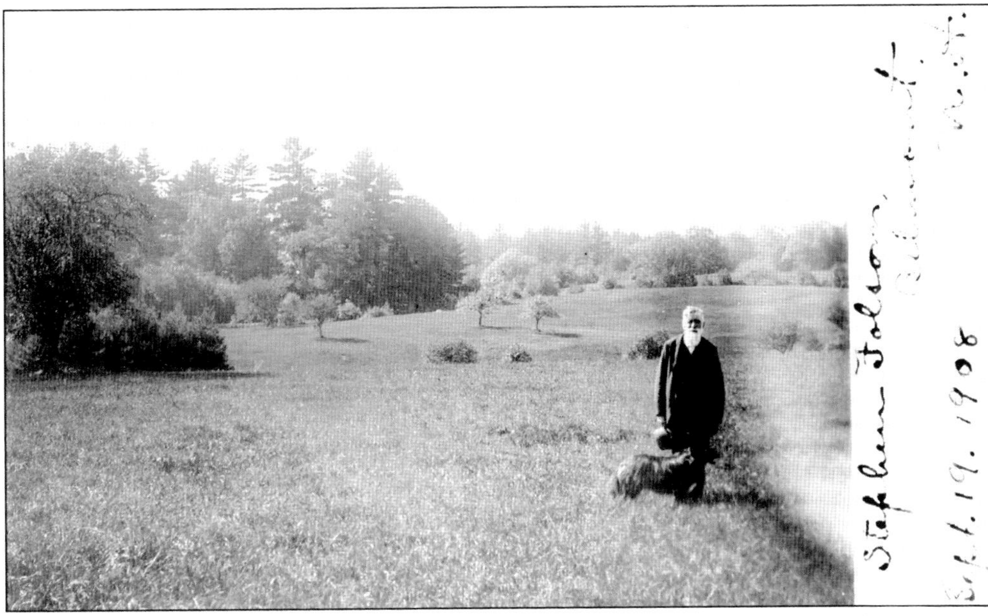

Stephen Folsom lived at the corner of Hurricane Road and Seavey Road. He was born in 1831 and died in 1912. After his death, the house that he lived in burned, but the barn that went with the property still stands on the opposite side of Hurricane Road. The story is told that he belonged to a religious sect that observed its Sabbath on Saturday, so he could be seen working his fields on Sunday when others were going to church. The same sect also thought it had determined the exact time of the end of the world, so when that day arrived the members went to hilltops to await the event. They apparently later came home disappointed. The barn is owned by Brett Riendeau and Jenny Vansen.

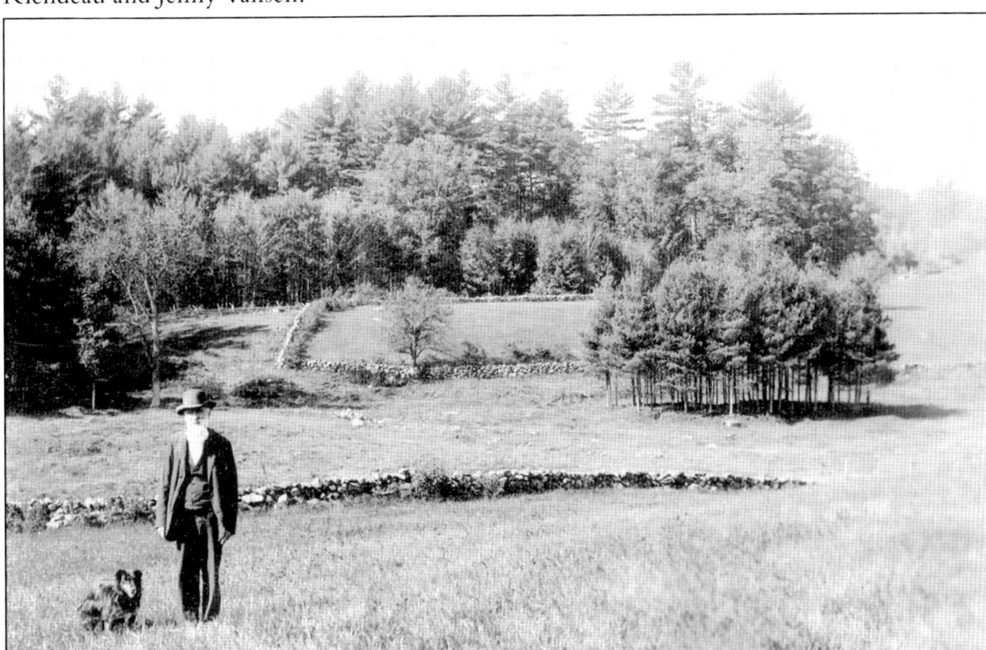